BEAUTY AND SENSIBILITY
IN THE THOUGHT OF
JONATHAN EDWARDS

BEAUTY AND SENSIBILITY
IN THE THOUGHT OF
JONATHAN EDWARDS

An Essay in Aesthetics and Theological Ethics

by

Roland André Delattre

New Haven and London, Yale University Press, 1968

for my wife, Susan
and my brother, Pierre

PREFACE

The conviction upon which this book rests and the validity of which it is designed to demonstrate is that the aesthetic aspect of Jonathan Edwards' thought and vision, which finds its definitive formulation in his concepts of beauty and sensibility, provides a larger purchase upon the essential and distinctive features of his thought than does any other aspect, such as the idealist, empiricist, sensationalist, Platonist, scholastic, Calvinist, or mystic. All of these labels have been applied to Edwards, singly or in varying combinations. None of the interpretations suggested by them is entirely without merit, and some of them touch upon dimensions of Edwards' thought that are absolutely indispensable to a full understanding of him. But it has become my conviction that, however important the matters illuminated by other approaches, none grasps the really distinctive quality of his thought or vision. Certainly beauty and sensibility do not provide the only significant purchase upon Edwards' thought, but they do provide a larger and wider and deeper one than does any of the alternatives, and they lead us to those dimensions of his thought most peculiarly his.

This book calls special attention to an aspect of Edwards' thought that so radically—at the roots—qualifies the whole that it gives him not only an important place—of that he is already well assured—but also a distinctive place in the full sweep of Christian thought. Although the unique is, except for the greatest of minds, more commonly secondary if not peripheral, it seems to me that in this case it is decisive for the whole. This may help to explain the difference between the character of his thought as I shall portray it and its actual historical impact. Those dimensions of his thought and vision that he shared with others—and they are of course substantial—were readily appropriated (if not always so profoundly understood) by friend and foe. But the really unique was never fully perceived. At least it was not perceived by the theologians, although, as Alan Heimert has demonstrated,[1] many ordinary

---

1. Alan Heimert, *Religion and the American Mind: From the Great Awakening to the Revolution* (Cambridge, Harvard University Press, 1966).

ministers (who were not always very ordinary at all) of the evangelical churches did understand and share a good part of that aspect of Edwards' vision with which I am concerned in this book. If from eighteenth-century New England he has a contribution to make to contemporary Christian— and not only to Christian—life and thought, it may well be by virtue of those aspects of his thought to which this essay is devoted.

In 1960 H. Richard Niebuhr wrote that if Christians are to "meet in our day the need which the church was founded to meet," it will not be by becoming more orthodox or more liberal, more biblical or more liturgical.

> Our old phrases are worn out; they have become cliches by means of which we can neither grasp nor communicate the reality of our existence before God. Retranslation is not enough; more precisely, retranslation of traditional terms—"Word of God," "redemption," "incarnation," "justification," "grace," "eternal life"—is not possible unless one has direct relations in the immediacy of personal life to the actualities to which people in another time referred with the aid of such symbols.

Niebuhr did not presume to know what sort of reformation to look for, but he could characterize the sort of development that in his view carried the most promise of faithful contemporary embodiment of "radical monotheism": "I look for a resymbolization . . . in pregnant word and in symbolic deeds . . . of the message and the life of faith in the One God."[2]

The present essay may be read as a step in the exploration of one such avenue of resymbolization suggested by the place of beauty and sensibility in the thought of Jonathan Edwards. It is primarily with the help of his own fresh conceptions of beauty and sensibility that he tried to apprehend and to communicate just those actualities of our existence before God with which Niebuhr was most concerned. Insofar as we make Niebuhr's concern also our own, it would therefore seem particularly appropriate to look to Edwards for guidance in such a reformation through resymbolization in word and deed, for it is his life and thought that provided Niebuhr with one of his most illuminating historical models of the radical monotheism at the center of his own thought. Insofar as contemporary relevance as well as historical understanding is our concern, the present essay attempts to clarify Edwards' conceptions of beauty and sensibility, with the primary focus on beauty, so that

2. H. E. Fey, ed., *How My Mind Has Changed* (New York, Meridian, 1961), 79–80.

these important aspects of his thought may become more readily accessible to all who are presently engaged in the work of theological ethics and moral philosophy.

This essay is a study of Edwards' thought, an effort to move toward a better understanding of him. But it has a second purpose as well. It is conceived as an effort to think not only about Edwards and his theological ethics but also with him about matters of continuing interest that his thought may illuminate. It is offered as a further step in a continuing and widening conversation with a man from whom contemporary theological ethics has much to learn. The time has finally come—and it is long overdue—when we are moving beyond the simple and pious reaffirmation of what everyone says—that Edwards is very likely the greatest American philosopher and theologian of (at least) the colonial period—to the more rewarding enterprise of taking Edwards seriously enough to think with him and to draw him into contributing to our own reflection.

Oxford, Ohio
October 1967

ACKNOWLEDGMENTS

It was the late H. Richard Niebuhr who first brought Jonathan Edwards to my attention in ways that led from my interest in the relationships between the aesthetic and the ethical dimensions of human existence toward my doctoral dissertation, which was the first version of this essay. He died before the project was very far along, but it would not have gotten under way without him, and my indebtedness to him as a scholar and teacher continues to grow substantially with the passing years.

I wish to thank John E. Smith for his help and encouragement during a critical period in the development of the project in the year following Niebuhr's death, and Sydney E. Ahlstrom for the intellectual excitement of his seminars on American religious thought and for his invaluable assistance, advice, and friendship while the dissertation was being completed. I want to take this opportunity to express my special gratitude to two of my other teachers at Yale: to Julian N. Hartt, from whom I learned much of the theology and aesthetics I have been able to bring to this essay, and to James M. Gustafson for his friendship as well as his illumination of the terrain of theological ethics. David D. Hall, with whom a friendship began in one of Ahlstrom's seminars, has contributed considerably to the improvement of this volume with many scholarly and editorial suggestions. I have benefited greatly from a perceptive reading of the manuscript by Wayland W. Schmitt of the Yale University Press; his advice was congenially offered as well as incisive. All who have studied Jonathan Edwards in recent years know how much I owe Thomas A. Schafer for his extraordinary labor in transcribing Edwards' "Miscellanies" and for his exemplary scholarship in editing them for their forthcoming appearance in the Yale edition of Edwards' complete works. He has been unfailingly generous both in giving me free access to his typescripts of the "Miscellanies" and in sharing his general knowledge of Edwards and his unique acquaintance with the "Miscellanies."

Those "Miscellanies," upon which I drew heavily for this essay, are deposited in the Beinecke Rare Book and Manuscript Library at Yale University. I am grateful to the staff of that library, and most especially to Miss Marjorie Wynne, for their cheerful and ready assistance, not only this year but also in earlier years when they were housed less spaciously in the Rare Book Room of the Sterling Memorial Library.

It is a pleasure to acknowledge the generous assistance of Miami University and its Faculty Research Committee, from whom I received a four-month Summer Research Appointment, together with supplemental research funds. They were indispensable in revising the dissertation from the form in which it was submitted to the Graduate School of Yale University.

Everybody says it, and the reader smiles, but I know it to be so: the writing of a book—this one at any rate—is a family enterprise, especially if one's wife is as gifted as mine in the many ways that not only make the writing of a book possible but also make the reading of it more rewarding. These and other incalculable debts to my wife, together with those to my brother, which are no less substantial and of considerably longer standing, are gratefully acknowledged in the dedication of this volume.

CONTENTS

LIST OF ABBREVIATIONS

Citations of works by Jonathan Edwards most frequently quoted in this study will be inserted directly into the text of the essay immediately following the quotation or reference. The citation will appear between square brackets and will consist of the code reference indicated below and the page references from the editions of these works listed below. In the cases of the "Miscellanies" and the "Notes on the Mind" the citations refer to number rather than page.

Unless otherwise indicated, all references to *Works,* either here or in the footnotes, are to *The Works of President Edwards,* a reprint of the Worcester Edition of 1808–09 with some additions (4 vols. New York, Leavitt & Allen, 1843).

Citations of works other than those listed here will appear as footnotes.

Code	Title
CF	*Charity and its Fruits,* ed. Tryon Edwards (New York, Robert Carter and Brothers, 1856).
EC	*Dissertation Concerning the End For Which God Created the World,* in *Works, 2,* 191–257.
FW	*Freedom of the Will,* ed. Paul Ramsey (New Haven, Yale University Press, 1957).
Grace	"A Treatise on Grace," in *Selections From the Unpublished Writings of Jonathan Edwards of America,* ed. A. B. Grosart (Edinburgh, 1865).
HA	*A Humble Attempt to Promote Explicit Agreement and Visible Union of God's People in Extraordinary Prayer,* in *Works, 3,* 427–508.
Images	*Images or Shadows of Divine Things,* ed. Perry Miller (New Haven, Yale University Press, 1948).
Mind	"Notes on the Mind," in Harvey G. Townsend, ed., *The Philosophy of Jonathan Edwards From His Private Notebooks* (Eugene, University of Oregon Press, 1955).

Misc.   "Miscellanies," Yale Collection of Edwards Manuscripts
             (Yale University Library).
OS   *The Great Christian Doctrine of Original Sin Defended*, in
             Works, 2, 305–510.
RA   *Religious Affections*, ed. John E. Smith (New Haven, Yale
             University Press, 1959).
Trinity   *An Unpublished Essay of Edwards on the Trinity*, ed. G. P.
             Fisher (New York, 1903).
TV   *The Nature of True Virtue* (Ann Arbor, University of
             Michigan Press, Ann Arbor Paperback, 1960).
WR   *A History of the Work of Redemption*, in *Works, 1*, 293–
             516.

1

INTRODUCTION

Beauty is one of the things Jonathan Edwards was most concerned with understanding. "It is what we are more concerned with than any thing else whatsoever: yea, we are concerned with nothing else" [Mind, 1].[1] If today we in turn wish to come to a full understanding and appreciation of his thought and vision, we must dare to take seriously his frequent suggestion that beauty is the central clue to the nature of reality. He does not suppose that he has completely penetrated either the eternal mysteries of the Divine Being or the ultimate order of the creation. What he does find, in ways this essay will try to elucidate, is that the concept of beauty, and the perception and enjoyment of spiritual beauty in particular, offers as deep a penetration of those mysteries and of that order as is available to men. The primary beauty of being's cordial consent to being and the image of such beauty in the secondary beauty of harmony and proportion provide him with the surest clue to the mysteries of the things that are and the things that are good and of Him in Whom, from Whom, and to Whom the orders of being and beauty are one. Edwards was convinced that beauty is the reality in terms of which the Divine Being and the moral and religious life of human beings as well as the order of the universal system of being, both moral and natural, can best be understood.

Beauty is fundamental to Edwards' understanding of being. It is the first principle of being, the inner, structural principle of being-itself, according

1. While the quoted passage refers to excellency, it is not inaccurate to refer it to beauty as well, for in this "Note," as elsewhere, Edwards uses excellency and beauty as interchangeable concepts.

> There has nothing been more without a definition than excellency, although it be what we are more concerned with than any thing else whatsoever: yea, we are concerned with nothing else. But what is this excellency? Wherein is one thing excellent and another evil; one beautiful and another deformed?

It is clear from the rest of this "Note" and from the parallelism of excellency and beauty, of evil and deformity, that it is with beauty that Edwards is concerned. See pp. 58–67 for a further development of the virtual identity of beauty and excellence in Edwards' thought.

to which the universal system of being is articulated. Beauty is also the measure and objective foundation of the perfection of being—of excellence, goodness, and value—and is, therefore, the basis for Edwards' way of affirming and construing the ultimate unity of being and good in God. Beauty is not the only kind of order he finds in reality. But as the first principle of both being and the perfection of being, it provides the primary model of order in terms of which Edwards attempts to understand all forms of order and disorder, concord and discord, in the whole system of being under God.

Beauty is also fundamental to Edwards' understanding of Divine Being: it is that "wherein the truest idea of divinity does consist" [RA 298];[2] it is first among the perfections of God; it constitutes in itself the perfection of all the other divine attributes; it provides a major clue to his doctrine of the Trinity; and it defines his understanding of the nature of the divine transcendence and immanence and of the relation between transcendence and immanence in God with respect to His creation, governance, and redemption of the world.

Finally, beauty is fundamental to Edwards' understanding of human being. It is spiritual beauty that constitutes the spiritual image of God in man, both individual and corporate man. Virtue, both natural and spiritual, and all varieties of justice and the fruits of conscience are understood by him as varieties and forms of beauty. He finds in beauty the central clue to the meaning of conversion, of the new life in Christ, and of the holiness and joy given in the indwelling of the Holy Spirit. Beauty provides the model in terms of which he understands the nature of community, social, civil, and religious. In sum, for Edwards beauty is the key to the structure and the dynamics of the moral and religious life and more particularly to the manner of the divine governance and its relation to human freedom and responsibility. For it is his view that God governs not by brute force but by the attractive power, that is, the beauty of the apparent good.

Edwards' interest in beauty is not something to which he is driven by the difficulty of the philosophical and theological problems to which he addresses himself, as one student of his thought has suggested.[3] He does not flee to

---

2. All references to frequently cited works by Edwards will be indicated in this fashion. Citations will appear immediately following the quotation using the letter code indicated in the "List of Abbreviations" and with page numbers referring to the edition listed there. In the cases of the "Miscellanies" and the "Notes on the Mind" the citations refer to number rather than page.

3. Harvey G. Townsend suggests that Edwards "found the resolution of his doubts in the hypothesis that the universe is beautiful. In the secret places of his experience, aesthetic resolutions offered peculiar satisfactions." *Philosophical Ideas in the United States* (New York, American Book, 1934), p. 55.

beauty in search of the private satisfactions of aestheticism or in quest of consolation in the face of despair. On the contrary, he begins with beauty, finding in it not an hypothesis for the resolution of his doubts but rather the foundation of his certainties. Beauty is related to his vision of the perfection of being rather than to the resolution of any private doubts about its imperfections. Beauty is not a refuge but a platform, and out of his encounter with beauty he tries to move toward theological, philosophical, and moral clarity.

No less important to Edwards' thought than his concept of beauty is his conception of sensibility. To the secondary beauty of harmony and proportion there is a corresponding natural sensibility, and to the primary beauty of being's cordial consent to being there is a corresponding spiritual sensibility. Just as "there is such a thing as good taste of natural beauty" [RA 282], so also there is "spiritual disposition and taste," which "guides a man in his behavior in the world" [RA 284]. "Spiritual understanding primarily consists in this sense, or taste of the moral beauty of divine things" [RA 273], and from it arises "all true experimental knowledge of religion" [RA 275]. "This spiritual sense," he concludes, "is infinitely more noble than . . . any other principle of discerning that a man naturally has, and the object of this sense infinitely greater and more important" [RA 275] than the object of any natural sensibility, for "the immediate object of it is the supreme beauty and excellency of the nature of divine things, as they are in themselves" [RA 271].

Taken together, beauty and sensibility may be said to be the objective and subjective components of the moral or spiritual life. They must be taken and considered together, for they are essentially and internally related, not only as sense of beauty and object of that sense but also as together constituting the more objective and the more subjective aspects of what Edwards calls the "inherent good," consisting in the possession and enjoyment of an "objective good."[4] For example, the communication of the Spirit of God to the creature may be spoken of by Edwards more objectively as the Holy Spirit dwelling in the heart to make the soul "a partaker of God's beauty and Christ's joy" [RA 210] or more subjectively as the communication of a "new spiritual sense, and the new dispositions that attend it," by which there is "a new foundation laid in the nature of the soul" [RA 206] for a new kind of exercise of both understanding and will. That is, the primary beauty,

4. See Ch. 4, pp. 80–84, for further explication of the terms objective good and inherent good.

which is the "moral or spiritual image" of God in man [RA 256, 258] is but
the more objective side of the same reality that is more subjectively expressed
as the spiritual sensibility that is the first essential gift of the Holy Spirit.[5] The
appropriateness of designating beauty as an objective rather than a subjective
determinant of the moral life will appear in Chapter 2, where Edwards' conception of beauty will be shown to be primarily objective, structural, and
relational rather than subjective, emotional, and relativist.

Recent studies of Jonathan Edwards have increasingly recognized the
enormous significance of the twin aesthetic concepts of beauty and sensibility
in his thought. In fact, this recognition constitutes one of the most important
achievements of recent Edwards scholarship. Especially relevant to the present study is the work of Perry Miller, John E. Smith, and Douglas Elwood.
The present state of our understanding of Edwards and the specific contribution to that understanding that this study is designed to provide can be best
described in connection with some brief observations on the work of these
three scholars.[6]

The contemporary reassessment of Edwards began with the seminal work
of Perry Miller, who has done more than any other single scholar to bring
about a recognition of the significance of beauty and sensibility in Edwards'
thought. A substantial portion of his intellectual biography of Edwards is
organized in terms of the antinomy between the objective good and the inherent good, an antinomy that Miller feels is resolved in Edwards' mind by
his vision of the grace of God by which "man is lifted into the perception of
a coincidence of the objective order of pleasure with the inherent order of
virtue, and discovers from afar that both converge in beauty."[7] He concludes

5. "The first effect of the power of God in the heart in REGENERATION is to give
the heart a Divine taste or sense; to cause it to have a relish of the loveliness and sweetness
of the supreme excellency of the Divine nature . . . He that is once brought to see, or
rather to taste, the superlative loveliness of the Divine Being, will need no more" [Grace
37].

6. Joseph Haroutunian, Alan Heimert, Clyde Holbrook, Paul Ramsey, and Thomas
Schafer have also made important contributions to an understanding of Edwards along
lines this study attempts to advance. See the Bibliography and Bibliographical Essay.

7. Perry Miller, *Jonathan Edwards* (New York, Meridian, 1959), p. 298. This major
theme in Miller's treatment of Edwards is of more abiding merit than the other central
theme running through this book—the theme of Edwards' idealism and empiricism in terms
of Locke and Newton. It is a curious thing that Miller should have been able to contribute
so much to our understanding of Edwards' despite a significant error in his formulation of
the objective and inherent good, which "converge in beauty." The two orders of good do in

that Edwards' conception of beauty is "the crown of his thought," though what he offers as justification for this judgment is more suggestive than systematic. He is no less aware of the importance of sensibility than of beauty to the aesthetic character of Edwards' thought. For example, he finds in aesthetics the key to Edwards' ethics not only because beauty and virtue stand under one rule—"the definition of the ethical is beauty"—but also because without the appropriate sensibility that one rule does not operate. In Miller's cryptic summary of the matter, "Grace is sensible."[8]

In his Introduction to the new Yale edition of the *Religious Affections* John E. Smith emphasizes the importance of sensibility in Edwards' analysis of the self; Edwards distinguishes in the self between the faculties of understanding and will and finds that "the affections are no other than the more vigorous and sensible exercises of the inclination and will of the soul" [RA 96]. Smith points out that the importance of the distinction between understanding and will gives us "no clear warrant for making this into an opposition between the two terms" and that therefore the identification of the affections with the will or inclination "gives us no reason for opposing understanding and affections." "The point almost invariably missed," he continues, "is that in Edwards' view the *inclination* . . . involves *both* the will and the mind." "The essential point," he concludes, "is that the affections manifest the center and unity of the self."[9]

Smith understands and in his analysis illuminates what I shall call Edwards' essentially aesthetic-affectional model of the moral or spiritual self. His analysis provides the essential elements for showing that according to this model sensibility is the key to the quality of understanding and to the quality of the will and is the measure of the unity of understanding and will in the self, that is, the measure of integrity in the self.

Smith shows that "by bringing sense within understanding, Edwards resolved some problems of long standing." By reinterpreting human understanding "so as to include a sensible element within it," Edwards was able to distinguish between mere notional understanding and spiritual understanding on the basis of an element internal to the concept of understanding itself

---

fact converge in Edwards' thought. But Miller is in error when, as in the passage quoted, he identifies pleasure with the objective rather than the inherent good. As I will show, the inherent good includes both pleasure and virtue (or beauty) and consists in the possession of an objective good, which, for Edwards, is always defined in terms of beauty or excellence.

8. Ibid., pp. 241, 290, 325.
9. RA, Intro., pp. 13, 14.

and to identify spiritual understanding "with the *new spiritual sense* or the sense which apprehends the beauty and moral excellence of divine things."[10]

Sensibility is also the key to the quality of the will or inclination. "In everything we do, wherein we act voluntarily, 'tis our inclination that governs us in our action" [RA 97]. But "the will never is in any exercise any further than it is affected" [RA 97], so the "more vigorous and sensible exercises of this faculty . . . are called the *affections*" [RA 97].

> Such is man's nature, that he is very inactive, any otherwise than he is influenced by some affection . . . We see the world of mankind to be exceedingly busy and active; and the affections of men are the springs of the motion: take away all love and hatred, all hope and fear, all anger, zeal and affectionate desire, and the world would be, in a great measure, motionless and dead. [RA 101]

The heart of the will or inclination, then, is in the affections. The heart of the affections, in turn, is in the sensibility, whether it is the sensibility of the natural man or the "new spiritual sense" [RA 206], the new "apprehension, idea or sensation of mind" [RA 207f] from which all truly spiritual and gracious affections arise.

According to Edwards' aesthetic-affectional model of the self, sensibility is also the measure of the unity of understanding and will in the self, that is, it is the measure of integrity in the self. As Smith points out at the beginning of his analysis of Edwards' conception of the affections and of their relation to understanding and will in the self:

> The first point to be stressed is that Edwards, for all his ability to draw clear distinctions, nevertheless struggled to preserve the unity and integrity of the self and to avoid compartmentalizing the human functions and powers.[11]

The sensible element to which Smith calls attention serves to distinguish not only between notional and spiritual understanding but also between the self in whom understanding and will are at odds with each other and the self[12] in whom there is integrity of understanding and will in the aesthetic-affectional unity of the self. Where the understanding in question is merely notional, the

10. Ibid., pp. 56, 46, 32.

11. Ibid., p. 11.

12. This may, of course, be the same person as the first, but at a different moment in time.

person remains "an indifferent unaffected spectator" [RA 96], and the faculties of understanding and will, of head and heart, may be said to operate with relative independence. But where the understanding is sensible, where the mind does not only "speculate and behold, but relishes and feels" [RA 272], approves or disapproves, likes or dislikes, loves or hates, consents or dissents, then there is in Edwards' view such an integrity in the self that no clear distinction can be made "between the two faculties of understanding and will, as acting distinctly and separately" [RA 272]. He therefore speaks of such "sensible knowledge" as consisting in "a sense of the heart," for "the heart is the proper subject of it, or the soul as a being that not only beholds, but has inclination, and is pleased or displeased" [RA 272]. The very experience of spiritual sensibility is for Edwards a mark of such integrity of head and heart in the self, for it consists in "a sensation of the mind which loves and rejoices" [RA 113]. Smith concludes at the end of his analysis of Edwards' argument regarding the fourth sign[13] of true religious affections:

> Edwards' chief purpose was to retain understanding in religion as furnishing a rational criterion, but also to redefine it as a *sensible* light involving direct sensible perception and the inclination of the heart. If this point is missed, the basic point of the *Affections* is lost and we shall be forced to rely upon that opposition between the head and the heart which bedeviled the polemics of the Revival and of Romanticism in later American life.[14]

It seems clear that although Edwards employs the terminology of faculty psychology, he does not see understanding and will as distinct faculties at all but rather as names for the manner of the self's engagement with reality as being and as good, respectively. Furthermore, it would seem that since man is inactive unless affected, complete indifference and a purely notional understanding must be regarded as ideal types without empirical exemplification. Insofar as reality is encountered at all, it is encountered by some measure of engagedness of an aesthetic-affectional self, and that engagement involves both the understanding and the will. The understanding is not properly speaking a faculty of the self but is rather Edwards' way of speaking about the self in its engagement with reality as being. This engagement of the un-

---

13. The fourth distinguishing sign of true religious affections reads: "Gracious affections do arise from the mind's being enlightened, rightly and spiritually to understand or apprehend divine things" [RA 266].

14. RA, Intro., p. 33.

derstanding is always to some degree coordinate with the will, which, again, is not a faculty of the self but is rather Edwards' way of speaking about the self in its engagement with reality as good or evil.

The relation between understanding and will in Edwards' aesthetic-affectional model of the self corresponds to the relation between being and good in his aesthetic model of the articulated system of being, which will be examined in Part I. Just as sensibility provides the key to both understanding and will as modes of the self's engagement with reality and the basis for the unity of understanding and will in the self, so beauty provides the key to both being and goodness as well as the foundation of the ultimate unity of being and good in God. Since his objective, structural concept of beauty constitutes Edwards' principal model for interpreting the relation of being to being, including the relation of moral agents to other beings, we shall see that beauty (or deformity) will provide a more objective characterization of moral agents and their relations, corresponding to the more subjective characterization in terms of sensibility.

Edwards' aesthetic-affectional model of the self in its engagement with reality may be represented by a simple figure, which I shall refine in Chapter 3.

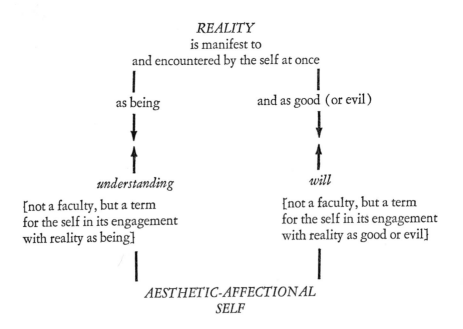

REALITY
is manifest to
and encountered by the self at once

as being   and as good (or evil)

understanding   will

[not a faculty, but a term   [not a faculty, but a term
for the self in its engagement   for the self in its engagement
with reality as being]   with reality as good or evil]

AESTHETIC-AFFECTIONAL
SELF

These and other closely related matters are illuminated by John Smith's analysis of Edwards' thought. But, like Perry Miller before him, Smith gives relatively little attention to an analysis of Edwards' conception of beauty—certainly nothing like the careful analysis he offers of sensibility. And what he does say on the subject is a little misleading, for he finds in the tenth sign of true religious affections "the most explicit evidence" of the "aesthetic side" of Edwards' doctrine of the affections.[15] But the beauty Edwards speaks of there is only the secondary beauty of symmetry and proportion, not the primary beauty of being's consent to being, with which he is more directly concerned in his analysis of the first five of the twelve signs and most especially of the third sign.[16]

In his study of *The Philosophical Theology of Jonathan Edwards* Douglas Elwood sets out "to reunite Edwards the theologian and Edwards the philosopher by locating the principle of correlation in his doctrine of immediacy."[17] He takes note of, though he does not fully exploit, the decisive significance of beauty and sensibility for understanding the distinctiveness of Edwards' thought in relation to the Reformed tradition.

> His stress on the primacy of the aesthetic element over the moral
> and legal in our experience of God places the old Calvinism on a
> very different footing. His neo-Calvinism [stress on the *neo*] ap-

15. The tenth sign reads: "Another thing wherein those affections that are truly gracious and holy, differ from those that are false, is beautiful symmetry and proportion" [RA 365].

16. Primary beauty rather than secondary beauty is central to Edwards' analysis of (especially) the first five signs, though it appears most explicitly only in his formulation of the third sign, which reads: "Those affections that are truly holy, are primarily founded on the loveliness of the moral excellency of divine things. Or (to express it otherwise), a love to divine things for the beauty and sweetness of their moral excellency, is the first beginning and spring of all holy affections" [RA 253f]. By assuming for the moment the virtual identification in his thought between beauty and excellence, which will be shown in Chapter 4 (see pp. 58–67), Edwards' formulation of the second sign can be read as no less explicit about the objective significance of beauty to his thought. It reads: "The first objective ground of gracious affections, is the transcendently excellent and amiable nature of divine things, as they are in themselves; and not any conceived relation they bear to self, or self-interest" [RA 240]. In his analysis of the third sign, Smith takes notice of "the aesthetic element and its importance in Edwards' thought" [RA, Intro., 29] but defers more direct discussion of it until he comes to consider the tenth sign. My suggestion is that Edwards' conception of beauty could have been better clarified by deferring instead in the other direction.

17. Douglas Elwood, *The Philosophical Theology of Jonathan Edwards* (New York, Columbia University Press, 1960), p. 3.

pears most prominently in his fundamental conception of God in terms of absolute *beauty* and not merely absolute *power,* and in his appeal to immediate experience in our knowledge of God. This difference of religious symbol is of the highest importance not merely for an understanding of Edwards but also for the rediscovery of the relevancy of the Christian understanding of God in the mid-twentieth century.

The continuity between Elwood's work and the present essay lies in the fact that what is given or communicated in that divine immediacy is primarily the divine beauty and a corresponding spiritual sensibility. His interest in Edwards' "doctrine of immediacy" leads Elwood to focus his attention upon the aesthetic dimension of sensibility, especially in his chapter on "A 'New Sense of Things.' " But he is also attentive to the significance of the other aesthetic dimension of beauty in Edwards' thought and vision. His examination of Edwards' "ontological realism" moves in the direction of an explicitly aesthetic interpretation of his philosophy of being and of his theology. The discovery of an "essential equation of being and beauty in God" and of an identification of "spiritual beauty as the primary essence of God" in Edwards' thought leads Elwood to move further than anyone else has toward a systematic exploration of the significance of beauty in Edwards' thought. One result of taking the significance of beauty even more radically than Elwood does will be to urge a modification of his characterization of Edwards' thought as "mystical-realist,"[18] at least to the extent of substituting the term aesthetic-realist for mystical-realist.

Although his work does not contribute directly to the sort of systematic analysis with which the present essay is concerned, mention should be made here of Alan Heimert's *Religion and the American Mind: From the Great Awakening to the Revolution.* As a cultural historian Heimert breaks new ground in the study of Edwards and the Edwardseans by showing, especially in the chapter on "The Beauty and Good Tendency of Union,"[19] the historical consequences of taking seriously precisely those dimensions of Edwards' thought and vision with which I am concerned. He sees and understands the implications of the fact that "it was not ratiocination, but an aesthetic perception of the good, that according to Edwards determined human action."

18. Ibid., pp. 9, 29, 30, 28, 25.

19. Alan Heimert, *Religion and the American Mind: From the Great Awakening to the Revolution* (Cambridge, Harvard University Press, 1966), pp. 94–158.

And he shows that in Edwards' view God's governance and redemption of the world depends upon no awful display of the divine power but rather upon the regeneration of human sensibility to the attractive power of the divine beauty. "What distinguished Edwardeanism from the moral system of his contemporaries," Heimert observes, "was his definition of virtue as 'love to being in general'—a definition which made heartfelt love of the beautiful society and active longing after its establishment the essence and test for Calvinists of the regenerate personality." But he overstates his case for the location of that divine beauty in human community when he concludes from his reading of *The Nature of True Virtue* that Edwards "made not God but men . . . the noblest object of Christian regard" or, put more bluntly, that "in substance, the God of Jonathan Edwards was a supremely excellent Christian commonwealth."[20] This is a humanistic reading of Edwards that obscures the radical monotheism so central to his whole programme. Love of being-in-general is not identical with—though it certainly does include—love of any society or commonwealth, however extensive or beautiful. Heimert's achievement is nonetheless significant: he appreciates and begins filling out the corporate dimensions of a Christian moral existence understood in terms of beauty and sensibility, a matter insufficiently stressed in previous interpretations of Edwards.

It is in some respects curious that although recent studies of Edwards have recognized the enormous significance of the twin aesthetic concepts of beauty and sensibility in his thought, such recognition has not as yet led to a systematic examination of his conception of beauty that can stand comparison with the careful attention devoted to his conception of the corresponding sensibility. Although much has been written about the sense of beauty, not nearly enough attention has been given to the object of that sense—to the beauty itself, as it is understood by Edwards and as it operates in his thought. The following chapters are therefore addressed specifically to this task in order to help right the balance in our understanding of the distinctively aesthetic dimensions of his thought and vision.

20. Ibid., pp. 194, 112, 104.

PART I

BEAUTY

2

A PRELIMINARY DEFINITION

Jonathan Edwards' conception of beauty is at once philosophical and theological. The preeminence of beauty among the divine perfections corresponds to the central place of beauty in his vision of reality as one grand system of being and good. When he speaks of God as "the foundation and fountain of all being and all beauty" [RA 15], he is not simply preaching or praising God or commending Him to men; he is giving expression to his understanding of the Divine Being as he has known and experienced Him, and he means to offer a philosophical as well as a religious view of the reality there encountered. All his systematic works, and many of his others as well, offer both theological and philosophical arguments for the positions he defends. He sees the two tasks as essentially one because their common object is in the end One. Ontology (the science of being) and theology (the science of Divine Being) have a common object. If we remember that the theological argument to which we will attend in Part II of this essay is the grander of the two, we may begin in Part I, as Edwards himself sometimes does, with the philosophical argument first, insofar as that can be separated from the theological argument in a system of thought that is so much of a single piece.

Edwards' entire theological-philosophical-moral enterprise is framed by his reverence for being, his love of beauty, and his faith in Him who is

> the foundation and fountain of all being and all beauty . . . of whom, and through whom, and to whom is all being and all perfection; and whose being and beauty are, as it were, the sum and comprehension of all existence and excellence. [TV 15]

This manner of expressing himself is typical of Edwards. According to his vision of reality, this is the broadest characterization that can be offered of it; we encounter and experience and know it at once as being and good, as existence and excellence, as being and perfection, or as being and beauty. The order of our investigation in Part I is set by this view of reality; in Chapter 3 we consider beauty as the first principle of being, in Chapter 4 as the measure and objective foundation of the perfection of being, and in

Chapter 5 as the principle of the ultimate unity of being and perfection, of being and good. But first we must undertake a preliminary delineation of Edwards' conception of beauty.

Beauty can be defined, even if only inadequately and for limited purposes, and Edwards was frequently at pains to define it. But definition is at best only a beginning, for beauty is certainly among those "things of this nature" Edwards had in mind when he said about divine love that "things of this nature are not properly capable of definition. They are better felt than defined" [Grace 36]. Elsewhere, in discussing "the glory of God" he takes note of the obscurity of definitions in such matters,

> perhaps an obscurity which is unavoidable, through the imperfection of language, and words being less fitted to express things of so sublime a nature. And therefore the thing may possibly be better understood by using many words and a variety of expressions, by a particular consideration of it, than by any short definition. [EC 253]

If we are to approach things of this nature discursively rather than directly through experience, we must proceed more by description than by definition. It should soon become clear that Edwards' reservations about the efficacy of definitions should not be taken as signs of anti-intellectualism or of non-cognitivism. In fact, he follows the above observation about things "better felt than defined" by noting immediately that:

> Love is a term as clear in its signification, and that does as naturally suggest to the mind the things signified by it, as any other term or terms that we can find out or substitute in its room. But yet there may be a great deal of benefit in descriptions that may be given of this heavenly principle though they are all imperfect. They may serve to limit the signification of the term and distinguish this principle from other things, and to exclude counterfeits, and also more clearly to explain some things that do appertain to its nature.
>   Divine Love, as it has God for its object may be thus described. [Grace 36]

He immediately launches his description by speaking of "the first thing in Divine Love" as "a relish of the supreme excellency of the Divine nature, inclining the heart to God as the chief good" [Grace 36]. We may profitably follow his example and, by attending to how he uses words, move descriptively and analytically toward an understanding of his conception of beauty.

There are two principal kinds of beauty; both of them are varieties of the single rule of beauty as agreement or consent, as opposed to discord and dissent.

> There are two sorts of agreement or consent of one thing to another. (1) There is a *cordial* agreement; that consists in concord and union of mind and heart . . . (2) There is a *natural* union or agreement; which, though some image of the other, is entirely a distinct thing; the will, disposition, or affections of the heart having no concern in it, but consisting only in uniformity and consent of nature, form, quality, etc. [TV 31, italics added]

Primary beauty, variously referred to as true, highest, moral, spiritual, divine, or original beauty, consists in one kind of consent or agreement: the cordial or heart-felt consent of being to being. It is essential to primary beauty that the will, disposition, or affection of the heart be involved in the consent. Secondary beauty, inferior to the former and otherwise referred to as natural beauty, consists in a very different sort of agreement or consent—although it may be an image or shadow of primary beauty—that is, "a mutual consent and agreement of different things, in form, manner, quantity, and visible end or design; called by the various names of regularity, order, uniformity, symmetry, proportion, harmony," and "uniformity in the midst of variety" [TV 28]. Edwards regards the visible fitness of a thing to its end or use as of this same sort of beauty or consent. He frequently speaks of these two kinds of beauty as spiritual beauty and natural beauty rather than as primary and secondary beauty.

Both primary and secondary beauty are forms of the one rule of consent. And both of them involve the relation of being to being. But it is not so clearly essential to secondary beauty—as it clearly is to primary beauty— that a relation of being to being be involved. Edwards does say that without consent there can be no beauty or excellency. But secondary beauty can be spoken of as internal to one being (unless the perceiving being is taken into account) in a sense that cannot be true of primary beauty; for primary beauty may be attributed to one being only by virtue of some relation between that being and some other being or beings, and in the final analysis primary beauty may be attributed to one being only by virtue of its relation to being-in-general or to "being simply considered." God, Who is being-in-general, both the sum and the fountain of all being, is the only being Who has primary beauty internal to Himself. " 'Tis peculiar to God that He has beauty within Himself" [Mind 45]. He alone both is being as such and consents to being as such. For all other beings a relation to being-in-general means a relation to other beings, although it should be noted that for Edwards this may be an internal relation of participation rather than a strictly external relation. Still, even in the Divine Being plurality is required, or there can be no consent in Him. "One alone cannot be excellent" or beautiful "inasmuch as in such case there can be no consent" [Misc. 117]. On this platform Edwards erects his ontological doctrine of the Trinity.[1]

One essential difference between primary and secondary beauty lies in the presence or absence of "cordiality" in the consent, that is, in whether or not the consent is given by a being that has a will—a spiritual being. Primary beauty is peculiar to spiritual beings, for they alone have wills, or rather, they alone are willing beings capable of giving consent or dissent. A clash of colors in a dress may detract from its beauty and may be spoken of as involving a relationship of dissent between the colors. But it is more properly a matter of disharmony than of dissent; the terms consent and dissent are borrowed from language about spiritual relations and can be applied to material relations only by analogy, for "there is no other *proper* consent but that of minds, even of their will" [Mind 45, italics added].

It should be noted in this connection that the object of consent is as essential to the definition of beauty as the character of the consenting being. In the case of primary or spiritual beauty, that object must be either other minds or other things. If the consent is "of minds towards minds, it is *love,* and when of minds towards other things, it is *choice*" [Mind 45, italics added]. Love and choice, then, are forms of consent and beauty.

While primary beauty is peculiar to spiritual beings, secondary beauty is found in all kinds of beings. Although the latter is distinct from and inferior to the former, it constitutes an image of primary beauty in that it too is a sort of consent. The two are nonsymmetrically related: everything that has primary beauty also has secondary beauty, but the reverse may or may not be true. Secondary beauty may be found in immaterial or spiritual things and relations as well as in external or material things and relations. Thus the secondary beauty of harmony and proportion is to be found in the very being

1. See Ch. 7.

and works of God [RA 365], and it is as "plain and sensible" in the order and harmony of society as it is in the proportions of a beautiful building [TV 35]. Edwards finds the secondary form of beauty not only in the proportions of the visible world, the harmonies of the audible world, or the tastes of the sensible world but also in social justice and personal virtue, in the fruits of conscience, and in the wisdom that consists in "the united tendency of thoughts, ideas and particular volitions, to one general purpose" [TV 36]. But even if volitions are involved—a condition essential to primary beauty—the beauty is still of a secondary kind if the object (the system of being to which their united consent is given) is some limited system of being rather than being-in-general.

If the beauty is to be primary rather than secondary, the consent must be to being simply considered, as being, and not for any qualifications of that being. Such a test can be met only by God Himself, for only to His "perfect vision" can being-in-general or being simply considered appear as an object, although Edwards himself recognizes the difficulties involved in suggesting that being can ever appear other than as qualified, determinate, or particular being.[2] An approach to such perfect vision consists in seeing things as they are and treating them accordingly, as opposed to seeing and treating them only as they are related to our own being, our own needs and interests. "True love to God primarily consists in a supreme regard to him for what he is in himself. The tendency of true virtue is to treat everything as it is, and according to its nature" [OS 332]. This would not require anything so pretentious as seeing all things. But it would involve a disposition to see things as they are in themselves, which for Edwards means seeing things at once in their particularity and as they are related in consent and dissent to the whole system of being, rather than seeing and treating them primarily in terms of their relation to our particular being or as they are related in consent and dissent to the limited communities of beings in which we have a special interest. Such a passion for objectivity is basic to Edwards' understanding of the nature of that true virtue that is a form of primary or spiritual beauty. This view of the relation between primary and secondary beauty constitutes the framework for Edwards' objectivist program against utilitarianism at every level.

In addition to the distinction between primary and secondary beauty, a second and closely related distinction with respect to beauty is important. Beauty

2. See pp. 97–99.

is either general or particular. Particular beauty may be affirmed of whatever "appears beautiful when considered only with regard to . . . a limited and private sphere" [TV 2]. General beauty may be affirmed only of what "appears beautiful when viewed most perfectly, comprehensively and universally with regard to its tendencies and connections" [TV 2f]. The essential thing to note here is the "limited and private sphere" with respect to which particular beauty is defined, in contrast to the wider "tendencies and connections" essential to the definition of general beauty.

A third distinction with regard to beauty must be joined to these two, for any particular beauty, when viewed as a part of some more comprehensive system of being, may be found to dissent from that larger system, in which case it must be pronounced false or confined beauty; otherwise, it is true beauty. The test is again a severe one: to pass muster as true beauty the consent must be to nothing short of the universal system of being!

> That which is beautiful considered by itself separately and deformed considered as a part of something else more extended, or beautiful only with respect to itself and a few other things and not as a part of that which contains all things—the universe—is *false beauty* and a *confined beauty*. That which is beautiful with respect to the universality of things has a generally extended excellence and a true beauty; and the more extended or limited its system is, the more confined or extended is its beauty. [Mind 14, italics added. Note the chiasmus at the end; otherwise the passage might be misread.]

Remembering that when Edwards speaks of true beauty his model is not the secondary beauty of harmony and proportion but the primary beauty of being's cordial consent to being will help keep the severity of this test in proper perspective. He does not mean that nothing can be regarded as beautiful unless it is viewed in relation to the universal system of being but only that if so viewed, what has appeared as beauty may appear as deformity with respect to a more extended system of being. He sometimes speaks of this distinction as one between universal beauty and partial beauty.

In sum, beauty may be distinguished as primary or secondary, spiritual or natural, as general or particular, as true or false, and as universal or partial. Primary beauty may be defined as the cordial consent of being to being-in-general or to particular being, with a regard to its tendencies and connections with the universal system of being.[3] Secondary beauty may be defined as harmony or proportion in either system of being, general or particular. Secondary or particular beauty may also be true beauty; but it is false or confined or partial beauty if when regarded as part of a larger system of being it appears as deformity or dissent from other being or beings.

Consent is the first thing in beauty, but it is not itself sufficient to the definition of beauty. The other elements progressively involved in the full definition of beauty may be represented as follows:

(1) *consent*
(2) consent *to being*
(3) consent *of being* to being
(4) *cordial* consent of being to being
(5) cordial consent of being *to being-in-general* (i.e. as being)

This simple mnemonic device may serve as the framework for a second way of summing up the elements essential to true, general, primary, spiritual beauty. (1) The most essential thing in beauty is whether it is defined by one or the other rule of consent, whether it is defined by the cordial consent of being to being or by proportion and harmony. (2) Primary or spiritual beauty is objectively defined, that is, it is defined by reference to the object of consent. If the consent is of mind toward minds, it is love, and if it is of mind toward things, it is choice. (3) The nature of the consenting being is essential to the definition of the beauty, and if it is to be primary or spiritual beauty, the consent must be given by intelligent or spiritual being. (4) The consent in spiritual beauty must be cordial, that is, heart-felt and willing consent and not merely rational assent. (5) The highest and ultimate determinant of beauty is being-in-general, both objectively (only consent that has being-in-general as its object constitutes perfect beauty) and subjectively (only being-in-general is perfectly beautiful). Only being-in-general both has perfect beauty and is the adequate object and norm of cordially consenting being.

This definition will suffice to get us on our way in the process of triangulating[4] Edwards' conception of beauty and its place in his thought.

3. The limitations of definition are clear at this point. See pp. 96–98 for an examination of the distinction (so important in Edwards' thought) between benevolence and complacence and between benevolent being and complacent being as the objects of benevolence and of complacence.

4. By triangulation I mean the location of one thing by relating it to at least two other things with which it is connected—in the present case the location and exploration of Edwards' conception of beauty with reference to his understanding of being and to his

Three additional principles may be distinguished as essential to Edwards' definition of beauty. Attending to them will help "to limit the signification of the term" and "to exclude counterfeits" as well as "to explain some things that do appertain to" [Grace 36] the nature of beauty as he understands it. It is important to anticipate possible misconceptions about his view of beauty —misconceptions flowing from apprehensions about presumed subjectivism attendant upon the intrusion of aesthetic notions into ethics or misconceptions flowing from the wide diversity of ways in which men have thought about beauty.

Beauty is objective. This does not mean that beauty is in the thing if the thing is finite, for only God has beauty in Himself. Nor is beauty only in the eye of the beholder. For although Edwards traces to the eye of the beholder much that passes for beauty and much that is only limited or partial beauty, he does not accept that as the only alternative to locating beauty as an immediate property of the object.[5] Beauty is objective in that it is constituted by objective relations of consent and dissent among beings, relations into which the subject (or beholder) may enter and participate but the beauty of which is defined by conformity to God (consent to being-in-general) rather than by degree of subjective pleasure.

Accordingly, it is Edwards' view that deformity rather than ugliness is the opposite of beauty. Although the notions of form and deformity involve the presence of a subject, deformity refers to the object and to objective relations, while ugliness refers to the subject and to subjective responses. If the measure of beauty is found to be primarily in the response of the subject, then the opposite of beauty will be designated as ugliness. Such is the case, for

---

understanding of that aspect of reality variously designated as goodness, excellence, or value. The term triangulation is borrowed from geometry and the vocabulary of the surveyor.

An instructive model for this procedure is offered by O. R. Jones' study of *The Concept of Holiness* (London, George Allen & Unwin, Ltd., 1961), in which he undertakes to illuminate that concept by examining it in connection with several concepts and notions with which it is intimately associated: fear, power, separateness, wholeness, goodness, divine personality, and what he calls "perfect vision." It is essentially the last of these concepts that, as Jones develops and makes use of it for philosophical analysis, lends originality to his study and offers interesting corroboration for some of the conclusions to which the present study will also come. The way in which he relates holiness and "perfect vision" is similar in some respects to the relations between beauty and sensibility in Edwards' thought.

5. Edwards, of course, rejects this view of what location is and what it means as well as the attendant notion of the relation between subject and object in experience.

example, with the subjectivist theory of beauty developed by Edmund Burke in Edwards' time.[6] But if the measure of beauty is found to be objectively determined by the relation of being to being, then the opposite of beauty will be designated as deformity. This is the case with Edwards' objectivist theory of beauty. Beauty is defined as the consent of being to being; dissent from being constitutes deformity.

It is important to remember in connection with Edwards' objectivism that beauty is as important as it is in his thought largely because it provides him with a model for what cannot be known without being enjoyed. The objectively determined moral life is one that in Edwards' view is endowed with what Kierkegaard calls subjectivity. For Edwards objectivity does not mean a lack of passion but rather a passion for seeing things as they are and responding accordingly. Disinterestedness does not mean for him an absence of interest or of subjectivity but rather a passionate interest in conforming the subjective order of pleasure to the objective order of beauty. Primary beauty is available not to the passive spectator but to the engaged man as a spiritual agent. It is perceived truly, not according to our capacity to stand back as before a painting but according to the inclination of our being, the core of which Edwards defines as sensibility. This is why it is important to remember that the primary model of beauty for Edwards is being's consent to being rather than proportion or harmony. The latter is real beauty, but it does not provide the primary model of beauty for his philosophical theology or for his interpretation of the moral and religious life. That is precisely why he rejected the moral theory of Hutcheson,[7] which took as its primary model and norm the proportion and harmony that Edwards found to be only secondary beauty.

Edwards tried to understand all things in relation to God. In settling upon beauty as the most distinguishing perfection or attribute of God he chose a concept that enabled him to conceive of God in objective, structural, and ontological terms and at the same time to make it philosophically (and not merely dogmatically) clear that (and why) God can be fully known only if He is the direct object of enjoyment—that man's knowledge of God is in part a function of his enjoyment of Him. With his objectivist concept of beauty Edwards can insist upon the objectivity of God while also affirming

6. Edmund Burke, *A Philosophical Enquiry Into the Origin of Ideas of the Sublime and Beautiful,* ed. J. T. Boulton (London, Routledge and Kegan Paul, 1958). The original publication date was 1757.

7. Francis Hutcheson, *An Inquiry Into the Original of Our Ideas of Beauty and Virtue* (London, 1725).

that God cannot be adequately known without being enjoyed. For beauty is objective with respect to the self, and yet it is available only in and through the enjoyment of it. It is not discernible to the indifferent eye. Though indifferent men may know many things about it, they do not and cannot know beauty itself.

Beauty is not self-contained. Beauty is objective in the above sense, but it is not essentially self-contained. The beauty of proportion and harmony is relatively self-contained, but the beauty of being's consent to being is not. Nothing is beautiful in a general way without regard to its "tendencies and connections," that is, without regard to its relations to being other than itself.

One way Edwards formulates this principle with regard to finite beings is in terms of consistency: secondary beauty lies in anyone's or anything's being consistent with itself; primary beauty lies in being consistent with other beings—ultimately with nothing less than "the great system, and . . . God who is the head of it" [TV 62f]—and is therefore not self-contained. For example, Edwards distinguishes "pure love," which "implies a disposition to feel, to desire, and to act as though others were one with ourselves," from "self-love," which "implies an inclination to feel and act as one with ourselves" [TV 61]. He finds that "natural conscience" is no more than an expression of such self-love or "self-union," for it is "a disposition in man to be uneasy in a consciousness of being inconsistent with himself" [TV 61].

> Thus approving of actions, because we therein act as in agreement with ourselves . . . is quite a different thing from approving or disapproving actions because in them we are united with being in general: which is loving or hating actions from a sense of the primary beauty of true virtue, and of the odiousness of sin. The former of these principles is private; the latter is public, and truly benevolent in the highest sense. The former—an inclination to agree with ourselves—is a natural principle: but the latter—an agreement or union of heart to the great system, and to God the head of it, who is all and all in it—is a divine principle. [TV 62f]

" 'Tis peculiar to God that He has beauty within Himself" [Mind 45], says Edwards. Yet even the beauty of God—and so also of being-in-general—is not self-contained, for it consists more properly in his effulgence and propensity to creative self-communication than in his self-sufficiency and in benevolence more than in complacence.[8]

8. See Ch. 7, pp. 168–70.

The corrective against aestheticism in Edwards' deployment of beauty as the primary model of order in the moral as well as the natural world lies in his objectivist definition of beauty and in his systematic insistence that virtue and holiness and spiritual beauty are founded not in consent to beauty but in consent to being. Beauty is the first principle of being, but it is ultimately to be resolved into being, rather than the reverse.

The model of beauty is the beautifying rather than the beautified. The distinction between the beautifying and the beautified corresponds to Edwards' distinction between primary and secondary beauty.[9] His conception of pri-

---

9. This distinction and order of priority correspond closely to Henry Nelson Wieman's distinction between creative and created good in *The Source of Human Good* (Chicago, University of Chicago Press, 1946) and even more closely to Alfred North Whitehead's distinction between the major and minor forms of beauty in *Adventures of Ideas* (New York, Macmillan, 1933).

The correspondence between Edwards' definition of beauty and Whitehead's is remarkable. Not only does Edwards' distinction between spiritual and natural beauty correspond closely to Whitehead's distinction between the major and minor forms of beauty, but Whitehead's view of both these forms of beauty as varieties of "mutual adaptation" corresponds to Edwards' view of spiritual and natural beauty as varieties of consent.

Whitehead defines beauty as "the mutual adaptation of the several factors in an occasion of experience" (*Adventures of Ideas,* p. 324). This is remarkably like Edwards' basic definition of beauty as being's consent to being. Whitehead then notes that adaptation implies an end and that therefore "beauty is only defined when the aim of the 'adaptation' has been analyzed" (p. 324). This move corresponds to Edwards' insistence that beauty cannot be defined apart from an analysis of the object or system of being to which the consent is given. Whitehead sees this object, end, or aim as twofold—to which there are two corresponding forms of beauty, according to the nature and object of the "mutual adaptation."

1. "It is in the first place, *the absence of mutual inhibition* among the various prehensions . . . When this aim is secured, there is the minor form of beauty, the absence of painful clash, the absence of vulgarity.

2. "In the second place, there is *the major form of Beauty.* This form presupposes the first form, and adds to it the condition that the conjunction in one synthesis of the various prehensions introduces new contrasts of objective content with objective content" (p. 324, italics added).

"The absence of mutual inhibition" is a mode of "mutual adaptation" that corresponds closely to Edwards' view of harmony and proportion as a secondary form of beauty. Whitehead's major form of beauty, like Edwards' primary beauty, involves moving beyond this confined mutual adaptation (Edwards: limited consent) to a reaching out toward larger systems of being—even to being-in-general. The creative, beautifying, major form of beauty "is more accurately to be considered as a definition of the term 'Beautiful'," says Whitehead, for "in all its senses, 'beautiful' means the inherent capacity for the promotion of Beauty" (pp. 328–29). Elsewhere he finds that "beauty, moral and aesthetic, is the aim of existence" (*Essays in Science and Philosophy* [New York, Philosophical Library, 1948], p. 8).

mary beauty is more fully exemplified by the creative and dynamic idea of
the beautifying, while his conception of secondary beauty corresponds more
closely to the more static and passive idea of the beautified. He would have
agreed with Shaftesbury that "the beautifying, not the beautified, is the really
beautiful,"[10] for beauty functions in his thought more as a formative principle of being than as a principle of well-formed being; it is more fully exhibited in bestowing beauty than in receiving it.

Because the primary model of beauty is provided by the beauty of being's
consent to being rather than by the beauty of harmony and proportion, it is
more properly and fully exhibited in creative spiritual relations of consent
than in created material relations of proportion. The latter is real beauty but
is ontologically and morally of a secondary nature. The beauty of the well-
formed is created more than it is creative, although Edwards does assign it an
important creative role in the divine economy.[11] But the real model of beauty
is the beautifying—that which has the power to consent to being, to beau-
tify, to bestow beauty. This makes for another count, so to speak, on which
God is most beautiful, for He is the fountain of all beauty, the beautifying One, the bestower of all beauty. He is both being-itself and beauty-itself,
both the powerfully beautiful subject and the attractively beautiful objective
Being, consent to Whom constitutes participation in beauty.

The continuity between the two basic varieties of beauty—spiritual and
natural—is as important to Edwards as their difference of definition, for it is
the analogy of harmony and proportion and form to the primary beauty of
being's consent to being that he has in mind when he speaks, for example, of
the "symmetry and beauty in God's workmanship" [RA 365] or of the "conformity to Christ" of "proportioned Christians" [CF 409]. That is, these
phrases are not simply conventional formulae of Christian morality or piety
but provide a systematic way of relating the elements of the Christian life to
"the things which are" and to Him Who Is.

10. Anthony Ashley Cooper [Third Earl of Shaftesbury], *The Moralist, a Philosophical Rhapsody* (Treatise Five of *Characteristics* [London, 1732]), p. 404. Edwards would
have disagreed, however, with Shaftesbury's reasons for coming to such a pregnant conclusion because he was not inclined to the same Platonic division between form and
matter.
11. See Ch. 8, esp. pp. 206f.

3

BEAUTY AND BEING

It would be impossible to get very far in discussing Edwards' conception of beauty and its place in his thought without discussing his concept of being. As Douglas Elwood has noted,

> reverence for Divine Being . . . remained throughout his life the fundamental disposition of his mind. Without an understanding of this [his] basic philosophy of being, the student of Edwards' thought reaches an impasse in any attempt to relate the many phases of his theophilosophic system.[1]

This is no less the case with respect to his ethics than it would be with respect to any other aspect of his thought, for ethics involves an understanding of human nature, and Edwards always remained true to an early admonition he directed to himself as a guide to his studies: "In treating of human nature, treat first of Being in general."[2] Our approach to his ethics has been through his conception of beauty, beginning with a look at consent as the first thing in beauty and proceeding immediately to the present consideration of beauty and being. The advisability of this route of approach to his understanding of the moral life is prefigured for us already in the words with which he concludes the first of his "Notes on the Mind," especially if we read them with his definition of primary beauty in mind: "Happiness strictly consists in the perception of these three things: of the consent of being to its own being; of its own consent to being; and of being's consent to being" [Mind 1]. Not only happiness but also virtue and holiness are forms of beauty, and love, which Edwards says "is certainly the perfection as well as the happiness of a spirit" [Misc. 117], is also a form of beauty.

The first thing to note is that Edwards' philosophy is a philosophy of being, and the articulation of that philosophy is the articulation of a system of

---

1. Elwood, *Philosophical Theology*, p. 25.
2. Edwards, *Works*, ed. Sereno E. Dwight (New York, 1829–30), *1*, 665.

being.[3] Being is the highest metaphysical concept for him. Nothing has a prior or higher ontological status. Even God is not beyond being. For example, God is not the One beyond being, as in some forms of Platonism and neo-Platonism, but is identified with being-itself.[4] The second thing to note is that if being is the highest ontological principle, not even beauty is above it or independent of it but is to be resolved into being.

Any philosophy of being must make some first move in the articulation of its ontology or metaphysics of being, and that first move will exercise a decisive influence upon the manner in which the entire system is articulated. Edwards' concept of beauty serves him in making that first move. Beauty is both ontologically and logically the first concept and category essential to the articulation of his system of being. "Without beauty what would become of being? Without being what would become of beauty?"[5] These words from the *Enneads* might well have been written by Edwards, so intimate is the relation between beauty and being in his vision of reality and in his thought. He finds that beauty provides the first and fullest and most adequate way of filling in the right-hand side of the equation "being is $\underline{x}$ " or "being consists in $\underline{x}$." Therefore, the pattern or manner in which his system of being is articulated bears the mark of the priority of beauty among the characteristics of being, for beauty has its own manner of articulation.[6]

3. No effort is made in this chapter to offer a thorough exposition and analysis of Edwards' doctrine of being. I undertake to say only as much about it as seems essential to the task at hand. A more thorough analysis will be found in Douglas Elwood, *The Philosophical Theology of Jonathan Edwards,* where Edwards' philosophy of being is developed in terms of the doctrine of divine immediacy, and in Thomas A. Schafer's even more extensive exposition and analysis in "The Concept of Being in the Thought of Jonathan Edwards" (unpublished Ph.D. dissertation, Duke University, 1951).

4. Edwards' graded system of being stands loosely in the Platonic tradition. But in this respect his position is to be distinguished from that of those Platonists such as Plotinus and Ficino who held that unity is ontologically prior to being and who therefore equated God with the One beyond being rather than with being-in-general or being as such.

It is interesting to note, in the light of the influence of the Florentine Platonists upon the Cambridge Platonists, who were in turn a major resource for Edwards' reflections on being, that Pico della Mirandola, Ficino's most eminent contemporary at Florence, took the opposite position from Ficino's on this matter—as had Augustine and Aquinas before him—and held that being is a higher metaphysical principle than unity.

5. Plotinus, *Enneads,* 5.8.9, quoted in Jacques Maritain, *Creative Intuition in Art and Poetry* (New York, Pantheon Books, 1953), p. 160.

6. See, e.g., Suzanne K. Langer's distinction between discursive and presentational symbolism, according to which the meaning and the elements of articulation in presentational symbolism are internal to the whole rather than strung out external to one another as in discourse, in *Philosophy in a New Key* (New York, New American Library, 1952), esp.

This statement contains the major theme for what is to follow in this chapter. And I call attention once again to the two elements of that theme: that beauty has its own manner of articulation and that the priority beauty will be shown to have among the characteristics of being decisively informs the pattern or manner in which Edwards' whole system of being is articulated.

Augustine and others have found that being as being is good and have used the concept of beauty to help spell out the meaning of their affirmation of the goodness of being. Edwards finds rather that being as being is beautiful or has beauty, and he uses such concepts as goodness to help spell out the meaning of his affirmation of its beauty.[7] Being as such consents to being. "Being or existence is what is necessarily agreeable to being" [Mind 62]. Because beauty has its own distinctive manner of articulation and because it provides Edwards with his fundamental model of order in terms of which to understand every other kind of order, his system of being is different in character from systems that, in terms of other primary models of order, attempt to derive all being from the plenitude and fullness and effulgence of being-itself. Many considerations shape Edwards' ontology, but none is more decisive than his concept of beauty and the fact that it provides him with his fundamental model of order. Beauty functions in his thought not only as a concept, then, but also as a category or a mode of order in terms of which all things are to be understood. By calling beauty a category I mean that it is a concept without which one could not give an adequate account of being. As such, it is at once a category of interpretation and a category of being, in which all

---

Ch. IV, "Discursive and Presentational Forms," pp. 63–83. The theory is given further development in *Feeling and Form* (New York, Scribner's, 1953).

7. The ontological priority of beauty in Edwards' thought suggests that his kinship with A. N. Whitehead may be at least as great as with Paul Tillich among contemporary figures. Like Tillich, Edwards tries to answer the ontological question: "What does it mean to be? What are the structures common to everything that is, to everything that participates in being?" (Tillich, *Love, Power, and Justice* [New York, Oxford University Press, 1954], p. 19). And like Tillich he understands ontology to be descriptive or analytic, not speculative: "It analyses the encountered reality trying to find the structural elements which enable a being to participate in being" (Tillich, p. 23). But like Whitehead, and unlike Tillich, who makes no significant use of the concept of beauty, when Edwards comes to characterize "the texture of being itself which is effective in everything that is" (Tillich, p. 20), he finds the concept of beauty to be the first one essential to the task. Not only does Edwards' conception of beauty closely resemble Whitehead's, but for both men the concept of beauty plays a similarly critical role in their thought by providing them with their primary model of order. In *Religion in the Making* (Cleveland, World Publishing Company, Meridian Books, 1960, p. 101) Whitehead finds "the foundation of the world in the aesthetic experience, rather than—as with Kant—in the cognitive and conceptive experience. All

things and events participate positively or negatively insofar as they have being—just as in the case of categories such as time, space, and causality.

The priority of beauty among the characteristics of being in Edwards' thought does not appear to be self-evident. At least the radical priority of beauty I am proposing is not self-evident.[8] The matter calls for systematic development. How does it appear that beauty is the primary characteristic of being, decisively shaping the manner in which his whole system of being is articulated? The most impressive evidence for this assertion is more theological than philosophical, having to do with the priority of beauty in the Divine Being. This theological evidence will be considered later, but its existence should be kept in mind as we consider the supporting philosophical evidence.

The philosophical evidence for the priority and formative significance of Edwards' conception of beauty for the articulation of his philosophy of being is given schematic formulation in Diagram A, which structures the relations among the essential concepts with which we must now be concerned.

Several things need to be said in explanation of the diagram itself and its basic rationale before we can explore more discursively some aspects of Edwards' thought that the diagram is intended to clarify. I have said that according to him we encounter reality as being and as good.[9] That provides the basic pattern for the lower half of the diagram, of "being as manifest and encountered." Edwards' principal model for interpreting reality manifest and encountered as being is the secondary beauty of proportion and harmony. Hence, all the terms under (a) in the diagram are, for him, forms of secondary beauty. His principal model for interpreting reality manifest and encountered as good is the primary beauty of being's consent to being. Hence, all the terms under (b) are forms of primary beauty.

---

order is therefore aesthetic order, and the moral order is merely certain aspects of aesthetic order. The actual world is the outcome of the aesthetic order, and the aesthetic order is derived from the immanence of God."

8. Neither Douglas Elwood nor Thomas Schafer, Edwards' most careful students in this matter, make this point in so many words, much less develop its significance systematically. However, Schafer comes very near doing so by his emphasis upon being as good, as distinguished from being as one and being as truth (Shafer, "The Concept of Being," esp. Ch. V, pp. 88–120). Elwood's whole treatment comes even nearer doing the job with his strong emphasis upon beauty among the divine perfections and upon the place of beauty, sensibility, and the aesthetic in Edwards' thought (Elwood, *Philosophical Theology*). My own proposals appear to me to be consistent with the best insight of Shafer, Elwood, and others regarding Edwards' complex philosophy of being, while going farther toward accurately representing the place of beauty in his system of being.

9. Where the context requires it, in accordance with Edwards' own vocabulary, I shall

DIAGRAM A

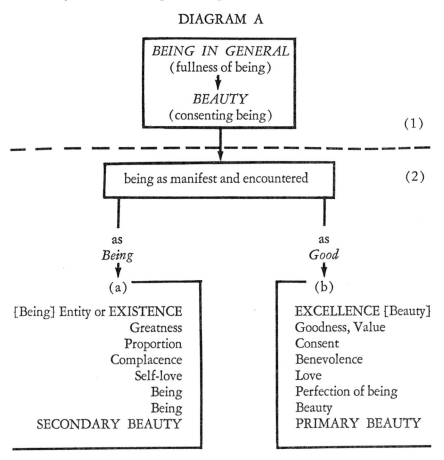

All the terms on side (a) of the diagram can be said to be correlative with each other because they have in common their interpretation by Edwards in terms of secondary beauty. All the terms on side (b) can be said to be correlative with each other for the same reason—they are all interpreted by Edwards in terms of primary beauty. On the other hand, each pair of terms that appear opposite each other in the diagram can be said to be coordinate or corresponding terms. For example, existence and excellence are coordinate with each other, as are greatness and goodness, being and beauty, and so on. This schematic representation of Edwards' thought on these matters was suggested

---

use the terms being-itself and being-in-general; where the context permits I shall use instead the term reality where the reference is to being irrespective of the distinction between being and good.

by his frequent use of these sets of terms in coordinate pairs as they appear in the diagram.

Primary beauty has greater ontological and moral weight than secondary beauty does. Therefore, in each coordinate set of terms in Diagram A the one on side (b) has the same kind of ontological (and, in some cases, moral) priority over its coordinate term on side (a) that primary beauty has over secondary beauty. Excellence has a higher ontological status than existence, goodness than greatness, and so on, though excellence is manifest only in existent being, goodness is encountered only where being has some measure of greatness, perfection is always perfection of some determinate being. Hence, the pairs of terms for being as manifest and encountered may appropriately be referred to as coordinate terms.

I have spoken so far only about the lower half of Diagram A. The upper half is intended to represent schematically the fact that ultimately beauty is resolved into being, and not the reverse, although in a context appropriate to the lower part of the diagram beauty as excellence has a higher ontological (and moral) status than being as existence or entity. Beauty is the first principle of being, not the reverse, as would appear to be the case if Edwards' thought were represented only by the lower half of the diagram.

The upper half of the diagram is intended to give schematic representation to the fact that Edwards uses the concepts "being" and "beauty" in two different but related ways. The difference and the relation can be seen in a preliminary way by attending first to the difference between being and beauty as they appear in the upper and lower parts of the diagram and second to the relationship of family resemblances between being as used in the upper half and the several correlative terms on side (a) of the lower half of the diagram and between beauty as used in the upper half and the several correlative terms on side (b) of the lower half.[10]

10. The relationship among beauty, holiness, excellence, goodness, and value and among their corresponding concepts is one of family resemblance (Ludwig Wittgenstein's term) rather than one of clear differentiation or of sub- and superordination such as could be diagrammed without remainder and without the diagram doubling back upon itself.

But this does not mean that these concepts have no referent or that their referents are not determinate, even though they do overlap and crisscross one another, as do the characteristics of members of a family. Nor does this mean that these concepts refer only to meanings and not to facts or to reality, to being, to existence. For example, Edwards asks not what the meaning of excellence is but wherein excellence consists—though the question of meaning and definition is not one he took to be sharply distinguishable from that of subsistence. And his answer to this question is ontological, not linguistic, though again the precarious relationship between language and reality continued to concern him to the end.

First, consider the relationship between the upper half of the diagram and the lower half. The problem this way of representing Edwards' thought is designed to cope with arises because sometimes he speaks of being and beauty as embracing all existence and excellence, all greatness and goodness, while at other times he speaks of being as the same thing as or correlative with entity or existence and of beauty as essentially the same as or correlative with excellence or goodness or perfection. In the first case beauty is resolved into being, even when, as he sometimes does, he uses the term excellence or goodness or perfection instead of beauty. But in the second case being as entity or existence is subordinate to, though not quite resolvable into, beauty as excellence.

The solution to understanding the intricate puzzle presented by such a complex fabric of being and such overlapping language about being is to propose that in the first case Edwards is speaking about being-in-general or being-itself, in which case beauty must be understood to resolve into being as its first principle; but in the second case he is referring to being as manifest to us and encountered by us, in which case beauty has a higher ontological status than being in the sense of entity or existence, as Edwards uses the terms. Therefore, in being as we encounter it, beauty is our principal clue to the nature of being-in-general and is the highest-order manifestation of being.

In these two cases, the first case refers to the upper box in Diagram A and the second case refers to the lower half of the diagram, that is, to the two orders in which all being is manifest to and encountered by intelligent perceiving being—the coordinate orders of existence and excellence or of greatness and goodness, and so on. No grading is intended by the order in which the concepts appear in either of the two lower groups.

The presence of the concept "beauty" inside the upper box, is intended to

---

The ever-present danger of language getting cut off from reality and experience, a possibility he felt had become an actuality in his own day, was one of the problems to which he most persistently addressed himself.

Edwards' answer to the question of wherein excellence consists was, I repeat, ontological rather than linguistic. Or it was both, but linguistic only on the way to being ontological. For example, to Edwards the beauty of the Divine Being is not simply the idea of the mutual consent between Father and Son but actually consists in that consent—consists in the Holy Spirit, Who *is* that mutual consent. The Holy Spirit does not simply express or communicate the divine love and beauty but is that love and beauty in a strong and—Edwards insists upon the word [Misc. 94]—substantial sense. It is this substantial reality as a new principle of being that constitutes the gift of the Holy Spirit as beauty and sensibility. See Ch. 7.

represent Edwards' view that beauty is internal to being-itself or being-in-general in a way that has priority over every other qualification of being, for it is the very structure of being and its first principle.

The appearance of the phrase "fullness of being" in connection with being-in-general will be explained later.[11] The phrase "consenting being" in connection with beauty is shorthand for the full definition of primary beauty. The phrase "being as manifest and encountered" in the diagram points to the two orders in which being is manifest to and encountered by intelligent perceiving being. The phrase is placed as it is in the diagram in order to represent Edwards' view that beauty, as the primary characteristic of being, shapes or informs the manner in which the entire system of being is articulated.

There is, then, as will be shown more fully in the sequel, a difference in the relationship between being and beauty according to whether the concepts are used in ways appropriate to the upper or to the lower half of the diagram, that is, according to whether the subject is being-in-general or being as manifest and encountered by intelligent perceiving being. But these different uses of the key concepts, beauty and being, are not unrelated.

The relatedness can be represented by pointing to some family resemblances among certain concepts. There is a family resemblance among the concepts within each of the two lower groups, (a) and (b). There is also a family resemblance and relationship between beauty as used in the upper half of the diagram and the several correlative concepts in group (b) of the lower half such that sometimes one of the latter is elevated by Edwards to be used interchangeably with beauty as the internal structure and principle of being-in-general. Or sometimes beauty may instead be brought down and used like the concepts in group (b), that is, the concept "beauty" may be used to represent merely one of the two orders in which being is manifest and encountered, as distinguished from its role in Edwards' thought as the principle according to which the whole system of being is articulated. On the same principle there is a corresponding relationship between the concept "being" as used in the upper half of the diagram and the several correlative terms in group (a) of the lower half.

There are at least six ways in which the schematic representation of the structure of Edwards' thought overcomes important problems of interpretation with respect to his use of language and helps to illuminate his use of these concepts as well as the relationships among them.

---

11. See Ch. 3, pp. 45–47, and Ch. 4, pp. 80–83.

It makes sense of his saying both that being-itself "is that into which all excellency is to be resolved" [Mind 62], and that "Being, if we examine narrowly, is nothing but proportion" [Mind 1]. Being, examined narrowly, is being-as-proportion—being in the sense in which it may be used as one of the terms in the lower group (a) of the diagram. In this mode being-as-proportion is ontologically inferior to, though coordinate with, being-as-excellence, or primary beauty, for as such it is a kind of secondary beauty.

The diagram also makes it possible to represent both the unity of being and beauty in God and their distinction in being as manifest and encountered. The diagram can accurately represent the logic of such central passages as this one quoted earlier in briefer form.

> God is not only infinitely greater and more excellent than all other being, but he is the head of the universal system of existence; the foundation and fountain of all being and all beauty; from whom all is perfectly derived, and on whom all is most absolutely and perfectly dependent; of whom, and through whom, and to whom is all being and all perfection; and whose being and beauty are, as it were, the sum and comprehension of all existence and excellence: much more than the sun is the fountain and summary comprehension of all the light and brightness of the day. [TV 15]

The diagram makes it possible to represent the fact that being is never manifest or encountered as only one or the other of the two orders but always as both being and good, for they are not independent realms of being but only coordinate orders of being. Being is encountered, then, never as only existence or only excellence but always as both existence and excellence, even where the excellence is almost nil, for there are—to use more recent terminology—no facts without values. Ultimately, as represented in the upper box of the diagram, beauty is resolved into being. But in all being as manifest and encountered in experience, being and beauty everywhere correspond as coordinate concepts and realities. In this latter sense, that is, as the terms being and beauty are used in the lower groups (a) and (b), being-as-existence or -entity or -proportion is essential to and coordinate with the corresponding manifestation of beauty-as-excellence or -goodness or -consent. Excellence and beauty are always grounded in the things that are—entity, existence, being.

The relationship between the coordinate concepts of self-love and love, greatness and excellence, and complacence and benevolence is essentially similar to the relationship we have seen obtains between proportion and consent. Self-love, for example, is "the entity of [a] thing" [Mind 1]—its being what it is. So self-love is a being in its mode as entity, existence, greatness, proportion, or secondary beauty. But each of these is, for Edwards, a capacity for its corresponding excellence. In fact, its very existence is enlarged or diminished according to that excellence, so that a thing's being or an event's being (in the larger sense of being) consists in a composition of its existence and excellence, its greatness and goodness, its being-as-entity and its beauty-as-excellence—its secondary and primary beauty.

Each of the concepts in group (a) is a capacity for its corresponding concept in group (b). All entity or existence is a capacity for excellence or beauty. "Greatness may be considered as a capacity for excellency" [Mind 62]. And self-love is in one place defined as "only a capacity of enjoyment or suffering" [Misc. 530]. Since the actualization of enjoyment can never exceed the capacity for it, self-love is essential to love. Self-love is a capacity for enjoyment; love is the actualization of enjoyment with respect to persons; and choice is the actualization of enjoyment with respect to things. In either case, no delight—even if God is its object—can exceed the capacity of the self for delight. So, for example, " 'Tis improper to say that our love to God is superior to our general capacity of delighting in anything," and "our delight in God's good can't be superior to our general capacity of delighting in anything" [Misc. 530]. Spiritual sloth or insensibility are as much the enemy of self-love as they are of love. Diagram A makes it possible to represent the relationship between self-love and love as it is understood by Edwards. They are not, properly understood, antithetical. On the contrary, self-love is essential to love, and the degree of love will correspond to the degree of self-love.

What reservations, however, are implied in the catch phrase "properly understood"? Two senses of self-love are distinguished by Edwards.

> Self-love is a man's love to his own good . . . Any good whatsoever
> that a man any way enjoys, or anything that he takes delight in—
> it makes it thereby his own good . . . 'Tis impossible that a man
> should delight in any good that is not his own, for to say that
> would be to say that he delights in that in which he does not de-
> light. [Misc. 530]

In this primary sense "self-love is not entirely distinct from love to God, but enters into its nature" [Misc. 530], provided that the delight is in God and His glory and the disposition is to consent to being-in-general. In this sense self-love is essential to and indistinguishable from any love at all, and if the meaning of self-love is loving one's own good, then it is absurd to suppose one has detracted anything from love by saying that all love is but self-love. But there is a second and narrower sense of self-love in common usage, according to which it means the love of some private or separate good. It is in that sense that self-love is merely "the entity of the thing" or its being what it is. Such self-love "is what arises simply and necessarily from the nature of a perceiving, willing being" and will take as its good "that which agrees immediately and directly with its own being" [Misc. 530].

The critical matter in distinguishing the two varieties of self-love is thus not whether a man will (or can ever be said to) love anything other than what he takes to be his own good, that is, what he delights in. Edwards finds that impossible, for it is a contradiction in terms. The critical question is rather whether the object of enjoyment will be a good or beauty defined according to the definition of secondary beauty or according to the definition of primary beauty. Or, to express the same idea differently, the critical question is whether the object of the will is found to have beauty or to be beautiful (delightful, lovely, good) by virtue of its agreement with one's own being (consistency with self, a form of secondary beauty) or whether the object of the will is found beautiful (delightful, lovely, good) by virtue of its agreement with being-in-general (primary beauty).

The confined sense of self-love is represented in Diagram A by self-love's standing opposite and ontologically inferior to pure love. But by virtue of its larger sense, self-love is also represented as taken up into the perfection of being along with pure love, as essential to and having a share in the latter. Edwards says in one of those passages that so radically set him apart from almost all those who took themselves to be his faithful disciples during the century following his death:

> Hence, 'tis impossible for any person to be willing to be perfectly and finally miserable for God's sake, for this supposes love to God is superior to self-love in the most general and extensive sense of self-love, which enters into the nature of love to God . . . So that this supposition, that a man can be willing to be perfectly and utterly miserable out of love to God, is inconsistent with itself. [Misc. 530]

In like manner, the beauty of proportion and harmony has a share in and is essential to the beauty of being's consent to being; and greatness has a share in and is essential to excellence; and complacence has a share in and is essential to benevolence.

Diagram A also makes it possible to represent both the relations in Edwards' thought between greatness and excellence (or goodness) and their common relation to being and beauty in the sense represented by the upper box in the diagram.

> Not only may greatness be considered as a capacity of excellency, but a being, by reason of his greatness considered alone, is the more excellent because he partakes more of being. Though if he be great, if he dissent from more general and extensive being or from universal being, he is the more odious for his greatness because the dissent or contradiction to being in general is so much the greater. [Mind 62]

The way in which greatness and excellence correspond so that they enlarge and diminish each other is summarily expressed in this passage. So also is the fact that the common and corresponding relation of greatness and excellence to the enlargement or diminution of being, that is, to the extensity or privation of being, consists essentially in their relation to and their participation in beauty. For, although the term beauty does not appear in this passage, the concepts of beauty and deformity are clearly present as consent and dissent from being-in-general.

The relation between excellence and greatness provides a good illustration and documentation of the rationale for Diagram A. How else are we to represent at once both of the following statements, coming as they do, not in widely separated contexts, but in successive pages of the "Notes on the Mind"?

   (i) "Existence or entity is that into which all excellency is to be resolved." [Mind 62]
   (ii) "Excellency may be distributed into greatness and beauty: the former is the degree of being; the latter is being's consent to being." [Mind 64]

As a corollary of the first statement Edwards concludes that God is excellent because He is "the infinite, universal, and all-comprehending existence" [Mind 62]. In the first of these two statements, as the very next sentence following it in the context makes clear, existence is used in the sense of "being," and thus excellency is resolved into existence as beauty is resolved into being-in-general in the upper box of the diagram. With regard to the second

statement, it is the family resemblance among certain of the concepts as represented in the diagram that makes it possible to give consistent formulation
to what Edwards says. Diagram A formulates the only way in which the second statement can be made consistent with the first one. In the second statement "excellency," by virtue of its family resemblance to beauty, functions
like the concept "beauty" in the upper box of the diagram, while greatness
and beauty designate the two orders in which being is manifest and encountered. "Greatness" designates the degree of being; "being" here functions as a
member of the family of concepts in group (a), while "beauty" functions as a
member of the family of concepts in group (b).

This reading of the matter depends a good deal upon the legitimacy and
accuracy of the family resemblances I have posited among the concepts
within each of the groups (a) and (b) in the diagram. This could be docu-
mented endlessly. One instance especially apposite to the present discussion
occurs in the course of Edwards' inquiry into the amount of regard or respect
due to any being. He concludes that in determining the regard due any
being "these two things are to be considered conjunctly, viz., greatness and
goodness, or the degree of existence and the degree of excellence" [Misc.
1208]. Not only is greatness equated with existence and goodness with excellence, but it is the two manifestations of being taken "conjunctly" that
determine the share of being or the ontological status of anything in the system of being. And this, too, the diagram adequately represents.

Diagram A, furthermore, makes it possible to represent accurately the relations in Edwards' thought between benevolence and complacence and what
he says about being and beauty in the course of discussing them. "The first
object of virtuous benevolence is being, simply considered" [TV 8]. Its second object or secondary object is "benevolent being" [TV 9], that is, "spiritual beauty" [TV 11]. "Loving a being on this [second] ground necessarily
arises from pure benevolence to being in general, and comes to the same
thing" [TV 10]. In other words, love of being for its beauty "necessarily
arises from . . . and comes to the same thing" as pure benevolence to being-
in-general. To have as one's object being-in-general is necessarily related to
and comes to the same thing as having as one's object beauty—consenting
being or spiritual beauty.

This necessary relation between being-in-general and beauty is represented
in the upper box of the diagram. It is because being-in-general and beauty are
thus related that benevolence necessarily carries with it complacence, that
is, that benevolence to being-in-general necessarily carries with it a corre-

sponding complacence in or delight in the beauty of being-in-general. For this
spiritual beauty which is but the secondary ground of virtuous benevolence is
precisely therein also the primary ground of complacence [TV 11]. "Therefore he that has true virtue, consisting in benevolence to being in general, and
in benevolence to virtuous being, must necessarily have a supreme love to
God, both of benevolence and complacence" [TV 15]. But there is more,
for the spiritual beauty that is so intimately and internally and necessarily
related to being-in-general consists "not in the simple proportion of the degree of benevolent affection seen, but in a proportion compounded of [a] the
greatness of the benevolent being, or the degree of being and [b] the degree
of benevolence" [TV 12]. In other words, spiritual beauty or primary beauty
in its primitive unity with being-in-general is articulated according to the
manner represented in the diagram and consists in a compound of greatness
and excellence or in a compound of the degree of being-as-existence and the
degree of beauty-as-excellence.

In the course of his discussion of benevolence and complacence in *The
Nature of True Virtue,* Edwards also says many other things that support the
rationale of Diagram A. For example, he says with respect to created beings
that

> benevolence or goodness in the divine Being is generally sup-
> posed, not only to be prior to the beauty of many of its objects,
> but to their existence; so as to be the ground both of their exist-
> ence and their beauty . . . as it is supposed that it is God's good-
> ness which moved him to give them both being and beauty. [TV 6]

It is evident that existence and being are here used as equivalent or correlative members of the family of concepts in group (a) and that in this sense
beauty is related to them as the corresponding or coordinate mode in which
being-in-general is manifest and encountered. Furthermore, these two orders
of being, whether referred to as existence and beauty or as being and beauty,
have their source in the "benevolence or goodness in the divine Being," and
that benevolence is precisely the primary beauty of the Divine Being. So once
again we see that Edwards' language conforms to the pattern represented
by the diagram.

The viability of the schema and diagram with which I here propose to
represent Edwards' philosophy of being and the critical role played by the
concept and category of beauty in the articulation of that system will rest
primarily upon its serviceability through the course of our investigation. But

this series of examples already shows something of how this manner of representing his thought is consistent with, and is helpful in clarifying, his use of the concepts with which we are primarily concerned. It shows the ways in which all excellence and beauty is ultimately resolved into being-in-general and the way in which the system of being is articulated according to the structure given by its first principle, beauty, in two coordinate orders of existence and excellence, greatness and goodness, proportion and consent, and so on. It also represents accurately Edwards' view that the natural order—without becoming other than what it is and without losing its own identity—is taken up into and fulfilled in the spiritual order, as is proportion into consent, greatness into goodness, self-love into love, complacence into benevolence, and existence into excellence.

Finally, Diagram A makes it possible to represent schematically how Edwards' psychology and theory of the self is related to his ontology. It provides a schema for representing how his theory of the aesthetic-affectional unity of the self, articulated through its primary activities of understanding and will, is related (in apprehension and encounter) to the aesthetic articulation of being manifest and communicated in its two modes of beauty as existence and excellence or as proportion and consent. There is a correspondence between his aesthetic model of order in the system of being and his aesthetic-affectional model of unity in the self. His model of the self is not constructed —either in the case of the Divine Being or in the case of human beings—by an analysis of any supposed faculties of understanding and will and of their powers, for he rejects the very notion that there are such faculties or that they have powers.

As a matter of linguistic convenience Edwards still speaks of faculties, but he is careful to avoid committing or encouraging the sort of confusion that caused John Locke to observe that "this way of speaking of *faculties* has misled many into a confused notion of so many distinct agents in us" and that "we may as properly say that it is the singing faculty sings, and the dancing faculty dances, as that the will chooses, or that the understanding conceives."[12] Edwards agrees with Locke and in the same spirit observes with respect to the will, for example, that:

> the will itself is not an agent that has a will . . . That which has
> the power of volition or choice is the man or the soul, and not the

12. Quoted in Paul Ramsey's Introduction to the FW, p. 47.

power of volition itself . . . We say with propriety, that a bird let
loose has power and liberty to fly; but not that the bird's power
of flying has a power and liberty of flying. [FW 163]

Accordingly, freedom "is the property of an agent, who is possessed of powers and faculties"; such things are "the properties of men or persons; and not
the properties of properties" [FW 163–64].

Edwards' model of the self is constructed, therefore, not upon an analysis
of these "properties"—the "powers and faculties" agents possess—but rather
upon an analysis of the engagement of the agent himself in his encounter
with reality. It is not by virtue of any reification of separate faculties in the
self but by virtue of a distinction between being and good in reality as encountered and apprehended by the self that Edwards speaks of understanding and
will in the agent. The terms understanding and will function in his vocabulary as names for the two principal modes of this engagement; they are not
themselves agents, nor do they operate independently of each other. They are
ways of speaking about the self as it confronts reality as at once both being
and good (or evil)—at once being and good, not first one and then the other
and certainly not either one or the other, for Edwards finds that there can be
no "clear distinction made between the two faculties of understanding and
will, as acting distinctly and separately" [RA 272], since it is not they but
the self that encounters reality.

If we recall now the analysis offered earlier[13] of the manner in which sensibility is the key to the quality of both understanding and will and the measure of the unity of understanding and will in the integrity of the self, I can
refine my earlier sketch of the aesthetic-affectional model of the self in its
correspondence with the aesthetic articulation of Edwards' system of being.
On the one hand, the self's cognitive encounter may be more or less success-
ful in understanding its object, with the fullest understanding consisting in a
"sensible knowledge" [RA 272]. Short of this fall "mere notional understanding" or "mere speculative knowledge" [RA 272], in which the self is
less fully engaged and the object is less sensibly, directly, or successfully encountered. On the other hand, since the heart of the will is in the affections
and the heart of the affections in turn is in the sensibility, the self's volitional
encounter with its object will be more or less willing as the self is more or
less sensibly affected and moved to love or hatred, attraction or repulsion,
consent or dissent. The volitional engagement of the self with its object as

13. See Ch. 1, pp. 3–8.

good (or evil) can be traced either in terms of sensibility or in terms of beauty, in ways that will be specified in Chapters 4 and 8. Of course, the object or reality encountered need not be single or simple and may indeed be a highly complex phenomenon. Edwards recognizes that the actual inclination of the self as will is likely to be defined by "compositions of inclinations" [Misc. 437; cf. FW 141–48]. With these refinements Edwards' aesthetic-affectional model of the self may be represented as shown in Diagram B. It will be noticed that both complacence (delight) and benevolence

DIAGRAM B

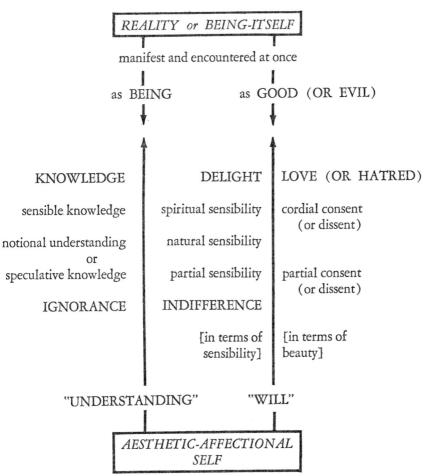

(love) pertain to the will in this model of the self but that in the object the self encounters, as represented in Diagram A, complacence is located in the order of being rather than of good because it is a form of secondary beauty. This reflects the radical unity of being and good in Edwards' system and the radical unity of understanding and will in his model of the self. It also demonstrates the limitations of schematic representations such as these, for they may appear to divide what they only intend to distinguish.[14]

Ultimately, being-in-general and beauty are essentially one in Edwards' ontology. This identity can be further elucidated by attending to the relation between the concepts of being and nothing. The fullness of unity between being and beauty is to be found only in God, Who is Himself the fullness and foundation and fountain of all being and beauty. But being and beauty also correspond throughout the entire graded system of being, from the fullness of being and beauty in God down through the negation or absence of being and beauty represented in Edwards' thought by the boundary concept "nothing."

The opposite of being is not becoming but nothing, although ontologically nothing is strictly a boundary concept, so that the threat to being is from other being or from dissension within being rather than from nonbeing.[15]

> A state of absolute nothing is a state of absolute contradiction. Absolute nothing is the aggregate of all the absurd contradictions in the world . . . When we go about to form an idea of perfect nothing we must . . . think of the same that the sleeping rocks dream of. And not till then shall we get a complete idea of nothing . . .
>
> There is such a thing as nothing with respect to this ink and paper . . . but there is no such thing as nothing with respect to entity,

14. Alan Heimert, in *Religion and the American Mind* (see esp. p. 110), does not, I think, master these difficulties. He correctly perceives the importance and the objectivist implications of Edwards' identification of happiness with holiness. But he misconstrues his model of the self when he identifies happiness with the understanding (as distinguished from holiness, which he rightly identifies with the will) and when, consistent with this error, he also identifies complacence with the understanding (as distinguished from benevolence, which he rightly identifies with the will).

15. It would be appropriate to speak of a threat (to determinate being) *of* nonbeing but not *from* nonbeing—as though nonbeing were a threatening agent rather than a possible condition for every determinate finite being. The threat of nonbeing comes from other being or from dissension within being rather than from nonbeing.

'being' absolutely considered. We don't know what we say if we
say we think it possible in itself that there should not be entity.[16]

So the opposite of both being and beauty is nothing. For, just as absolute
being consents to being and hence is beautiful, so "absolute nothing is
the essence of all contradiction" [Misc. 27a], "a dreadful contradiction"
[Mind 30], and is therefore, as dissent from being, the opposite of beauty as
well as of being. Or rather, absolute nothing is the opposite of being precisely because it is the opposite of beauty. "Disproportion or inconsistency is
contrary to being" [Mind 1].

Beauty is to being as deformity is to nothing. Good and evil are measured
on this same scale running from the fullness of being and beauty toward
nothing. "Disagreement or contrariety to being is evidently an approach to
nothing, or a degree of nothing . . . and the greatest and only evil; and entity is the greatest and only good" [Mind 1]. So the scales of consent and
dissent, being and nothing, good and evil, beauty and deformity—all these
scales—correspond to each other ontologically in Edwards' system of being.

These relationships may, for certain purposes, be conveniently represented as they are in Diagram C. Since beauty and sensibility correspond
throughout the system of what Edwards calls "intelligent perceiving being,"
the corresponding relations in the order of sensibility are also represented in
Diagram C. Only God and being-in-general exhibit absolute consent, being,
beauty, and goodness; and the essence of nothing is absolute dissent, contradiction, deformity, and evil. In the corresponding order of sensibility, which
pertains throughout the system of intelligent perceiving being, only God
exhibits perfect love and delight; and the essence of nothing is insensibility
and death. The beauty of any being designates its ontological weight, its
distance from nonbeing or "nothing." And conversely, the beauty of any
being designates its share of participation in the "fullness of being." Beauty is
the measure throughout the articulated system of being.

Being is what stands against "nothing." But it is not therefore an empty
universal—simply anything as opposed to nothing. Being is the fullest universal, for it stands against nothing by virtue of its beauty—its consent to
being. Beauty may, then, be said to be not only the fundamental structure of
being but also the power of being. Beauty is that by virtue of which being is
creative, for it is the beautifying rather than the beautified that is most truly

---

16. "Of Being," in Harvey G. Townsend, ed, *The Philosophy of Jonathan Edwards:
From His Private Notebooks* (Eugene, University of Oregon Press, 1955), p. 9.

DIAGRAM C

A WORKING REPRESENTATION OF SOME RELATIONS IN JE'S THOUGHT

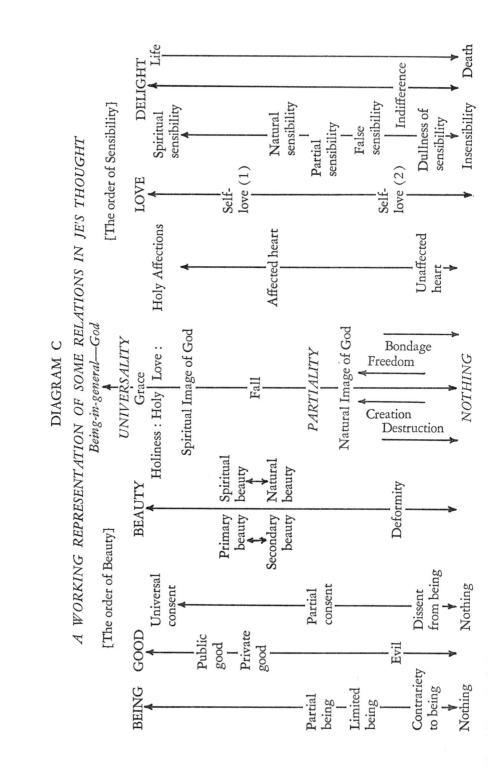

beautiful. And beauty is that by virtue of which all that has being bestowed upon it resists disintegration into nothing.[17] By virtue of beauty, being is; according to its measure of beauty, any particular thing or event has being and remains in being.

If beauty is taken seriously as the primary category of being, by virtue of which anything has being, it would seem that no choice need necessarily be made between the notions of creation *ad extra* and creation *ex nihilo*. For if "nothing" is understood as a boundary concept representing absolute contradiction and dissent from being, then it comes to the same thing to say that beings are brought into being out of nothing—out of dissent from being and contradiction of being—or that being is bestowed upon them and they are brought into being out of the fullness of being—out of the creative fullness and effulgence of being's cordial consent to being, that is, out of the beauty of being. To bestow beauty is (at once) to take out of nothing and to give being; and the greater the beauty, the greater the being.

While beauty is objective with respect to the self, the perception of it is a function of the self-disposition of the subject (person, self). Furthermore,

---

17. Hannah Arendt makes the same point with respect to a more confined realm of being—man's cultural world. In *The Human Condition* (Garden City, N.Y., Doubleday, Anchor Books, 1960, p. 153) she argues that

> the man-made world of things, the human artifice erected by *homo faber,* becomes a home for mortal men, whose stability will endure and outlast the ever-changing movement of their lives and actions, only insomuch as it transcends both the sheer functionalism of things produced for consumption and the sheer utility of objects produced for use.

She finds in beauty the measure of that transcendence and therefore the condition for the persistence in being and relative stability of the world as a scene for human action and spiritual freedom. In *Between Past and Future* (New York, Viking Press, 1961, p. 218) she argues that

> beauty is the very manifestation of imperishability. The fleeting greatness of word and deed can endure in the world to the extent that beauty is bestowed upon it. Without the beauty, that is, the radiant glory in which potential immortality is made manifest in the human world, all human life would be futile and no greatness could endure.

It is then, according to Hannah Arendt, beauty that bestows, supports, and even defines both the capacity of the cultural world that man creates to endure against the natural cycles of renewal and disintegration in his environment and the capacity of the deeds and words he performs and speaks in that world to survive the intrinsic frailty of human action. Edwards applies the same principle not only to the human cultural world but also to the universal system of being.

any apprehension of beauty must be immediate or direct, because it is given to perception (Edwards sometimes calls it intuition) rather than to reflection. To be known it must be itself experienced or encountered. It is not to be known at second-hand; nor is it discernible to the indifferent eye, or, more precisely, to the indifferent self, since it is the self rather than the eye that apprehends primary beauty, and even with respect to secondary beauty it is only a manner of speaking to say that it is apprehended by the eye. Beauty is available only in and through the enjoyment of it. Though indifferent men may know many things about beauty, they do not and cannot know beauty itself. The same goes for reflective but unperceptive men. Beauty is objective with respect to the self, and yet it is manifest to and encountered by persons according to their self-disposition.

The decisive manner in which Edwards' conception of beauty informs the development of his system of being is especially evident at this point. Edwards found in the concept of beauty the model for the articulation of his whole system of being because he wanted to say about being-in-general, and about being as manifest and encountered, precisely what has just been said about beauty. Being, too, is objective with respect to the self (in fact the being of the self presupposes the system of being), and yet the perception of or the encounter with being is a function of the self-disposition of the subject (person, self). Nothing is more immediately given to us than being; and the fullness of being is, if manifest and encountered, most immediately and directly given of all. To be known, being must itself be experienced or encountered. It is not to be known at second-hand; nor is it discernible to the indifferent eye or self. Being, like beauty, is available only in and through the enjoyment of it. Indifference is, in fact, an expression in the order of sensibility of that same privation of being and beauty and that movement toward nothing that he finds in dissent from and contrariety to being. To absolutely indifferent being, being is absolutely unavailable—neither manifest nor encountered.[18] Though relatively indifferent men may know many things about being and the system of being, they do not and cannot know being-

18. Indifference so absolute as to dissolve the indifferent being into nothingness does not mean that the being in question would physically disappear but only that he would disappear and be as nothing with respect to that part of his being about which relative attachment and indifference can be predicated. It makes sense to say that such an indifferent being, if utterly indifferent, becomes as nothing insofar as his being an agent with perception and will is concerned, even though in his physical being he may continue to behave (though not act) and may survive such constructed existence—perhaps under the care of an appropriate institution.

itself or the essential structure of being, which is beauty. The same goes for reflective but unperceptive men. Being-itself is objective with respect to the self, and yet it is manifest to and encountered by persons according to their self-disposition. The essential structure of being (primary beauty) and the fullness of being-in-general and of God are manifest to and encountered as present living realities only according to the degree to which men find in them their entire joy and happiness, the fulfillment of their aesthetic-affectional being.

This internal relation between the spiritual condition of the subject and the spiritual dimensions of the object in which the subject finds some measure of beauty runs through Edwards' entire system of being. It may be expressed with the focus on either the subject or the object; the self-disposition that is essential to the apprehension of any form of secondary beauty (even if among spiritual beings) is itself a corresponding form of secondary beauty and consists in either partial consent to being or consent to partial being. This formula may also be expressed as either limited consent to being or consent to limited being. All that is required for the apprehension of secondary beauty is a disposition to agreement with oneself or to agreement with some limited sphere of being. To such self-disposition being is manifest and encountered in terms defined by the concepts in group (a) of Diagram A. The true greatness of a being, even of the Divine Being, may, for example, be manifest and encountered as a living reality in the absence of any apprehension of the true goodness or excellence or beauty of that same being.[19] What is essential, on the other hand, to the apprehension of primary beauty—and therefore of being-itself—is a self-disposition that is itself a form of primary beauty, namely a being disposed to consent cordially to being as being. This last formula could also be expressed as a person's being at the disposal of being as it makes its claims on him. But that should not be mistaken for a passive state, since in Edwards' view it is precisely the definition of the most vital agency of any being that it be governed by a disposition to and sensible perception of things as they are in their own being and in relation to the universal system of being (their being in God), rather than as they are only in relation to the being of the agent in question.[20]

19. See Ch. 6, pp. 123–29, for further elaboration.
20.
We have reason to think . . . that He [God] is infinitely the most intelligent and sensible being of all; that He is more perceiving than any; that *His perception is so much more sensible and lively and perfect* that created minds are, in comparison of

Just as the knowledge of beauty provides Edwards with the model for all real knowledge—direct, sensible perception or intuition—so also beauty provides him with the model for all being as the object of any knowledge.[21] Nothing is rightly known until its beauty (or deformity) is known, and nothing is adequately known until its beauty is sensibly (rather than only notionally) known. Therefore, the knowledge of beauty provides the model for the apprehension of all being to which we are related directly or immediately rather than indirectly as by reflection, and the knowledge of beauty provides the model for the apprehension of all being to the extent that we apprehend something of its fullness and excellence. It is, for example, *as* beauty and *to* sensibility that the Divine Being is most immediately and powerfully present.[22] Or, to put it the other way around, it is by a sensible participation in the divine beauty, in what constitutes the divine beauty—his holiness, his Holy Spirit—that we are most immediately related to the Divine Being and are transformed into the spiritual likeness or image of God.

The matter of beauty as the object of sensibility raises one more point to be made respecting beauty and the immediacy of being. It has to do with beauty and the power of the definite. One of the most important things to note about the way the concept of beauty functions in Edwards' thought is that beauty—even the beauty of holiness[23]—is given in and through experience of an encounter with definite, concrete, substantial being and not in and through the abstract, ethereal, incommunicable, or untouchable. Beauty of holiness is a divine reality, but it is given as a present reality to men *as men*—and,

---

Him, like dead, senseless, unperceiving substances; and that He infinitely more exceeds them in the sensibility and life and height (if I may so speak) of His perception than the sun exceeds the planets in the intensive degree of his brightness . . . *And as He is more sensible, so He is,* as I may express it, *more voluntary* than created minds. He acts more of Himself, infinitely *more purely active.* [Misc. 749, italics added]

21. For Edwards all "reasoning is only of use to us in the consequence of the paucity of our ideas" [Mind 10] and especially because of the paucity of our ideas and experience of the objective order of being and beauty.

22.

The first effect of the *power of God* in the heart in REGENERATION is to give the heart a Divine taste of sense; to cause it to have a *relish of the loveliness* and sweetness *of the supreme excellency* of the Divine nature; and indeed *this is all the immediate effect of the Divine Power that there is,* this is all the Spirit of God needs to do, in order to a production of all good effects in the soul [Grace 37, italics added].

23. Edwards' use of the phrase "the beauty of holiness" in no way hangs on that magnificent and shop-worn mistranslation of the Old Testament text in the King James Version. See p. 118, n. 1.

at that, to ordinary "men of mean capacities" rather than to some gnostic company of intellectual or aesthetic elite. No "angelism" is to be found in Edwards' theological or philosophical employment of the concept of beauty.[24] Beauty is given to men as men, not to angels alone, nor even to men only insofar as they can be angels or angelic, but to men in their humanity. In fact, Edwards speculates that while angels may be above the saints in greatness, the saints are above the angels in beauty [Misc. 824].[25] Consent to being and dissent from being are not less, but rather more, particular and concrete and substantial because they are spiritual rather than material realities. As we have seen, the difference between primary and secondary beauty has nothing to do with the one being spiritual (in any angelic sense) and the other being material but has rather to do with the nature of the consenting relationship involved. The contrast is between spirit and nature, not between spirit and matter.

Beauty is an appropriate model for the development of a system of being in which absolute being-in-general is immediately related to every part of the system rather than mediately down through levels of being or links in some chain of being. This immediacy of being may be expressed summarily by saying that being is present in the manner in which beauty is present—in the particularity of things and events as we know and experience them. Insofar as the beauty or the being is apprehended in things or events, it is *there* and not simply hovering over them. Just as particular beauty is not self-contained, neither is particular being. But their real being and beauty is not, therefore, somewhere else, external to their particularity. They are not encountered by taking particular beauty or being only as a clue to ascend upward somewhere higher in the scale of being. For both beauty and being are given in rather than only through being as encountered and manifest in its rich particularity —or else they are not available at all.

The ontological priority of beauty over all other qualifications of being such as unity, truth, and goodness, shapes the very manner in which these

24. The term angelism is employed here as it is used by William F. Lynch in *Christ and Apollo: The Dimensions of the Literary Imagination* (New York, Sheed and Ward, 1960). It is from Father Lynch that I have also taken the phrase "the power of the definite" (p. 3). Beauty and insight, he says, are not to be located "in the sky" (p. 14). "There are no shortcuts to beauty or to insight. We must go *through* the finite, the limited, the definite, omitting none of it lest we omit some of the potencies of being-in-the-flesh . . . We waste our time if we try to go around or above or under the definite; we must literally go through it" (p. 7).

25. See Ch. 8, pp. 202f., for a discussion of this "Miscellany."

other qualifications are conceived and articulated in Edwards' thought. The schematic formulation offered in Diagram A makes it easier to deliver an explanation of this aspect of his philosophy of being than by approaching his theory of the essential qualifications of being, as Thomas Schafer does, by taking as a point of departure the classical tradition of philosophies of being. Schafer begins his analysis in this way.

> There are three aspects or modes of being as such which correspond to the "transcendentals" of medieval philosophy and which, in some form or other, are the starting point for any metaphysics of being. Expressed as logical concepts, they are: a. *Identity:* a thing is what it is. b. *Sufficient reason:* everything which is, to the extent that it is, has a sufficient reason for its being and its being what it is. c. *Finality:* potentiality tends to actuality, or, every agent acts in view of an end. The aspects of being as such to which these refer are: a. Being is *one.* b. Being is *truth.* c. Being is *good.*[26]

There is considerable merit in thus relating Edwards' doctrine of being to these logical concepts and aspects of being, for Edwards himself develops a good part of his doctrine of being in terms of a similar three-fold distinction between being as such, being as the object of understanding, and being as the object of the will or delight. But it is difficult, within the framework provided by this approach, to show the decisive way in which beauty shapes the conception and articulation of these three aspects of being.

The difficulty is illustrated by the contemporary effort of Jacques Maritain[27] to grant to beauty a somewhat higher ontological status than unity, truth, and goodness but to do so within the framework provided by the same tradition that Schafer takes as a point of departure. Jacques Maritain holds a high estimate of the ontological status of beauty, which is comparable and even compatible in many respects with Edwards'.[28] Formulated in terms of a philosophy that recognizes a "realm of transcendentals," his high estimate

26. Schafer, "The Concept of Being," p. 104.

27. Jacques Maritain, *Creative Intuition in Art and Poetry,* especially the section on "The Philosophical Concept of Beauty" in Ch. V, "Poetry and Beauty," pp. 160–67.

28. The same can be said of the relation between Maritain's concept of "knowledge through inclination" (*Man and the State* [Chicago, University of Chicago Press, 1951], p. 91) and Edwards' concept of "sensible knowledge." For Edwards, "sensible knowledge" is a function of the self-disposition or inclination of the subject, though it remains knowledge because it relates the subject cognitively to an objective order whose first principle is the beauty of being's consent to being—which beauty is precisely the peculiar object of spiritual sensibility. For Maritain, "knowledge through inclination" is also a function of the self-disposition or inclination of the subject, though it, too, remains knowledge be-

of the ontological status of beauty is expressed by distinguishing transcendental from aesthetic beauty and making of transcendental beauty not only one of the transcendentals but a sort of transcendental above all transcendentals: "Beauty is the radiance of all transcendentals united." But this elevation of beauty is achieved at the price of vacuousness as to content and structure and of irrelevance to that "province of beauty in which senses and sense perception play an essential part,"[29] which is relegated by Maritain to aesthetic beauty alone. Beauty ascends the throne like a constitutional monarch—to reign but not to rule.

> Beauty belongs in the realm of transcendentals, of those 'passions or properties of being,' as the Schoolmen said—Unity, Truth, Goodness—which are but various aspects of Being—Being as undivided, Being as confronting the power of knowledge, Being as confronting the power of desire—and which are, in actual fact, one with Being, and as infinite as Being itself, in so far as they are considered in their metaphysical reality. It may be said that Beauty is the radiance of all transcendentals united.[30]

It appears that beauty can be given such high ontological status within this framework of the transcendentals only by emptying it of all its content. Transcendental beauty has certain characteristics, to be sure.[31] But once it

---

cause it relates the subject cognitively to the Natural Law of an objective moral order. Maritain argues that according to Thomas Aquinas, "human reason discovers the regulations of natural law through the guidance of the *inclinations* of human nature" and that

> the very mode or manner in which human reason knows natural law is not rational knowledge, but knowledge *through inclination*. That kind of knowledge is not clear knowledge through concepts and conceptual judgments; it is obscure, unsystematic, vital knowledge by connaturality or congeniality, in which the intellect, in order to bear judgment, consults and listens to the inner melody that the vibrating strings of abiding tendencies make present in the subject (*Man and the State*, pp. 91–92).

29. Maritain, *Creative Intuition*, pp. 162, 163–64.

30. Ibid., p. 162.

31. Ibid., p. 161. Maritain's designation of the essential characteristics of beauty is apposite.

> The three essential characteristics or integral elements traditionally recognized in beauty: *integrity*, because the intellect is pleased in fullness of Being; *proportion or consonance*, because the intellect is pleased in order and unity; and *radiance or clarity*, because the intellect is pleased in light, or in that which, emanating from things, causes intelligence to see (*Creative Intuition*, p. 161).

"Beauty," he says, "consists of intuitive knowledge, and delight. Beauty makes us delighted in the very act of knowing" (p. 161). The similarities and compatibilities between Maritain

is distinguished from aesthetic beauty, there is little left to it by way of structure or content. Transcendental beauty appears to be nothing in particular, of which there are innumerable particular determinations. Aesthetic beauty is one such particular determination; it is "transcendental beauty confronting the sense as imbued with intelligence, or intellection as engaged in sense perception."[32] What is there left to distinguish transcendental beauty, even as the object of intuition by pure spirit? Maritain seems to want to give more substance to the notion of transcendental beauty than he is able to give within the framework of this philosophy of being. But it cannot be said that his conception of transcendental beauty—insofar as he is even left with such a concept—shapes in any decisive way his conception of the other transcendentals. If we now want to represent the manner in which Edwards' conception of the ontological priority of beauty does exercise a decisive formative influence upon his conception of the other essential attributes of being and of the Divine Being, we would do well to avoid the classical framework based on the transcendentals.

The three essential aspects of being as such to which the three transcendentals of Thomist philosophy refer—unity, truth, and goodness—have a place in Edwards' ontology, of course. But that place and their content is shaped by the ontological priority of beauty. The next chapter will specify how this is the case with respect to being as good, so I shall consider here only the unity and truth of being. All other possible candidates for the position of ontological priority occupied by beauty will then, in Edwards' view, have been effectively dealt with. For it is his view that all other attributes of being and of the Divine Being can be reduced to these three, and all three are shaped by his concept of beauty.

Edwards says with respect to the Divine Being that there can be no more than these three attributes, and his conception of them is best represented by a schema and diagram such as I have proposed.

> 'Tis evident that there are no more than these three, really distinct in God—God, and His idea, and His love and delight. We can't conceive of any further distinctions. If you say there is the

---

and Edwards in these matters are more striking at first than after more careful examination, but it would take us too far afield to explore the matter here.

32. Ibid., p. 164.

power of God, I answer, the power of a being, even in creatures is nothing distinct from the being itself besides a mere relation to an effect. If you say there is the infiniteness, eternity of God, and immutability of God—they are mere modes or manners of exist- ence. If you say there is the wisdom of God—that is the idea of God. If you say there is the holiness of God—that is not different from His love, as we have shown, and is the Holy Spirit. If you say there is the goodness and mercy of God—they are included in His love, they are His love with a relation . . .

There is, in resemblance to this threefold distinction in God, a threefold distinction in a created spirit—namely, the spirit itself, and its understanding, and its will or inclination or love. And this indeed is all the real distinction there is in created spirits. [Misc. 259]

In this scheme the notion of being as truth is displaced by or subsumed under the notion of being as existence and as idea. Being-in-general is seen to be articulated not as truth and goodness but as idea and love or delight or as existence and excellence or goodness. It is more properly as existence and idea than as truth that being is encountered as the object of the understand- ing. To stress truth as the object is to overintellectualize this aspect of the human encounter with being. The truth is more in the encounter and the rela- tion of perceiving being to being perceived, than it is in the object. That in the object on which the truth rests is the thing's being as it is, its existence. "Truth [is] the agreement of our ideas with the things as they are" [Mind 10]. "Truth is the agreement of our ideas with existence" [Mind 15]. That in the subject that is essential to the having of truth—or, more forcefully, being *in* the truth—is an inclination to perceive things as they are.

The mere perception of being is agreeable to perceiving being, as well as being's consent to being . . . Hence there is in the mind an inclination to perceive the things that are, or the desire of truth. [Mind 49]

In other words, not only beauty but also being, not only being as excellence but also being as existence, is agreeable to perceiving being.

At the end of his "Notes on the Mind" Edwards proposes to himself a subject for future inquiry: "whether beauty . . . be not the only object of the will, or whether truth be not also the object of the will."[33] The answer would seem to be that both beauty and truth are objects of the will. For although being-itself is ontologically prior to primary beauty and is what primary beauty is the first principle of, being as manifest in the order of existence, idea, truth, and greatness is ontologically subordinate to being as manifest in the order of excellence, beauty, and goodness—subordinate, but still a form of beauty. Therefore truth as well as beauty is an object of the will, for truth apprehended is itself a form of secondary beauty. Being as truth or idea is a special case of being as beauty.

We have seen that unity is not, for Edwards, a higher metaphysical principle than being. Unity is not "beyond" being, but it is certainly essential to being. And the model of unity in his thought is provided by beauty. Absolute unity is rejected, even in being-itself or the Divine Being. It is rejected because if beauty is to be attributed to being-in-general or to the Divine Being—and any ontology that would not permit this would have made no sense to Edwards either theologically or philosophically—then there must be diversity at the very heart of being. "One alone cannot be excellent, inasmuch as, in such case, there can be no consent. Therefore, if God is excellent, there must be a plurality in God; otherwise there can be no consent in Him" [Misc. 117]. The principle applies to all being, and not only to God. If being is to have excellence at all, its excellence must be seen as shaping its unity, and not vice versa.

> One alone without any reference to any more cannot be excellent; for, in such case, there can be no manner of relation no way, and therefore no such thing as consent. Indeed, what we call 'one' may be excellent because of a consent of parts, or some consent of those in that being that are distinguished into a plurality some way or other. But in a being that is absolutely without any plurality there cannot be excellency, for there can be no such thing as consent or agreement. [Mind 1]

Thus unity is essential to being, but the model of unity is provided by beauty. The ontological priority of beauty as the structure of being shapes the manner in which the unity of being is conceived and articulated in

33. No. 56 of the "subjects" listed by Edwards at the end of the "Notes on the Mind."

Edwards' system. Two kinds of unity are essential to being—internal unity and unity with a system of being. Internal unity, or consent to and consistency with one's own being, is a form of secondary beauty. But internal consent or unity is not sufficient, even though necessary, to being. Without some unity among beings, without some measure of consent to other being(s) nothing can remain in being. For beings are not given in isolation but are only given in a system of being. And this unity with a system of being(s) may exhibit either primary or secondary beauty, depending upon the nature of the consent and upon the reach of the system to which consent is given.

4

BEAUTY AND EXCELLENCE, GOODNESS, AND VALUE

Having established consent as the first thing in beauty and beauty as the first thing in being, I turn now to a consideration of the ways in which beauty is first with respect to the perfection of being. We shall be concerned with the family of concepts in Diagram A having to do with the perfection of being: beauty, excellence, goodness, and value.[1] These terms all have a wider than moral or religious reference. Excellence and goodness especially are more nearly ontological and structural concepts as well as moral and religious ones; and it is by virtue of that that they are so intimately related to Edwards' concept of beauty. My objective in this chapter is to enrich our understanding of his conception of beauty and the ways in which it functions in his thought by examining it in relation to those concepts of the perfection of being with which it is so closely related.

BEAUTY AND EXCELLENCE

If there is a first word in this third step in the process of triangulating Edwards' concept of beauty it is either excellence or excellency. In the very first of his "Notes on the Mind," a note entitled "Excellency," he begins with a virtual equation of excellency and beauty.

> There has nothing been more without a definition than excellency, although it be what we are more concerned with than anything else whatsoever; yea, we are concerned with nothing else. But what is this excellency? Wherein is one thing excellent and another evil; one beautiful and another deformed? [Mind 1]

He asks what excellency is, but his search for the answer takes the form of a discussion of beauty. His inquiry leads him to find excellency and beauty first

1. Holiness and love also belong properly to this group of concepts, but since they are primarily religious and moral concepts, they will be reserved for fuller consideration (in Part II) in relation to beauty in the Divine Being and in human being.

in equality,[2] then in proportion,[3] and finally in consent: "This is an universal definition of excellency: The consent of being to being, or being's consent to entity. The more the consent is, and the more extensive, the greater is the excellency" [Mind 1]. In "Note" 14 he puts the equation of excellency and beauty more directly and concludes with a rule for the degree of true beauty that (allowing for the chiasmus) conforms exactly to the above rule for the degree of excellency.

> Excellence, to put it in other words, is that which is beautiful and lovely . . . That which is beautiful with respect to the universality of things has a generally extended excellence and a true beauty; and the more extended or limited its system is, the more confined or extended is its beauty. [Mind 14]

Interwoven with this inquiry into excellency and beauty in terms of objective relations of equality, proportion, and consent among beings is a parallel investigation that comes to the same conclusions in terms of perceiving being. The relation between these two arguments is interesting, for it shows that while beauty and excellency do not have their being apart from perceiving mind, they are objectively rather than subjectively determined and defined. But the two arguments are so closely interwoven in Edwards' own mind that he himself does not clearly distinguish them. The argument in terms of objective relations has already been summarized.

For the argument in terms of perceiving being we must return to the same opening paragraph of the first "Note on the Mind" with which I began this discussion of beauty and excellence. After asking wherein one thing is excellent and another evil, one beautiful and another deformed, he continues:

> Some have said that all excellency is harmony, symmetry, or proportion; but they have not yet explained it. We would know, why proportion is more excellent than disproportion; that is, why proportion is pleasant to the mind and disproportion unpleasant. [Mind 1]

There he introduces the second line of investigation. Pleasantness to the mind is taken as a specification of excellence. And just as the answer to the question of "why proportion is more excellent than disproportion" leads him

2. "Excellency therefore seems to consist in equality," which "may be called simple beauty" [Mind 1].
3. "Proportion is complex beauty" [Mind 1].

to find excellency and beauty to consist most simply in equality, then in proportion, and most universally in consent, so also the answer to the question
about pleasantness to the mind leads him through the same series of answers
—for the question is to him very much the same in both cases.

The argument from pleasantness to perceiving being also begins with
equality and proportion and is summarized:

> The reason why equality thus pleases the mind, and inequality is
> unpleasing, is because disproportion or inconsistency is contrary
> to being. For being, if we examine narrowly, is nothing else but
> proportion. [Mind 1]

Passing on, then, from equality and proportion to consent as the ground of
pleasantness, he says, "I can conceive of no other reason why equality and
proportion should be pleasing to him that perceives but only that it has an
appearance of consent" [Mind 63].

Just as the universal definition of excellency in terms of objective relations
is beauty—"the consent of being to being, or being's consent to entity"—so
the definition of excellence in terms of pleasantness to perceiving being is
grounded in beauty: "Pleasedness to perceiving being always arises either
from a perception of consent to being in general or of consent to that being
that perceives" [Mind 1].

Both lines of inquiry into that in which excellency or beauty consists—the
one based upon objective relations among beings and the one based upon
pleasantness to perceiving being—resolve themselves into the nature of being itself.

> Being or existence is what is necessarily agreeable to being; and
> when being perceives it, it will be an agreeable perception. And
> any contradiction to being or existence is what being, when it per-
> ceives, abhors. If being, in itself considered, were not pleasing,
> being's consent to being would not be pleasing nor would being's
> disagreement with being be displeasing. [Mind 62]

However interwoven the two lines of argument or inquiry may be, it is
the one based upon objective relations among beings that is primary and
that constitutes the basis of the other. The second argument bears to the first
one such an "of course" relationship of implication in Edwards' mind that he
is less analytically scrupulous about it than he is about other matters. One
such "of course" passage indicates why the two arguments are so interwoven
and also why, in the final analysis, the discernment of excellency and beauty

must involve critically seeking out the objective relations among beings rather than relying upon pleasantness to perceiving being. Edwards observes that where being disagrees with being there is deformity and then goes on to affirm that such disagreement

> must undoubtedly be disagreeable to perceiving being, because what disagrees with being must necessarily be disagreeable to being in general, to everything that partakes of entity, and of course to perceiving being; and what agrees with being must be agreeable to being in general, and therefore to perceiving being. But agreeableness to perceiving being is pleasure, and disagreeableness is pain. [Mind 1]

The basis of the "of course" is that being-in-general is for Edwards intelligent, perceiving, spiritual being. Hence the "undoubtedly," the "of course," and the "therefore."

An important reason why objective relations among beings are more reliable than pleasantness to perceiving being as a guide to excellency or beauty is given in the passage quoted a moment ago to the effect that pleasantness to perceiving being may arise from a perception of consent to self, "to that being that perceives" (or to some larger but still confined or private system of being), as well as from a perception of consent to being-in-general. In other words, pleasantness to perceiving being may arise from a perception of secondary beauty (consent to self or to any private system of being) as well as from a perception of primary beauty. Such pleasantness or pleasure is therefore, by itself, an unreliable guide to true spiritual beauty. For primary beauty is defined objectively by conformity to God rather than subjectively by the degree of pleasure in finite perceiving being. Only in God and in the redeemed, the saints, do the two determinants of beauty actually correspond. For them, pleasantness to perceiving being not only may but does arise only from "a perception of consent to being in general."

To be sure, objective relations among beings may also be falsely discerned. Neither true virtue nor the fact that one is numbered among the company of the saints carries any guarantee that men will see things as they really are. But to have one's perception of how things are and of wherein they are good or evil governed by a disposition to be pleased according to whether things consent not to being-in-general or to God but rather according to one's own being or to some other partial or confined system of being is to be systematically denied a perception of things as they are and of their true beauty or real deformity. An emphasis upon this objective aspect of excellency and beauty may operate as a check upon subjectivism and aestheticism of taste as to what constitutes goodness or excellence or beauty by reminding us that for Edwards, what is critical for the determination of beauty and excellence is whether the consent that yields pleasantness to perceiving being is consent to being-in-general or to some private system of being. The objective relations that define the character of this consent may be falsely discerned. But at least they are more publicly available and open to critical examination than their subjective counterparts in the "pleasantness to perceiving being."

Excellency of objective relations, then, is a more reliable guide to beauty than is the pleasure of perceiving being, although both have a share in it (since the disposition to be pleased with being-in-general and with the good of the universal system of being is itself a form of primary beauty). This nonsymmetrical relation between the two determinations of beauty and excellency is spelled out in some detail by Edwards. For example, in his early sermon on "God Glorified in Man's Dependence" he distinguishes the good the redeemed have in God as either objective or inherent good. "The glorious excellencies and beauty of God" constitute that objective good. The inherent good consists in the possession and enjoyment of that objective good. "The inherent good," he says, "is twofold: it is either excellency or pleasure." The saints or the redeemed have this "spiritual excellency and joy by a kind of participation of God" in which they are "made excellent by a communication of God's excellency: God puts his own beauty, that is, his beautiful likeness upon their soul."[4] Or again it is "by a kind of effusion of God on the soul" that they partake of this spiritual joy and pleasure. These examples illustrate Edwards' view that while joy and pleasure constitute a portion of the inherent good, excellency and beauty are constitutive of both the inherent good and of the objective good on which that inherent good rests. This further documents Edwards' objectivism and supports the present case for the priority of objective relations among beings over pleasantness to perceiving being in the determination of beauty and excellency.

This priority of excellency over pleasure in the determination of beauty is important to an understanding of the objectivist character of Edwards' conception of beauty. But it should not be allowed to obscure the intimate internal relation between excellence and pleasure, between beauty and sensibility, in his thought. The relations seen in his early sermon on "God Glorified in Man's Dependence" continue to hold for his thought, as can be seen in his discussion of the "fulness of all possible good in God" in his posthumously

4. "God Glorified," *Works, 4,* 174.

published *Dissertation on the End For Which God Created the World.*
There he sums up the fullness of good in God as consisting in three things:
"light and knowledge," "holiness, moral excellence, and beauty," and "joy
and happiness" [EC 206]. Note that he speaks not of three classes of things
but of three things, so that here again beauty is identified or equated with and
not merely classed with holiness and moral excellence. "Holiness, moral
excellence, and beauty" are not merely the same kind of thing; they are the
same thing.

Of these three things, Edwards then designates the first as a natural good in
God, while the second and third are bracketed together as comprising the
moral good in God, which is "either excellence or happiness" [EC 206, n. 1].
Here the term is happiness rather than pleasure, as in the earlier sermon, but
the meaning is the same. Excellence and pleasure are internally related as
together definitive of the moral good in God. The contrast between natural
and moral good is not the same as that between objective and inherent good.
To avoid confusion, therefore, I return to the point made earlier—that while
joy and pleasure constitute a portion of the inherent good, excellency and
beauty are constitutive of both the inherent good and the objective good on
which that inherent good rests. That point may be put in another way in
order to emphasize the internal relation between excellency and pleasure
rather than the priority of excellency over pleasure in the determination of
spiritual beauty. That is, it may also be said that for Edwards excellency alone
is sufficient to the determination or definition of the objective good but that
both excellency and pleasure are essential to the definition of the inherent
good. It is this internal relation between excellency and pleasure in the inherent good that constitutes the rationale for the radically interwoven character of his two lines of inquiry into the constitution and definition of beauty
and excellency with which I began the present discussion—the inquiry based
upon objective relations among beings and the inquiry based upon pleasantness to perceiving being.[5]

The identity in definition between beauty and excellence, a closer identity
than we will find between beauty and any of the other terms in Edwards'
vocabulary of the perfection of being supports an objectivist interpretation

---

5. The *internal relation* between excellency and pleasure is a form of the internal relation between beauty and sensibility in Edwards' thought that provides the structure for
the present essay. And the *priority* of excellency over pleasure is a form of the priority of
beauty over sensibility in his thought that provides the rationale for my focusing primarily
upon beauty rather than upon sensibility.

of his conception of beauty. For excellence is most fundamentally a structural and not simply an evaluative concept: excellence "is, in its prime and proper sense, being's consent to being" [Mind 45]; it is defined principally by objective relations of consent among beings.

Edwards always finds in beauty and consent the structure and substance of excellence. In "Note" 45 he alludes to his earlier "Note" 1, which we have already examined in some detail,[6] and then picks up the inquiry in order to further specify that it is in primary beauty that excellence most properly consists.

> Excellence. 1. When we spake of excellence in bodies we were obliged to borrow the word 'consent' from spiritual things. But excellence in and among spirits is, in its prime and proper sense, being's consent to being. There is no other proper consent but that of minds, even of their will; which, when it is of minds towards minds, it is love, and when of minds towards other things, it is choice. Wherefore all the primary and original beauty or excellence that is among minds is love; and into this may all be resolved that is found among them. [Mind 45]

All other applications of the term consent can be only by analogy according to the nature of the beings involved, as he says in "Note" 62.

> As bodies, the objects of our external senses, are but the shadows of beings, that harmony wherein consists sensible excellency and beauty is but the shadow of excellency. That is, it is pleasant to the mind because it is a shadow of love. [Mind 62][7]

However generic the concept of excellence may be for Edwards—and it is a generic concept for him, in the same way "arête" was for the Greeks[8]—every effort to specify its content turns back upon beauty, whether as being's consent to being or as love (a form of beauty or of consent to being). Beauty is fundamental to both being and the perfection of being.

It would appear that it is the objective and structural aspect of beauty that

6. See pp. 58–61.

7. Notice the interweaving of the two lines of argument—from objective relations among beings and from pleasantness to perceiving being.

8. Arête, often translated as virtue, is more properly translated as excellence. See H. D. F. Kitto, *The Greeks* (Baltimore, Penguin Books, 1957), pp. 171–72: " 'Virtue', at least in modern English, is almost entirely a moral word; arête on the other hand is used indifferently in all the categories and means simply 'excellence'."

Edwards has in mind in his common use of the two terms beauty and excellence in tandem. He frequently employs the two terms as a pair, not as though by using both concepts he meant to say two distinct things but as though to reinforce and underline his meaning by supporting one concept with the other. To cite a few examples from several different sources, he says that "God's holiness is the infinite beauty and excellence of his nature" [Trinity, 97], that "as God is infinitely the greatest Being, so he is allowed to be infinitely the most beautiful and excellent" [TV 14], that the Holy Spirit "is that divine excellency and beauty itself" [Trinity, 119], that the immediate object of "spiritual understanding" is "the supreme beauty and excellency of the nature of divine things" [RA 271], that "the perceiving of spiritual beauty and excellency no more belongs to reason, than it belongs to the sense of feeling to perceive colors,"[9] and that in the redemption of the elect God "intended to bring them to perfect excellency and beauty in his [Christ's] image" [WR 304]. He also speaks of original righteousness as consisting in man's having "the highest relish of those things that were most excellent and beautiful, a disposition to have the quickest and highest delight in those things that were most worthy of it" [OS 387]. In all these and similar cases the terms beauty and excellence support one another in their usage and reference, and the character of the support given is primarily to emphasize the objective and structural aspect of beauty insofar as they can be distinguished from the evaluative and (perhaps) more subjective possibilities inherent in such a largely aesthetic concept as beauty. If such an emphasis upon the objective and structural aspect of beauty is not a part of the meaning to be found in this supportive use of the term excellence in connection with beauty, then one would expect Edwards to be quite as likely to use in the same way the other terms from his vocabulary for the perfection of being and to speak in the same contexts of "beauty and goodness" or of "beauty and value." But he does not; his use of these alternative pairs always has a less objectivist reference. Not much of a case could be made to hang on such an analysis of patterns alone, but as supportive evidence it is not without interest and merit.

One problem remains to be considered regarding the relation between beauty and excellence in Edwards' thought. If beauty and excellence are so nearly identical, what are we to make of "Note" 64? It reads in its entirety: "Excellency may be distributed into greatness and beauty: the former is the degree of being; the latter is being's consent to being" [Mind 64]. Here

9. "A Divine and Supernatural Light," *Works, 4,* 448.

beauty is not the structure or inner principle of excellence but appears to be only one of two modes or components of excellence. This statement, though it is not as extensively unpacked as are the "Notes" surrounding it, sharply poses the problem of accounting for the undeniable fluidity of Edwards' vocabulary.   .

The solution, I suggest, lies in some schema like the one summarized in Diagram A. Just as love is for Edwards both one of the Christian virtues and the sum and fountain of all Christian virtue, so excellence is both one of the two orders in which the whole system of being is articulated (greatness and goodness, existence and excellence, etc.) and the principle of the ultimate unity of those two orders. By virtue of its family resemblance and even its identity of definition with beauty, the term excellency is elevated in this "Note" to serve (as the concept beauty more commonly does) as the first principle of the system of being-in-general, as the generic concept of which greatness and beauty are the species. In this context, then, the degree of being and the degree of beauty together may be said to constitute the degree of excellency. By the same token, beauty, the primary function of which is as the first principle of being-in-general according to which the whole system of being is articulated, appears here as simply one of the two orders of that system.

Excellency is, in this "Note," distributed into "greatness and beauty." But clearly excellency has more to do with the latter than with the former. In fact, only two "Notes" earlier Edwards says that "greatness is a capacity for excellence" [Mind 62]—though it is a capacity that may go either way: "a being by greatness alone is more excellent" if it consents to being, because it "partakes of more being" and hence gives more consent [Mind 62];[10] but conversely, "a being, by greatness alone is more odious in dissent to being in general" [Mind 62] for the same reasons. Beauty and excellence, then, even in this formulation, retain their essential identity of definition in Edwards' thought. The problem posed by "Note" 64 is resolved by showing that the concept of excellence functions here as elsewhere in his thought according to the same logic that has already been shown for the concept of beauty. But even when excellence functions as the more generic concept, it is beauty that provides the model for what excellence is. It is always the concept of beauty that must be joined to that of being if excellency is to be understood.

10. A corollary Edwards deduces from this is that "hence God infinitely loves Himself because His being is infinite. He is in Himself, if I may so say, an infinite quantity of existence" [Mind 62].

Edwards continues to equate beauty and excellence to the very end. The opening sentence of the posthumously published treatise on *The Nature of True Virtue* begins, as did the first of his early "Notes on the Mind," with just that equation by speaking of virtue as "something beautiful, or rather some kind of beauty or excellency" [TV 1]. At the early stage of his thought represented by "Note" 64 he is inclined to use the concept of excellence as the bridge category for relating the two orders of being and of the perfection of being, the orders of being and of being good. But as his thought matures, he increasingly stresses the concept of beauty as the generic and bridge category for interpreting and relating the two orders of being and perfection of being and confines his use of the term excellence to its role as designating one of the two orders in which the whole system of being is articulated. As the first principle of that system of being, the concept of beauty is given fuller and richer development in his thought than is the concept of excellence. This suggests the answer to one further question.

If beauty and excellence are so identical in Edwards' thought, then why, it might be asked, designate one rather than the other as more fundamental? And then why beauty rather than excellence? The question is legitimate, but it can be answered briefly. One reason is that Edwards' concept of beauty has a wider reach than does his concept of excellence because he gives it a richer articulation—as a concept, as a category of interpretation, and as a mode of order. His usage must be our principal guide here, and he increasingly places beauty at the center of his thought about both being and the perfection of being in a way that is matched by the concept of excellence only with respect to the more objective and structural aspects of beauty—a matter of such importance, to be sure, in his thought that the concept of beauty is clearly more fully identical with that of excellence than it is with either goodness or value. A second reason for designating beauty rather than excellence as the primary concept in terms of which he interprets the perfection of being is that, unlike the term excellence, it is clearly the appropriate objective counterpart to the subjective order of sensibility. Beauty and sensibility, both largely aesthetic terms, together define the perfection of being and the quality of the moral and spiritual life.

BEAUTY AND GOODNESS

Goodness is next in importance after beauty and excellence in the rich family of concepts with which Edwards interprets the perfection of being. Excellence must be judged to be a concept virtually identical with beauty in his thought, lacking only the fuller development he gives the concept of beauty, for even the variations in their use and meaning conform to the same rules. The relation between beauty and goodness is not nearly so clear or easy to determine. I shall begin by suggesting the complexity of the relation between beauty and goodness in Edwards' thought and then advance three propositions, the elucidation of which should lead to a clearer understanding both of the relation between beauty and goodness and of the terms related. It will soon become evident that by establishing the virtual identification of beauty with excellence we have already taken a long step in that direction.

In the first place, unlike beauty and excellence, beauty and goodness are not virtually identical for Edwards. The nearest he comes to equating them is in a sermon on "The Excellency of Christ," in which he says not only that goodness is "excellent in whatever subject it be found" but also that goodness "*is* beauty and excellency itself, and renders all excellent that are possessed of it." But he immediately takes something back from this ecstatic identification of goodness with beauty or excellency by adding that goodness "is yet more excellent when joined with greatness."[11] If greatness adds to the excellency or beauty of goodness, then goodness alone is not the same as excellency or beauty. Here we have goodness in one breath fully equated with beauty and excellency, while in the next it is found to be but one of the two orders—goodness and greatness—that together compose the articulated system of being and beauty. It is in fact the structure and thesis of the whole sermon under discussion that it is the greatness and goodness of Christ that combine to constitute his excellency or beauty.

> In Christ, infinite greatness and infinite goodness meet together, and receive lustre and glory one from another. His greatness is rendered lovely by his goodness. The greater any one is without goodness, so much the greater evil; but when infinite goodness is joined with greatness, it renders it a glorious and adorable greatness. So, on the other hand, his infinite goodness receives lustre from his greatness. He that is of great understanding and ability, and is withal of a good and excellent disposition, is deservedly more esteemed than a lower and lesser being, with the same kind inclination and good will. Indeed, goodness is excellent in whatever subject it be found; it is beauty and excellency itself, and

11. "The Excellency of Christ," *Works, 4,* 197, italics added.

renders all excellent that are possessed of it; and yet more excellent
when joined with greatness.[12]

Since this sermon is perhaps as near as Edwards comes to equating beauty and
goodness, we can hardly conclude that they are identical, however closely
related they are.

That they are closely related is clear from their frequent appearance to
Edwards as a mutually illuminating and supportive pair of concepts and
realities, in much the same manner in which beauty and excellence appear.
He says, for example, that true virtue "is the general goodness and beauty of
the disposition and its exercise" [TV 3]. But he pairs goodness in a similar
fashion with excellence and with glory, value, virtue, and love. Not much
can therefore be deduced from this except a strong family resemblance and
considerable overlap in meaning among these concepts and an intimate relation among the realities to which they refer. Such a family resemblance, apparent among certain groups of concepts in his thought, is not a function of
loose thought; it is, instead, a function and expression of his view of reality as
consisting of internally related beings and systems of being rather than of
discrete and disconnected items.

If beauty and goodness are not identical but are closely related, the question naturally arises as to whether one is subordinate to the other. Is goodness a form or aspect of beauty, on the one hand, or, on the other hand, is
beauty a form or aspect—perhaps even the highest form or aspect—of goodness? If the question is put in this way, considerable evidence could be mus-
tered to support either of the two positions. But a weighing of the evidence
will show that there is no clear-cut linear relation of sub- and superordination
in either direction between beauty and goodness.

The principal reason is that it is not beauty and goodness as such or in the
abstract that are in some way related to each other but always determinate
goods and beauties, always the beauty and goodness of some determinate
being or system of beings. It will be important to keep this in mind lest, in
our immediate concern to clarify certain relations among concepts, we are
seduced into obscuring the actualism of Edwards' thought. Beauty and excellence, goodness and value, are not abstract eternal essences but are constituted by and consist in actual relations and tendencies among determinate
beings. This should be clear from the very definition of beauty as the cordial

12. Ibid.

consent of being to being, just as it will shortly be evident from the relational character of goodness. Spiritual beauty and goodness are, furthermore, fully as determinate, substantial and concrete as natural beauty and goodness—even more so, in Edwards' view. Certainly spiritual relations are no less determinate for being spiritual than are material relations, even though it may prove far more difficult to determine in any given case just what the actual spiritual relations are.

Since it is always determinate beauty and goodness, beauties and goods, that are somehow related for Edwards, and since there is no one-way relation of sub- and superordination between them, we should expect to find beauty and goodness internally related as elements in the rich fabric of being. The complexity of this interrelation and the pattern of this fabric can be suggested briefly by looking at two representative texts. In *The Nature of True Virtue* it appears that beauty in the creature is grounded in goodness in the Creator, or, to generalize the proposition, that beauty at one level of the system of being is derived from goodness at some higher level in the system. "Benevolence or goodness in the divine Being" is not only prior to both the beauty and existence of its objects "so as to be the ground both of their existence and their beauty," but it is also "God's goodness which moved him to give them both being and beauty" [TV 6]. But when, as in the *Religious Affections,* Edwards comes to "locate" and interpret the goodness of God, he finds that God's goodness is in turn grounded in His beauty and excellency. "God's goodness," he finds, is "part of the beauty of his nature" [RA 248], and—expressing the same thing in terms of excellency as well as beauty—the "infinite excellency of the divine nature, as it is in itself, is the true ground of all that is good in God in any respect" [RA 243].

With beauty and goodness so interwoven in the fabric of being, we should not expect to come too quickly upon any single formulation of the relation between them. The complicating factors for our understanding of the relation in Edwards' thought between beauty and goodness are essentially two: first, that we have always to do with determinate beauty and goodness—with a diversity of goods and beauties woven together into the richly textured fabric of being—rather than with a pair of abstract eternal essences, and second, that this interrelation in reality is reflected in the strong family resemblances among certain concepts, particularly beauty and goodness. Complications? It would be better to say that these are two essential ingredients to a correct understanding of Edwards' interpretation of the perfection of being. Despite these complexities, beauty can still be said to provide the model for his understanding of goodness and of the many kinds of good relative to the moral and religious life. Certain characteristic relations emerge from a study of his work, and something can be learned about his vision of beauty and its formative place in his thought by attending to some of them. Douglas Elwood is right that for Edwards beauty is a wider concept than goodness.[13] This is the best single spatial image of their relationship. It will be best, however, not to settle immediately upon it but to earn our way back to it by elucidating the following three propositions.

I shall first state three guiding propositions together in summary form, then enlarge upon each of them in turn, in order to show the ways in which they qualify and lend substance to the judgment that for Edwards beauty is a wider concept than goodness and is the model for his understanding of the goodness of being.

Beauty is the measure of goodness. It is itself the highest good and is the distinguishing mark that designates whatever is highest in goodness, especially moral goodness. It reaches beyond goodness to embrace and measure also that for which the concept of goodness alone is inadequate, constituting thereby the model also for holiness and the divine glory. In the apprehension of any good, beauty is at once the measure of the existential character of the apprehension and the measure of the reality of the good apprehended.

Beauty designates what is most objective in goodness—the objective element and foundation of goodness. It is in connection with this that the virtual identification of beauty and excellence is most important.

Beauty designates what is most attractive in goodness—the attractive power of any good, by virtue of which it becomes the apparent good of intelligent perceiving being and makes strong its claim upon the sensibility and subjectivity of moral agents. Beauty therefore also designates and constitutes the creative power of goodness and of being. It designates that which, being good, is most effectively united with power. It designates where and in what manner being and good are one. Spiritual or primary beauty may then be said to be the law governing the moral world, just as the secondary and derivative beauty of proportion and harmony may be said to be the law governing the natural world. Beauty is the model of order for both moral and natural worlds, and the relation between the two basic kinds of beauty (consent and proportion) is the assurance that the two orders are ultimately one under the sovereign pleasure of God.

13. Elwood, *Philosophical Theology,* p. 28.

Beauty is the measure of goodness in several respects. In order to see how this is so, we should begin by noting that as Edwards seeks to understand what is good, what forms goodness takes, and what the relations of the many goods encountered are, both among themselves and between the many and the One source of all good, he employs several distinctions respecting the good. In addition to the distinction between good and evil, he distinguishes intrinsic from instrumental good, that is, *bonum formosum* from *bonum utile,* or beautiful good from profitable good. He distinguishes natural from moral good and moral from spiritual good, public or general good from private or separate good, objective from inherent good, fullness of good from partial good, and, with respect to the apparent good, he distinguishes real or true from false good. His conception of beauty provides the unity of vision among these various perspectives on the good. For all of them it is beauty that provides the measure in some respects, the objective foundation in others, and the attractive and creative power of the good in others. Taken together, these several considerations find beauty emerging not as the only good but as a wider concept than goodness and essential to our understanding of it and participation in it.

We may begin with the very apprehension of something as good and consider in turn the distinctions respecting what is good, noting the ways in which beauty is in each case essential to the larger or greater good. "There are," says Edwards in one of his private notes, "two ways in which the mind can be said to be sensible that anything is good or excellent."

> 1. When the mind . . . [is] maturely convinced in judgment that a thing is according to the meaning of the word 'good,' as that word is generally applied.
>
> 2. . . . when it is so *sensible of the beauty* and amiableness of the thing that 'tis sensible of pleasure and delight in the presence of the idea of it. This kind of sensibleness of good carries in it an act of the will or inclination, or spirit of the mind, as well as the understanding. [Misc. 489, italics added]

The key to this second kind of sensibleness of good is that the mind is "sensible of the beauty and amiableness of the thing." This apprehension is distinguished also by its involving pleasure and delight and will or inclination, whereas the first kind of apprehension of good involves only the understanding, that is, it involves a more limited or partial engagement of the mind with its object as good. What this means is that the apprehension of beauty is essential to the fullest existential knowledge of any real good.

This theme is further unfolded in his sermon on "A Divine and Supernatural Light." In this sermon the "two-fold understanding or knowledge of good that God has made the mind of man capable of" is distinguished as a "merely speculative and notional" understanding, on the one hand, and a "sense of the heart," on the other.[14] His concern here is primarily with the knowledge of God, but the above relation between the knowledge of anything as good and having a sense of its beauty remains generalized in order to apply to the knowledge of any being as good. For Edwards, no real good is fully known until its beauty is known and enjoyed and beauty is neither known nor enjoyed until it is sensibly apprehended and "taken to heart" by a "sense of the heart."

In this sermon, as elsewhere, that beauty is the measure of goodness and the mark of the more existential of the two kinds of apprehension of anything as good is reflected in the vocabulary with which Edwards designates the object of apprehension. He says that the goodness and existence—and even the excellence—of a thing may be the object of the first kind of apprehension of good, while the second kind always has beauty as its object.

> There is not only a rational belief that God is holy, and that holiness is a *good* thing, but there is a sense of the *loveliness* of God's holiness . . .

> There is a difference between having an opinion that God *is* holy and gracious, and having a sense of the loveliness and *beauty* of that holiness and grace . . .

> There is a wide difference between mere speculative rational judging anything to be *excellent,* and having a sense of its sweetness and *beauty*.[15]

Once again, such patterns of vocabulary might not by themselves sustain my argument about the relation between beauty and goodness in Edwards' thought. But as supportive evidence they provide an interesting instance of the way in which his view of the priority of beauty is reflected even in his vocabulary. The distinction between reason and sense, of course, does not

14. *Works, 4,* 442.
15. Ibid., pp. 441–42, italics added.

mean that reason is not involved in the perception of beauty but only that reason does not itself give the perception of it. As he says later in this same sermon:

> Reason indeed is necessary to it . . . But if we take reason strictly, not for the faculty of mental perception in general, but for ratiocination . . . the perceiving of spiritual beauty and excellency no more belongs to reason than it belongs to the sense of feeling to perceive colors . . . It is out of reason's province to perceive the beauty or loveliness of anything . . . Reason's work is to perceive truth and not excellency . . . Reason may determine that a countenance is beautiful to others, it may determine that honey is sweet to others; but it will never give me a perception of its sweetness.[16]

So far I have distinguished the apprehension that something is good from the perception of its goodness and shown that what distinguishes the latter from the former is the knowledge and enjoyment of its beauty. The perception of beauty provides Edwards with his model and measure for the fullest apprehension of any good.

But the perception of the beauty of a thing does not yet guarantee that the existential engagement with that good is for its intrinsic goodness rather than for its instrumental goodness. Beauty is also the measure for determining the answer to this question, since beauty characterizes both of these kinds of goodness; an instrumental good has at best only secondary beauty, while the intrinsic good alone has primary beauty. Any good may appear lovely in either way—even such a real good as the grace of God.

> The grace of God may appear lovely two ways: either as *bonum utile,* a profitable good to me, that which greatly serves my interest, and so suits my self-love; or as *bonum formosum,* a beautiful good in itself, and part of the moral and spiritual excellency of the divine nature. In this latter respect it is that the true saints have their hearts affected, and love captivated by the free grace of God in the first place. [RA 262f]

There are two closely related aspects to the distinction drawn here. One is between an instrumental and an intrinsic good; the other is between a thing's being good by virtue of some conceived relation it bears to self and to

16. Ibid., p. 448.

self-interest and its being good or "appearing lovely" by virtue of a beauty it has in itself. The latter may be rephrased as Edwards' distinction between a private or "proper and separate good" and a public or general good, to which I shall return shortly.

Instrumental or profitable goods are not to be scorned, but attachment to them is truly virtuous or a sign of truly holy affections only if subordinate to one's being captivated in the first place [RA 263] with their beauty. Actually, beauty characterizes both instrumental and intrinsic goodness, for a thing's being regarded as good at all consists in its appearing lovely or beautiful. But in the first case the beauty consists in the object's being agreeable to or consenting to some limited system of being, whether it is the self or some larger system in which the self is interested; in the other case the beauty consists in the object's own nature, what it is in itself. In the first case, that of the *bonum utile,* the beauty may or may not be at odds with being in general, and accordingly attachment to it because of this beauty is "no certain sign of grace" [RA 263] or mark of virtue. In the other case, that of the *bonum formosum,* its appearing lovely to me does constitute a sign of true holiness and virtue, because its so appearing to me consists in my consenting to its being as it *is* and not as it is *useful,* which is simply another way of saying that it appears lovely to me because of its consent to being-in-general, that is, to being unqualified by any special or partial or private interest.

Only the *bonum formosum* is beautiful by a general or spiritual beauty. Spiritual beauty, then, is Edwards' model of the intrinsic good, that which simply by being is absolutely good and is its own excuse for being. Instrumental goods also appear lovely but have at best only a secondary beauty; and such apparent goods are real goods only by relation to and in subordination to an intrinsic beautiful good. Implicit in taking the "beautiful good" as the model for understanding what is intrinsincally good is Edward's view that true goodness is creative rather than static, formative and self-giving rather than self-contained and self-sufficient.

Since "the moral world is," for Edwards "the end of the natural world" [FW 251], such an intrinsic "beautiful good" will be primarily a moral or spiritual good rather than a natural good, although his notion of the "fullness of good"[17] embraces both natural and moral good. Between natural and moral good there obtains the same relation as between natural and moral or spiritual beauty.

17. See pp. 80–83.

Edwards' own efforts at distinguishing natural and moral good are something less than triumphs of clarity if they are read as essays at definition, in which case they would be either tautological or simply definitions by exclusion. They should be read instead as essays at description or distinction, rather than definition. His first attempt is in the now well-known "Miscellany" 782 on the "Sense of the Heart."

> By natural good and evil I mean all that good or evil which is agreeable or disagreeable to human nature as such, without regard to the moral disposition; as all natural beauty and deformity, such as a visible sensible proportion or disproportion in figures, sounds, and beauty of colors; any good or evil that is the object of the external senses; and all that good or evil which arises from gratifying or crossing any of the natural appetites; all that good and evil which consists in gratifying or crossing a principle of self-love. [Misc. 782]

By spiritual good, on the other hand, he means

> all real moral beauty and excellency, and all those acts of the will, or that sense of the heart that relates to it, and the idea of which involves it; as all relish for it and desires of it, and delight in it, and happiness consisting in it, etc. [Misc. 782]

By spiritual evil, he means all that stands contrary to this standard of primary beauty. His concept of the natural good appears to be essentially a residual category for all that does not qualify as a moral or spiritual good because it does not involve that spiritual sensibility that has as its distinctive object a primary "beauty and excellency."

When he comes to the subject again, in the *Religious Affections,* his concern has shifted somewhat from one of distinguishing primarily between the objects of natural and spiritual sensibilities to one of distinguishing between the natural and moral perfections of God and of man. Moral evil is first distinguished from natural evil. By the former he means "the evil of sin, or that evil which is against duty, and contrary to what is right and ought to be" [RA 254]. By the latter he means "that which is contrary to mere nature, without any respect to a rule of duty" [RA 254]. Moral good is then said to mean

> that which is contrary to sin, or that good in beings who have will and choice, whereby, as voluntary agents, they are, and act, as it

becomes 'em to be and to act, or so as is most fit, and suitable, and lovely. [RA 254]

And by natural good he means

> that good that is entirely of a different kind from holiness or virtue, viz. that which perfects or suits nature, considering nature abstractly from any holy or unholy qualifications, and without any relation to any rule or measure of right and wrong. [RA 254]

He then enumerates some of those natural goods: pleasure, honor, strength, "speculative knowledge, human learning, and policy" [RA 255]. And then he concludes, as though to confirm the view that he has been engaged in descriptive distinction rather than definition: "Thus there is a distinction to be made between the natural good that men are possessed of, and their moral good" [RA 255].

Beauty, then, is the measure of both natural and moral goodness and of the relation between them. Once again this interpretation finds support in the very vocabulary and diction of his discussions of beauty and goodness. The following statement is typical of his tendency to use the term "good" in referring to the natural good in something even while using the term "beauty" in referring to a corresponding moral or spiritual good:

> Thus in that great goodness of God to sinners, and the wonderful dying love of Christ, there is a *natural good,* which all men love, as they love themselves; as well as *a spiritual and holy beauty,* which is seen only by the regenerate. [RA 277, italics added]

The more substantial the goodness, the more likely he is to refer to it in terms of beauty, even though, strictly speaking, both varieties of goodness are forms of beauty.

Closely related to Edwards' distinction between instrumental and intrinsic good is his distinction between private and public good. Once again beauty is the measure of the distinction and of the relation between the goods distinguished. By public good he does not mean the good of the society as a whole, nor the good of mankind, nor even the good of the whole community of the living—for even reverence for life reaches to but a small part of the universal system of being, the good of which is alone truly public and general. The public good is measured by the exacting standard of primary beauty—the cordial consent of being to being in general. Any good, such as human benevolence and affection, is essentially private rather than public unless it conforms to this rule of beauty and "arise[s] from [a] temper of benevolence to being in general" [TV 86]. Private affections are not by any means enjoined or demeaned; they may have the secondary beauty of harmony and proportion and hence be "beautiful within their own private sphere" [TV 87]. But they will be truly good only if on a larger view they also meet the higher standard of primary beauty.

> No affection limited to any private system, not dependent on, nor subordinate to being in general, can be of the nature of true virtue; and this, whatever the private system be, let it be more or less extensive. [TV 22]

It is only natural for anything to seek its own good, in the sense of a "separate good" [Misc. 530], while it is virtuous to seek the good of some larger system of being—natural virtue if the good sought is defined by the rule of secondary beauty and hence is still private and true moral or spiritual virtue if the good sought measures up to the rule of primary beauty.

Beauty is the measure and norm for distinguishing and comparing the various kinds of good with each other. But good is also to be compared with evil, and there too it is beauty that provides the measure of good and evil throughout the whole graded system of being. A taste or relish for "that which has in it true moral beauty" is what "discerns and distinguishes between good and evil" [RA 281]. "Disagreement or contrariety to being is evidently an approach to nothing, or a degree of nothing . . . and the greatest and only evil; and entity [or being] is the greatest and only good" [Mind 1]. Dissent from being is the opposite of both being and beauty.[18] The scales of good and evil, being and nothing, consent and dissent, beauty and deformity, all correspond to each other ontologically as well as morally in Edwards' grand system of being, which runs from the "fullness of being" and beauty in God toward "absolute nothing," his boundary concept for that which is "the essence of all contradiction" [Misc. 27a].

Beauty is the measure of goodness in all these ways because beauty is itself the highest good and the first principle of being, which is "the greatest and only good" [Mind 1]. There are places where Edwards can be read as saying that beauty is not simply the highest good or the measure of goodness but that there is also in beauty something even higher than goodness. This is the

18. See pp. 44–47.

case at least with respect to his understanding of God. Beauty has such a special place among the divine perfections that it is the one among these perfections that cannot be simply classified as either a natural or a moral attribute of God. But this is a special case, for it is precisely and only in God, the fountain of both being and beauty, that the orders of being and being-good are fully one; and beauty is the principle of that unity. Generally speaking, it is enough to say that beauty is the highest good and the measure of goodness, and it is not necessary to insist that beauty is somehow higher than goodness in Edwards' vision of things. For beauty is not the only good. And even with respect to God there are occasions when goodness appears as a more richly articulated concept than beauty, as in the case of the "fullness of good" in God,[19] of which beauty is only a part—though the most important, objective, and highest part. Such formulations must be weighed in the balance together with such other formulations of the relation between beauty and goodness as the view that "God's goodness" is but a "part of the beauty of his nature" [RA 248]. Again it must be remembered that such a dialectical interdependence between beauty and goodness is to be found in Edwards' thought because he is dealing always with determinate goods and beauties, with determinate goodness and beauty, and with whole systems of these, and not with eternal essences.

Upon weighing the evidence with this in mind, considering the close kinship between his conceptions of beauty and goodness and the fluidity of his vocabulary about the perfection of being, it would indeed be rash to urge any simple linear relationship of sub- and superordination between beauty and goodness in his thought. And yet the principles of beauty do emerge as the more central and critical ones, especially for his constructive theological and moral reflections. Certainly the concept of goodness is never invoked as a category of interpretation for an understanding of beauty. Though beauty and goodness overlap considerably in their meaning, it is ultimately beauty that is the measure of goodness, and not the other way around.

Beauty is the objective foundation of goodness. This point is closely related to the virtual identity of definition already established between beauty and excellence as essentially structural, ontological, and objective (rather than primarily evaluative, moral, and subjective) conceptions of the perfection of being. We may begin to see how this is so by recalling the place

---

19. See pp. 80–83.

of beauty in Edwards' distinction between the objective and inherent portions of the good the redeemed have in God, first drawn in his early sermon on "God Glorified in Man's Dependence." Beauty and excellence constitute both the objective and the inherent good, whether in God or communicated to the creature. Beauty plays the more substantial part in defining the objective good, which consists of "the glorious excellencies and beauty of God." Its role in defining or constituting the inherent good is less comprehensive though no less important, for the inherent good, which is the possession and enjoyment of the objective good, "is two-fold: it is either excellency or pleasure," and it is received as "God puts his own beauty" upon the creature.[20] This two-foldness of the inherent good corresponds to the internal relation between the two coordinate orders of beauty and sensibility.

The term "fullness" is one frequently employed by Edwards in discussing the good of which beauty is the objective foundation. It is obviously a term of considerable significance to him, for he frequently gives himself to reflection about and restatement of its meaning, especially in connection with its use in Scripture. An examination of its meaning for him will serve to bring some order into the relationships among several distinctions in goodness he strongly insists upon.

He sometimes speaks of God's fullness as signifying his "beauty and happiness," as in the *Religious Affections,* where he argues that it is God's fullness that is given in truly spiritual and gracious religious affections.

> Not that the saints are made partakers of the essence of God, and so are "Godded" with God, and "Christed" with Christ, according to the abominable and blasphemous language and notions of some heretics; but, to use the Scripture phrase, they are made partakers of God's fullness (Eph. 3:17–19; John 1:16), that is, of God's spiritual beauty and happiness, according to the measure and capacity of a creature; for so it is evident the word "fullness" signifies in Scripture language. [RA 203]

At other times he uses the concept of the "fullness of good in God" in a somewhat larger sense as consisting in beauty and happiness together with a third component, the knowledge of God; in the *Dissertation on the End for Which God Created the World* he specifies that the fullness of good in God

20. "God Glorified," *Works, 4,* 174.

consists in three things: "light and knowledge," "holiness, moral excellence and beauty," and "joy and happiness" [EC 206].

The former of these two conceptions of the fullness of good corresponds to his conception of the inherent good; the latter is more inclusive. In fact, the narrower conception of "God's fullness" seems to be identical in content and definition with his conception of the "inherent good in God." The inherent good is defined as the possession of the objective good, and God's fullness is defined in the same way: "By fullness, as the term is used in Scripture, as may easily be seen by looking over the texts that mention it, is intended the good that any one possesses" [Grace 48].[21] The difference in content between the narrower and the wider conceptions of God's fullness may be adequately accounted for by assuming that when he employs it in its narrower meaning, Edwards has in mind specifically the moral or spiritual good in God, as distinguished from the natural good. This supposition is supported by the following footnote explaining his wider use of the term "fullness" in the *Dissertation on the End for Which God Created the World,* in which he distinguishes between the natural and the moral good and, within the moral good, between excellence and happiness:

> I shall often use the phrase *God's fulness,* as signifying and comprehending all the good which is in God natural and moral, either excellence or happiness; partly because I know of no better phrase to be used in this general meaning; and partly because I am led hereto by some of the inspired writers, particularly the apostle Paul, who often uses the phrase in this sense. [EC 206n]

Accordingly, Edwards' conception of the good in God may be represented as in Diagram D. The narrower meaning of "God's fullness" is represented as corresponding to his conception of the "inherent good in God," with both of these consisting of the two-fold moral good (beauty and happiness), which is distinguished by Edwards from the other portion (knowledge) of the wider conception of God's fullness. Also represented is the critical place of beauty

21. Cf. Edwards' "Notes on the Bible" 235: "By fullness, according to the apostle's use of the phrase, is signified the good of any being; all that by which any being is excellent and happy; including its perfection, beauty, riches, joy, and pleasure" (*Works,* ed. Sereno E. Dwight [New York, 1829–30], 9, 527).

DIAGRAM D

THE GOOD IN GOD

1. *Objective good:* beauty, excellence

   "the glorious excellencies and beauty of God."[22]

   "The infinite excellency [or beauty] of the divine
   nature as it is in itself [objectively], is the
   ground of all that is good in God in any respect." [RA 243]

2. *Inherent good:* (i.e. the possession of the objective good)

   (a) beauty   (b) happiness
       excellence   pleasure
                            joy
                            delight

3. *God's fullness:* (i.e. "the good that any one possesses")

   (a) beauty   (b) happiness   (c) knowledge
       excellence   pleasure   light
       holiness   joy
       love (of   delight (love of
          benevolence)   complacence)

MORAL OR SPIRITUAL GOOD   NATURAL GOOD

in this entire conception of the good in God, together with the relationship
between the order of beauty and the order of sensibility as the two coordinate
components of the spiritual and moral good in God.[23]

22. "God Glorified," *Works, 4,* 174.

23. Cf. the working representation of some relationships in Edwards' thought about
these two orders of beauty and sensibility in Diagram C. Edwards' more theological definition of God's fullness as consisting in the Holy Spirit will be considered in Ch. 7. He
says, e.g. that "God's fulness does consist in the Holy Spirit" [Grace 48], that "the fulness
of God consists in the holiness and happiness of the Deity" [Grace 48], and that "the
holiness and happiness of God consists in the Holy Spirit" [Grace 56]. Edwards' conception of the manner in which this fullness of good in God is communicated to the creature
will be considered in Ch. 8.

This formulation also conforms to Edwards' view of the "two ways in which the mind

It can be seen that we are now more explicitly concerned than before with the aspect of the moral and spiritual life that is represented by portion (b) of the inherent good or the fullness of good that the redeemed have in God —or, for that matter, that any man has in the possession of what he takes to be his objective good. Edwards finds that the realities represented by the terms in portions (a) and (b) of the inherent good are inseparably and internally related to each other in the moral and spiritual life, whether in God Himself or in the creature. Beauty and happiness, excellence and pleasure, holiness and joy, love (of benevolence) and delight (love of complacence) are inseparable and coordinate components of the moral and spiritual life. He measures the quality of such a life by reference to these two summary or definitive components, emblematic of the coordinate and corresponding orders of beauty and sensibility. One could begin with either order, so reliably do they correspond throughout the whole system of being. But ultimately it is the objective order of beauty rather than the subjective order of sensibility that provides the surest guide, for the latter is ontologically, morally, and conceptually dependent upon or secondary to the former. That is to say, in the present instance the realities of the moral life that are designated by the terms in portion (b) of the inherent good are ultimately dependent upon the realities designated by their coordinate terms in portion (a). Or to put it more radically, the (a) and (b) portions of the inherent good taken together (both beauty and joy) are ontologically dependent upon the reality of the objective good (beauty or excellence).

The two orders do, however, correspond so reliably that Edwards himself is sometimes hard put to resolve the question of whether their relationship is best described as one of a correspondence between them or of a priority of one over the other. This can be seen most clearly in his running debate with himself over whether a love of complacence is prior to or dependent upon a love of benevolence. Although he wavers at times, he ends up finally where he began as early as in the "Notes on the Mind"—in favor of the priority of benevolence over complacence.

If the question of priority must be answered, it is surely essential to the integrity of Edwards' whole philosophical-theological-moral program that the love of benevolence should be seen as having both moral and ontological

---

can be sensible that anything is good" [Misc. 489]: in judgment, according to the understanding, and in a more existential and fuller engagement of the self, a response and involvement of the will or inclination as well as the understanding, founded upon an apprehension of "the beauty and amiableness of the thing," and yielding a sense of "pleasure and delight in the presence of the idea of it" [Misc. 489].

priority over the love of complacence. But in some respects that is the wrong question. Or at any rate it is not the only question. For the correspondence of portion (b) to portion (a) of the inherent good and the correspondence of the subjective order of sensibility to the objective order of beauty are as important as the ontological and moral priority of the latter in each of these cases. This will be further clarified when I consider Edwards' analysis of the will.

Beauty is for Edwards the touchstone of objectivity in our relations with things as good or evil—the measure of objectivity or disinterestedness in the apprehension of anything as good. To be affected with the primary beauty of any real good is the very model of objectivity, as against the partiality of being affected with things as good by virtue of some relation they bear to a private interest of the self. To love something is to be attracted to it as good: "A holy love has a holy object: the holiness of love consists especially in this that it is the love of that which is holy, as holy, or for its holiness" [RA 260]. More particularly, it is the beauty of holiness that attracts such a holy love, for holiness is the beauty of divine things. The most objectivist terms in Edwards' vocabulary for the perfection of being are stressed in his discussions of the foundation of true love and holy affections toward anything as good.

> 'Tis unreasonable to think otherwise, than that the first foundation of a true love to God, is that whereby he is in himself lovely, or worthy to be loved, or the supreme loveliness of his nature. This is certainly what makes him chiefly amiable. What chiefly makes a man, or any creature lovely, is his excellency; and so what chiefly renders God lovely, and must undoubtedly be the chief ground of true love, is his excellency. God's nature, or the divinity, is infinitely excellent; yea 'tis infinite beauty, brightness, and glory itself. But how can that be true love of this excellent and lovely nature, which is not built on the foundation of its true loveliness? How can that be true love of beauty and brightness, which is not for beauty and brightness' sake? [RA 242f]

A true love of God will rest in the first instance upon objective beauty and excellence, as a *bonum formosum,* not as an instrumental good but as an intrinsic good, "the original good, and the true fountain of all good, the first fountain of all loveliness of every kind, and so the foundation of all true love" [RA 243]. On the other hand, "they whose affection to God is founded first on his profitableness to them, their affection begins at the wrong end" [RA 243]. Of these two foundations of a love to God, one constitutes a more objective determination of the self because it finds God to be good by virtue of His nature as it is in itself, while the other finds Him to be good primarily by virtue of some conceived relation to the self. One is founded on God, the other is founded on self. For Edwards as for Augustine, it is on such diverse objective foundations that are erected the city of God and the city of man.

> In the love of the true saints God is the lowest foundation; the love of the excellency of his nature is the foundation of all the affections which come afterwards, wherein self-love is concerned as an handmaid: on the contrary, the hypocrite lays himself at the bottom of all, as the first foundation, and lays on God as the superstructure; and even his acknowledgment of God's glory itself, depends on his regard to his private interest. [RA 246]

In sum, as Edwards declares in his opening statement of the third sign of holy affections:

> Those affections that are truly holy, are primarily founded on the loveliness of the moral excellency of divine things. Or (to express it otherwise), a love to divine things for the beauty and sweetness of their moral excellency, is the first beginning and spring of all holy affections. [RA 253f]

Or, as he says in the opening sermon of his 1738 series on *Charity and its Fruits:* "When God is loved aright, he is loved for his excellency, and the beauty of his nature, especially the holiness of his nature" [CF 7].

Beauty is the attractive power of the good—that by virtue of which any good, and most especially any real good, becomes the apparent good of intelligent perceiving being and makes strong its claim upon the sensibility and subjectivity of free and responsible moral agents. Beauty therefore also designates and constitutes the creative power of goodness and of being. It designates what, being good, is most effectively united with power and does in fact make strong its claim (the claim of the objective good) upon the creature with such power as to draw (rather than force) him into a participation in that good as also his inherent good. The real good of the creature, then, is not only good for us and over us but it is also attractive to us and before us. And beauty designates this attractive power of the good. It is beauty as the attractive power of the good that is the key to the way in which Edwards holds together the sovereign power of the Creator and the freedom and responsibility of moral creatures, for beauty is the rule according to which God governs the moral world.

We may begin by considering Edwards' famous definition of the will: "The will always is as the greatest apparent good is" [FW 142]. What is most important for showing beauty to be the attractive power of the good is the "is as" portion of this definition. Unlike the definitions of the will offered by some of Edwards' opponents in the controversy that occasioned the publication of his *Freedom of the Will,* this is not a causal but rather a descriptive definition of the will. Edwards rejects as an "absurd inconsistent notion" the idea that the essence of the moral good or evil of the will "lies not in their nature, but in their cause" [FW 341].

> 'Tis a certain beauty or deformity that are *inherent* in that good
> or evil will, which is the *soul* of virtue and vice (and not in the
> *occasion* of it) which is their worthiness of esteem or disesteem,
> praise or dispraise, according to the common sense of mankind.
> [FW 340, italics Edwards'.]

He does not say that the will is determined by the apparent good or by anything else besides its own pleasure but that it is as the apparent good is. The will is neither autonomously indeterminate nor heteronomously determined by something outside itself. Rather, the will is in correspondence with its object, the apparent good. It is as a good the very being of which, as apparent good, is in large part a function of the affectional disposition of the perceiving self. (It must, of course, be remembered that for Edwards the will is not a faculty of the self but is a manner of speaking about the self as a whole in its affectional engagement with reality as good or evil).

The two sides of this "is as" equation are the "will" and the "greatest apparent good"; and beauty is essential to a determination of both sides, that is, to a determination of both the spiritual or moral condition of the will and the attractive power of the apparent good. In his discussion of his key definition in the opening pages of the *Freedom of the Will,* Edwards first specifies two things important to an understanding of his meaning and to which I shall need to refer below. First he says: "I use the term 'good' . . . as of the same import with 'agreeable.' To appear good to the mind, as I use the

phrase, is the same as to appear agreeable, or seem pleasing to the mind"
[FW 143]. Then he says that he is speaking of direct and immediate and
not of indirect agreeableness: "I speak of the direct and immediate object
of the act of volition; and not some object that the act of will has not an immediate, but only an indirect and remote respect to" [FW 142]. Then he is
quite explicit about the importance of the "is as" terminology in saying that
"the will always is as the greatest apparent good is."

> I have rather chosen to express myself thus, that the will *is* as the
> the greatest apparent good, or as what appears most agreeable is,
> than to say that the will is *determined* by the greatest apparent
> good, or by what seems most agreeable; because an appearing most
> agreeable or pleasing to the mind, and the mind's preferring and
> choosing, seem hardly to be properly and perfectly distinct. [FW
> 144, italics Edwards']

He immediately proceeds to offer an alternative formulation of his reasons
for so choosing to express himself, drawing on the distinction—a critical one
for his position—between voluntary action and the act of volition proper of
which that action is a consequence.

> If strict propriety of speech be insisted on, it may more properly be
> said, that the voluntary action which is the immediate consequence
> and fruit of the mind's volition or choice, is determined by that
> which appears most agreeable, than the preference or choice itself;
> but that the act of volition itself is always determined by that in or
> about the mind's view of the object, which causes it to appear most
> agreeable. I say, in or about the mind's view of the object, because
> what has influence to render an object in view agreeable, is not
> only what appears in the object viewed, but also the manner of the
> view, and the state and circumstances of the mind that views.
> [FW 144]

Three sorts of things, then, lend strength to the agreeableness of an object
in view, or, to express it otherwise, contribute to the attractive power of anything as good: "what appears in the object viewed," "the manner of the
view," and "the state and circumstances of the mind that views." Edwards
admits that "it would perhaps be hard to make a perfect enumeration of"
these things and that it "might [even] require a treatise by itself" [FW 142,
145]. But he does nevertheless undertake to "mention some things in gen-

eral" regarding each of these three categories of things. In each case beauty
emerges as a critical and definitive component of the volitional equation.

The first thing Edwards mentions with respect to "what appears in the object" itself is the beauty or deformity which it has in itself.

> There are various things of this sort that have an hand in rendering
> it more or less agreeable; as: 1. That which appears in the object
> which renders it beautiful and pleasant, or deformed and irksome
> to the mind; viewing it as it is in itself. [FW 145]

Two other things are enumerated under this head: the apparent pleasantness
or troublesomeness of the "concomitants and consequences" attendant upon
the object [FW 145] and "the apparent probability or certainty of that good"
[FW 146]. But beauty remains the first objective determinant of the will, as
it is (for the same reasons) of the affections and of moral virtue and vice.
Here it can be seen why Edwards insists that in his "is as" equation he is speaking of the direct and immediate object of the will. For beauty is only apprehended directly by "immediate sensation" or perception, and not indirectly by
reflection. As he says in *The Nature of True Virtue,* "that form or quality is
called beautiful, which appears in itself agreeable or comely, or the view of
which is immediately pleasant to the mind" [TV 98].

> Indirect agreeableness . . . is not beauty. But when a form or qual-
> ity appears lovely, pleasing and delightful in itself, then it is called
> beautiful; and this agreeableness or gratefulness of the idea is
> beauty. It is evident that the way we come by the idea of beauty is
> by immediate sensation of the gratefulness of the idea called beau-
> tiful; and not by finding out by argumentation any consequences,
> or other things with which it stands connected; any more than
> testing the sweetness of honey, or perceiving the harmony of a tune
> is by argumentation on connections and consequences. [TV 98f]

It is by a direct sensation or immediate experience of the beauty or deformity in the object that anything becomes to the self its own apparent good or
evil. And the spiritual and moral condition of the self can be measured, according to Edwards, in accordance with the objective standard provided by
attending first to the beauty in the object. It is beauty that will primarily qualify the good as apparent good. But what kind of beauty? The primary beauty
of being's cordial consent to being in general? The secondary beauty of harmony and proportion? The limited and partial beauty of consent to and har-

mony with only a private or confined realm of being? Or perhaps it is the false beauty that is really, on a wider view of things, a deformity, for it stands in dissent against a larger good and a wider realm of being. Or again, is the beauty found in the object one that is defined by the nature of the object itself as inherent good, *bonum formosum?* Or is it rather a secondary, partial, and perhaps even false beauty defined by its harmony or conformity with self or with some wider though still private realm of being in which the self is interested?

Such questions about the kind of beauty by virtue of which something is taken as the apparent good of moral agents are central to Edwards' phenomenology of the moral and spiritual life. "Various kinds of creatures," he observes in the *Religious Affections,* "show the difference of their natures, very much, in the different things they relish as their proper good, one delighting in that which another abhors" [RA 262]. The questions are designed primarily to be put to oneself and not to others. But his extensive and systematic exploration of them testifies to his objectivist conviction that the rules of beauty are objective and written into the nature of things rather than subjective in the sense of an arbitrary function of mere convention and social or cultural "taste," that true beauty consists in conformity to God and consent to being in general rather than in conformity to self or consent to any confined realm of being, however extensive, and that men can, therefore, both put and answer such questions more successfully if they study and discuss them together and in public.

> By this you may examine your love to God, and to Jesus Christ, and to the Word of God, and your joy in them, and also your love to the people of God, and your desires after heaven; whether they be from a supreme delight in this sort of beauty [as *bonum formosum,* a beautiful good in itself], without being primarily moved from your imagined interest in them, or expectations from 'em. [RA 262]

Essentially the same questions as are here proposed by Edwards specifically with respect to the love of God may properly be put respecting the nature of the beauty by virtue of which anything else is constituted as one's apparent good. For, as it is beauty that establishes any good as one's apparent good, so it is by the nature of that beauty that one can measure the moral or spiritual quality of the will, which is the other side of Edwards' "is as" equation.

The second sort of thing that contributes to the agreeableness of an object in view or to the power of its attractiveness as the apparent good is "the manner of view." Here Edwards has in mind primarily "the liveliness of the idea the mind has, of that good" [FW 146]. This has an influence because "the ideas we have of sensible things by immediate sensation, are usually much more lively than those we have by mere imagination, or by contemplation of them when absent" [FW 146]. And beauty is just such a sensible thing respecting which he had said in his sermon on "A Divine and Supernatural Light" that "there is a difference between having an opinion . . . and having a sense" or "between having a rational judgment . . . and having a sense."

> There is a wide difference between mere speculative rational judging any thing to be excellent, and having a sense of its sweetness and beauty. The former rests only in the head, speculation only is concerned in it; but the heart is concerned in the latter. When the heart is sensible of the beauty and amiableness of a thing, it necessarily feels pleasure in the apprehension. It is implied in a person's being heartily sensible of the loveliness of a thing, that the idea of it is sweet and pleasant to his soul; which is a far different thing from having a rational opinion that it is excellent.[24]

The difference between having a rational judgment that something is beautiful and having a sense of that beauty is crucial in the determination of the will by the beauty of the apparent good. The attractive power of the apparent good will be liveliest when the "manner of view" is sensible rather than notional, speculative, or rational. As Edwards observes in one of the "Notes" that contributed to the preparation of his treatise on the *Freedom of the Will:*

> Merely the rationally judging that a thing is lovely in itself, without a sensibleness of the beauty and pleasantness of it, signifies nothing towards influencing the will . . . Therefore, if a man has only a rational judgment that a thing is beautiful and lovely, without any sensibleness of the beauty . . . he will never choose it. [Misc. 436][25]

24. *Works, 4,* 442.
25. Edwards makes one exception to this statement, about which it may be worth inserting an explanation here. In this "Miscellany" he distinguishes between the "rational will" and the "will of appetite." The "whole will compounded of these two . . . is always a free agent," but in the fallen creature the two components of the whole will may be divided against each other. In such a conflict of motives it is always the will of appetite

Such a sense of the beauty of the thing, if it is in fact a lively sense, will prevail in the determination of the will even over a rational judgment to the contrary. But, as he goes on to urge in the sermon quoted above, this sense of beauty and excellence, far from standing in opposition to reason, "removes the hindrances of reason [and] positively helps reason." With respect to divine things in particular:

> It makes even the speculative notions the more lively . . . The beauty and sweetness of the objects draws on the faculties, and draws forth their exercises: so that reason itself is under far greater advantages for its proper and free exercises, and to attain its proper end, free of darkness and delusion.[26]

He does not set sense against understanding or sentiment against reason, as did most of his contemporaries on both sides of the controversy over the

---

that prevails in the immediate act of volition, so that a person may, from a "sensibleness of the good," will something that is contrary to his own rational judgment of what is good or best for himself. On the other hand, a man may will what is good in itself not because of any direct sensibleness of the beauty that is in such a good but because of a rational judgment that it is beautiful or good—a more indirect process. This would be what might (with Kant in mind) be called an accidentally rather than essentially virtuous exercise of the will by a person whose will is not at its center (the "will of appetite") virtuous. It is this possibility that is the exception Edwards makes to the statement as cited in the body of the text above. With this explanation, that statement may now be read more comprehensively in its wider setting:

> When I say, his judgment of what is best for himself, I don't mean his judgment of what is best absolutely, and most lovely in itself; for the mind's sense of the absolute loveliness of a thing directly influences only the will of appetite. If the soul wills it merely because it appears lovely in itself, it will be because the loveliness draws the appetition of the soul. It may indirectly influence what I call the rational will, or the judgment may be convinced that what is most lovely in itself will be best for him and most for his happiness. Merely the rationally judging that a thing is lovely in itself, without a sensibleness of the beauty and pleasantness of it, signifies nothing towards influencing the will except it be this indirect way, that he thinks it will therefore be best some way or other for himself—most for his good. Therefore, if a man has only a rational judgment that a thing is beautiful and lovely, without any sensibleness of the beauty, and at the same time don't think it best for himself, he will never choose it. Though, if he be sensible of the beauty of it to a strong degree, he may will it though he thinks 'tis not best for himself. Persons, from a sensibleness of the good and pleasantness of sense enjoyments, will them though they are convinced they are not best for themselves. Hence it follows that a person with respect to his rational will may be perfectly free, and yet may refuse that which he at the same time rationally judges to be in itself most lovely and becoming, and will that which he rationally knows to be hateful. [Misc. 436]

26. "A Divine and Supernatural Light," *Works, 4,* 443.

Great Awakening. Instead he sets "sensible knowledge" against "mere speculative knowledge" or "mere notional understanding" and finds that "spiritual
understanding" is of the nature of "sensible knowledge" rather than of "speculative knowledge," for in it "the mind don't only speculate and behold, but
relishes and feels" [RA 272]. Spiritual understanding "primarily consists in
this sense or taste of the moral beauty of divine things" and "includes all
that discerning and knowledge of things of religion, which depends upon,
and flows from such a sense" [RA 273].

The attractive power of the apparent good is in part, then, a function not
only of the apprehension of the beauty in that good but also of the manner
of view of that beauty, whether "sensible" and grounded in personal experience or "notional" and acquired at second-hand.

The third kind of thing that Edwards feels contributes to the attractive
power of the apparent good is "the state and circumstances of the mind that
views." His understanding of this is related to what has just been observed
about his conception of "spiritual understanding." The last chapter in *The
Nature of True Virtue* is entitled: "In What Respects Virtue or Moral Good
Is Founded in Sentiment; and How Far It Is Founded in the Reason and
Nature of Things." It is addressed not so much to the controversy over the
place of reason and emotion in the religion of New England as it is to the
strikingly parallel controversy among contemporary moralists in England
and Scotland over contending claims regarding the rightful priority of reason
or sentiment in the moral life. As in the controversy over the Great Awakening, Edwards finds it necessary to develop a redefinition of the very terms of
the controversy and to offer a conception of the self, the moral agent, in
which what had been torn apart is reunited. His answer to the question asked
in the chapter title is accordingly—both/and in character.

> *The manner of being affected* with the immediate presence of the
> beautiful idea, depends not on any reasonings about the idea after
> we have it, before we can find out whether it be beautiful or not;
> but *on the frame of our minds* whereby they are so made that such
> an idea, as soon as we have it, is grateful, or appears beautiful. [TV
> 99, italics added]

But the particular frame of mind or spiritual sense "whereby the mind is
disposed to delight in the idea of true virtue" [TV 99] is "not arbitrarily
given, without any foundation in the nature of things" [TV 102] or reason.
For such a frame of mind is itself virtuous. And virtue, as Edwards again

reminds his reader, "is a certain kind of beautiful nature, form, or quality" [TV 98] and "consists in the cordial consent or union of being to being in general" [TV 99]. "Now certainly agreement itself to being in general must necessarily agree better with general existence, than opposition or contrariety to it" [TV 100]. In these and other closely related arguments Edwards finds an explanation of "why that spiritual and divine sense, by which those who are truly virtuous and holy perceive the excellency of true virtue, is in the sacred scriptures called by the name of light, knowledge, understanding, etc." [TV 102], and why, on the other hand, "the want of this spiritual sense, and the prevalence of those dispositions which are contrary to it, tends to darken and distract the mind, and dreadfully to delude and confound men's understandings" [TV 103].

Though he finds it useful sometimes to speak in this way of the "frame of mind" as contributing to the attractive power of anything as an apparent good, Edwards expresses some doubt as to whether this really adds anything to what is already included under the "manner of view" and "what appears in the object viewed." In the pages of the *Freedom of the Will* where he lists these three kinds of things he gives only brief attention to the third and then suggests:

> But possibly 'tis needless and improper, to mention the frame and state of the mind, as a distinct ground of the agreeableness of objects from the other two mentioned before; viz. the apparent nature and circumstances of the object viewed, and the manner of the view: perhaps if we strictly consider the matter, the different temper and state of the mind makes no alteration as to the agreeableness of the objects, any other way, than as it [1] makes the objects themselves appear differently beautiful or deformed, having apparent pleasure or pain attending them: and as it [2] occasions the manner of the view to be different, causes the idea of beauty or deformity, pleasure or uneasiness to be more or less lively. [FW 147]

The reservations expressed here seem well founded. Although no harm is done by adding the frame of mind as a third consideration, to do so amounts really to speaking once again and at the same time of both sides of the "is as" equation. In fact, since it is an equation, to speak of a second side is already but to speak of the first in different terms, although the additional terms add substantially to the descriptive value of the analysis of that equation.

As we have seen, the common denominator into which the terms of that equation may be resolved is beauty—objectively in the apparent good, inherently in the will, or the affectional inclination of the moral agent. It is to the concept of beauty that Edwards turns for the central category of interpretation in his analysis of the attractive power of anything as good. It is the quality of beauty to be found in them—primary, secondary, or partial beauty or the deformity of dissent from being—that constitutes the measure, the objective foundation, and the attractive power of both the apparent good and the goodness of the will which "is as" such an apparent good. If the will always is as the apparent good, it can be good only by virtue of the creative presence of God as Himself the beauty that is the common denominator of the volitional "is as" equation of the redeemed. According to Edwards, God[27] is present to his creation in the manner in which beauty is present. In Jesus Christ God presents Himself as an object of sensibility in Whom man's real good is manifest as the apparent good. On the other side of the equation, as it were, God presents Himself subjectively or inherently as the beauty of holiness and of spiritual sensibility, that is, as the beauty and delight that is the Holy Spirit. The good in God is conceived by Edwards as primarily before men (in the beauty of Jesus Christ) and in them (in the beauty of the Holy Spirit) rather than over them or behind them as a law. God's moral governance of his spiritual creatures is conceived by Edwards as exercised objectively through the attractive power of the apparent good (in the beauty of Jesus Christ before them) and subjectively through the creative power of the good (the inherent good dwelling in them as the beauty and joy of the Holy Spirit).

As the good become apparent and attractive, beauty is the link between the objective and subjective definitions of goodness. We have seen that in Edwards' understanding of beauty and excellence there is interwoven an objective definition of them in terms of objective relations of consent and dissent among beings and a more subjective definition of both beauty and excellence in terms of pleasantness to perceiving being. The two definitions are internally related and interdependent, although the fundamentally objectivist character of Edwards' thought is disclosed in the greater reliability and ultimate priority of the objective over the subjective definition as a guide to beauty and excellence in any being.

27. As will be shown in the chapters of Part II.

The same pattern has been found when beauty is considered in relation to goodness. Beauty is in a general way the measure of goodness and the highest good, and primary beauty is the model of the intrinsic good (*bonum formosum*) as distinguished from the instrumental good (*bonum utile*). It is primarily through the objectively defined beauty of the apparent good that it exercises its attractive power over the subject, drawing the will of the moral creature into conformity and consent with itself by the subject's receiving the communicated good as its inherent good (both beauty and delight). But the interdependence and correspondence of the inherent good in the subject with the objective good in the object as apparent good is such that the relation between the objective and subjective definitions of goodness must be descriptively expressed as one of an actual "is as" correspondence, as well as of an ultimate and ontological priority of the objective over the subjective component. Accordingly, beauty is first of all the model of what is intrinsically and objectively good in itself (by virtue of its consent to being-in-general); and it is beauty that provides the measure of the departure from this norm in any lesser good.

In order to be good something must not only be good but must also appear good. Therefore goodness, like beauty and excellence, also has its more subjective definition, according to which good means "that which agrees with the inclination and disposition of the mind" [Mind 60]. The good must appear in order to be good, for "things are neither good nor bad but only with relation to perception" [Misc. 749]. He even goes so far as to say in one of his earliest "Notes" that without intelligent perceiving beings in the world, "all the world would be without any good at all" [Misc. gg]. Beauty is the model of such a conception of goodness because although it is primarily defined by objective relations of consent and harmony among beings, its appearance is nevertheless essential to its very being as beauty. It might even be said that it is Edwards' primarily objectivist definition of beauty that saves this view of goodness from leading to moral relativism and subjectivism. His subjective definition of goodness in terms of perception does not mean that things are good or bad only according to arbitrary personal or private taste, for there is an objective and structural standard of perception provided by beauty. To love is to be attracted to something as good, and "all love arises from a perception, either of consent to being-in-general or a consent to that being that perceives" [Misc. 117]. Things are perceived or appear good, then, by virtue of a primary or a secondary beauty that is in them.

The beauty of the apparent good is the link between the objective and subjective definitions of the moral goodness of virtuous love grounded in such a perception. It constitutes the bond between the disinterested, objective, and virtuous love of benevolence ("a disposition to love being in general") and such interested and subjective love of complacence ("delight in beauty") as is virtuous. For the beauty of the apparent good is at once the secondary ground of virtuous benevolence and the primary ground of virtuous complacence.

Beauty is the secondary rather than the primary ground of moral goodness or virtuous love because, "if virtue be the beauty of an intelligent being, and virtue consists in love, then it is a plain inconsistency," Edwards argues in the opening pages of *The Nature of True Virtue,* "to suppose that virtue primarily consists in any love to its object for its beauty" [TV 6]. "For that would be to suppose, that the beauty of intelligent beings primarily consists in the love of beauty," in which case beauty, the thing loved, must also consist in the love of beauty, so that virtue would consist in the love of the love of the love of beauty, "and so on in infinitum" [TV 7]. But virtue is not prior to itself any more than the apparent good is causally prior to the good will, as Edwards is careful to point out in explaining the importance of the precise way in which he has expressed himself in formulating his volitional "is as" equation. Virtue is not prior to itself, for its objective foundation lies not in something causally prior to itself but in something with which it "is as" in correspondence or consent. If the virtue in question is true virtue, it will be in such an "is as" correspondence with things as they are in themselves and according to their place in the universal system of being. "The tendency of true virtue is to treat everything as it is, and according to its nature" [OS 332]. Therefore, "the first object of a virtuous benevolence is being, simply considered" [TV 8], or being-in-general. But beauty enters as a secondary ground or object of virtuous benevolence because:

> loving a being on this ground necessarily arises from a pure benevolence to being in general, and *comes to the same thing* . . . A spirit of consent to being must agree with consent to being." [TV 10, italics added]

I hold that the beauty of the apparent good is the link between the objective definition of goodness in terms of relations of consent among beings and the subjective definition of goodness in terms of delight and pleasantness to perceiving being.

This spiritual beauty, which is but a secondary ground of virtuous benevolence, is the ground not only of benevolence, but complacence, and is the primary ground of the latter; that is, when the
complacence is truly virtuous. [TV 11]

The love of being for its primary beauty is so firmly connected for Edwards
with the love of being "simply considered" that it comes to the same thing,
since, as we have seen, primary beauty is itself the first principle of being.
And delight in beauty is no less firmly linked with the love of any being for
its beauty because delight in beauty is essential to the very perception of
beauty; such goodness will be the apparent good only of one whose goodness
is such as to enjoy and find beauty in it.

The correspondences between virtuous complacence (delight in beauty)
and benevolence (love of being and beauty) and, within benevolence, between being and beauty as the primary and secondary objects of virtuous
benevolence are important to Edwards' conception of the relations between
being and being good or between being and the perfection of being. Though
God's own "communicative goodness" is absolutely "independent and self-
moved" [EC 221]:

Creatures, even the most gracious of them, are not so independent
and self-moved in their goodness, but that in all exercises of it,
they are excited by some object that they find, something appearing good. [EC 221]

The determination of the will of moral creatures is a matter, then, of particular relations among determinate beings out of which there emerges "something appearing good." It is in keeping with the objectivism and actualism of
his thought that Edwards should speak of true virtue not only as benevolence to being-in-general but also—and interchangeably—as a propensity or
disposition or inclination to such a benevolence to being-in-general.[28] To the
perfect vision of God, being-in-general is an object of perception. But not
even virtuous man is granted any such vision. The creature encounters and
perceives reality not as being-in-general but always as determinate (even if
mysterious) beings in relations of consent and dissent, of harmony and dis-

28. For example, in the material now under discussion: "The first object of a virtuous
benevolence is being, simply considered; . . . and what it has an ultimate *propensity* to is
the highest good of being in general" [TV 8, italics added]. "The second object of a
virtuous *propensity* of heart is benevolent being" [TV 9, italics added].

harmony. Accordingly, while men should have a propensity or disposition or inclination to consent to being-in-general, what they will actually encounter and perceive will always be something less than being-in-general.

> When I say true virtue consists in love to being in general, I shall *not* be likely to be understood [as saying], that no one act of the mind or exercise of love is of the nature of true virtue, but *what has being in general,* or the great system of universal existence, *for its direct and immediate object:* so that no exercise of love, or kind affection to any one particular being, that is but a small part of this whole, has any thing of the nature of true virtue. *But* that the nature of true virtue consists in *a disposition* to benevolence towards being in general; though *from such a disposition* may arise exercises of *love to particular beings,* as objects are presented and occasions arise. [TV 4f, italics added]

Even true virtue in the creature does not have being-in-general for its direct and immediate object. Therefore, "under the conditions of finitude" true virtue, consisting in love of being-in-general, takes the form of a disposition to benevolence toward being-in-general that issues in and expresses itself in love of particular beings. Since every particular being stands in some relationship of consent or dissent, harmony or disharmony, rather than of indifference toward being-in-general, this means that being always presents itself to the creature in some determinate form of beauty or deformity. Being does not present itself to the creature as being-in-general but is always given to him in and through and as particular and determinate consenting and dissenting being, that is, being articulated as beauty and deformity.

It is crucial, therefore, that according to Edwards loving a being for the spiritual beauty that is in it arises necessarily from and comes to the same thing as "pure benevolence to being in general" [TV 10]. On no other terms could the real good become the apparent good of intelligent perceiving creatures. On those terms the severe standard of true virtue becomes not only a critical principle but also a substantive principle relevant to the circumstances of finite creatures. "The tendency of true virtue is to treat everything as it is, and according to its nature" [OS 332]. The surest guide to such treatment of things as they are is the perception and delight in things according to the measure of primary beauty or deformity that is in them.

In all that men encounter in the articulated system of being, Edwards is saying, it is the primary beauty of being's cordial consent to being and the shadow or image of such beauty in the secondary beauty of harmony and proportion that provides them with their surest clue to and the deepest penetration of the mystery of the things that are and the things that are good.

BEAUTY AND VALUE

Value is a term of considerably less significance in Edwards' vocabulary for the perfection of being than beauty, excellence, and goodness—or than holiness, which will be considered in Part II. The term value appears frequently enough in his writings, but unlike the other terms it does not carry us to the center of his thought; it is not one of the really characteristic terms of discourse into which his thought can be resolved. But there appear to be reasons for this that do take us to the center of his thought. The very peripheral place of the term value in his vocabulary illustrates and supports what has been said about the importance of understanding the objectivist character of his thought if the place of the largely aesthetic categories of beauty and sensibility in his thought and vision are to be understood. The relative insignificance of the term value in Edwards' thought is precisely its significance for the present essay.

Edwards sometimes employs the term value in tandem with beauty, in much the same way that we have seen him employ the terms excellence and goodness, using the expressions "beauty and value," "beauty and goodness," or "beauty and excellence." For example: "Holiness in the creature arises from a sense of holiness; 'tis a sense of the value and beauty of it that inclines the heart to it" [Misc. 1127]. Here value appears with beauty as mutually supportive attributes or as essentially identical and interchangeable terms. He also sometimes employs the terms value and goodness, or valuable and good, as synonymous, so that where he says in one place that the "infinite excellency of the divine nature, as it is in itself, is the true ground of all that is *good* in God in any respect" [RA 243, italics added], he says elsewhere that the excellency of God's nature, as it is in itself, "is the foundation of all that is *valuable* in him in any respect" [OS 332, italics added]. Accordingly, he sometimes uses these terms also in mutually supportive tandem, as in speaking of God's end in creation as "simply and absolutely good and valuable in itself" [EC 203].

More commonly, the term value hovers on the edge of his vocabulary for the perfection of being, while beauty, excellence and goodness are at the center of it. Value is introduced generally as a secondary terminology. For example, in an important sermon on Matthew 5:8 ("Blessed are the pure in heart, for they shall see God"):

> Intellectual pleasures consist in the beholding of spiritual ex-
> cellencies and beauties, but the glorious excellency and beauty of
> God are far the greatest. God's excellence is the supreme excel-
> lence. When the understanding of the reasonable creature dwells
> here, it dwells at the fountain, and swims in a boundless, bottom-
> less ocean. The love of God is also the most suitable entertainment
> of the soul of man, which naturally desires the happiness of so-
> ciety, or of union with some other being. The love of so glorious a
> being is infinitely *valuable,* and the discoveries of it are capable of
> ravishing the soul above all other love.[29]

Or again, in a sermon on "The Excellency of Christ," it is only at the very end of a long passage in which he has been expounding upon the goodness and greatness, the beauty and excellency of Christ, that he introduces the term value into his discussion.

> Indeed goodness is excellent in whatever subject it be found, it is
> beauty and excellency itself, and renders all excellent that are pos-
> sessed of it; and yet more excellent when joined with greatness; as
> the very same excellent qualities of gold do render the body in
> which they are inherent more precious, and of greater *value,* when
> joined with greater than when with lesser dimensions.[30]

One further example will serve the immediate purpose. It is taken from *The Nature of True Virtue,* in the first chapter of which he does not even employ the term value until the final page [TV 12], although he finds all the other related terms essential and central to his discussion. His basic thesis has already been carefully laid out before the term value is even introduced. Immediately following its introduction, the final paragraph, which begins by saying that "it is impossible that any one should truly relish this beauty, con-sisting in general benevolence, who has not that temper himself" [TV 12], concludes, two sentences later:

> For if a being destitute of benevolence, should love benevolence to
> being in general, it would prize and seek that for which it had no

---

29. *Works,* ed. S. E. Dwight (New York, 1829–30), *8,* 287, italics added.
30. "The Excellency of Christ," *Works, 4,* 197, italics added.

value. For how should one love and value a disposition to a thing, or a tendency to promote it, and for that very reason, when the thing itself is what he is regardless of, and has no value for, nor desires to have promoted. [TV 12f]

In the first sentence of this passage value is employed as a synonym for relish, taste, or even inclination rather than for their object. In the second sentence it is employed first as a synonym for the verb to love and then as a synonym for regard, desire, or relish. Perhaps one could even say that it serves in the last instance as a synonym for "use." In all these instances the term value has a family resemblance to the subjective terms bearing upon the order of sensibility (sense, relish, taste, temper, desire, inclination, disposition, love, delight, etc.) rather than to those bearing upon the more objective order (beauty, excellence, goodness) apprehended by those forms of sensibility. And the pattern displayed in these examples of an essentially peripheral place for the term value in his vocabulary for interpreting the perfection of being is characteristic of Edwards' thought.

Where his concern is teleological, as in the companion piece to *The Nature of True Virtue*, the essay on *The End For Which God Created the World*, the term value plays a more prominent role, although as we shall see, its role even there is secondary and derivative rather than formative or characteristic of his thought. In this context its meaning is close to that of other terms for the object sought (end, goal, objective good, value). For example, "an ultimate end" is defined as one in which "the aim of the agent stops and rests (without going further), being come to the good which he esteems a recompense of its pursuit for its own value" [EC 194]. But the meaning of value is even more closely and clearly related to that of other terms for the response of the subject (esteeming, regarding, loving, relishing, delighting in, valuing) to whom the object appears good (lovely, worthy, excellent, beautiful, valuable). Consider, for example, two of the passages richest in their invocation of the term value.

The first passage is taken from the more philosophical discussion in the opening chapter.

We must suppose from the perfection of God's nature, that whatsoever is valuable and amiable in itself, simply and absolutely considered, God values simply for itself; it is agreeable to him absolutely on its own account, because God's judgment and esteem are according to truth. He values and loves things, accordingly, as they are worthy to be valued and loved. But if God values a thing sim-

ply, and absolutely, for itself, and on its own account, then it is the
ultimate object of his value; he does not value it merely for the
sake of a farther end to be attained by it. [EC 203]

The second passage is from the closing pages of the final chapter, where
Edwards is discussing "the emanation or communication of the divine ful-
ness, consisting in the knowledge of God, love to God, and joy in God"
[EC 255]. He is arguing that "though it be true that God has respect to the
creature in these things; yet his respect to himself and to the creature in this
matter, are not properly to be looked upon as a double and divided respect of
God's heart" [EC 255], because the good of the creature and the glory of
God are one. He then concludes:

> It was this value for himself that caused him to value and seek that
> his internal glory should flow forth from himself. It was from his
> value for his glorious perfections of wisdom and righteousness, etc.,
> that he valued the proper exercise and effect of these perfections,
> in wise and righteous acts and effects. It was from his infinite value
> for his internal glory and fulness, that he valued the thing itself,
> which is communicated, because he infinitely values his own glory,
> consisting in the knowledge of himself, love to himself, and com-
> placence and joy in himself; he therefore valued the image, com-
> munication or participation of these, in the creature. And it is be-
> cause he values himself, that he delights in the knowledge, and
> love, and joy of the creature; as being himself the object of this
> knowledge, love and complacence. [EC 255–256]

In the first passage the idea of value appears initially as an adjective—
valuable—respecting the object. But in every subsequent appearance value
is a verb or a synonym for love, esteem, or prize as verbs. Especially is this
so in the second passage, where the term value appears entirely as a part of
the vocabulary bearing upon the order of sensibility rather than as a part of
the vocabulary bearing upon the objective order apprehended by it. These
passages carry us to the center of Edwards' thought, but the concept of value
appears to have played no significant part in the actual conception of the
ideas there displayed.

Nowhere, in fact, does Edwards give the concept of value the sort of analytic attention and development we have seen him give the concepts of

beauty, excellence, and goodness.[31] More particularly, and even more important, is the fact that what is lacking in his concept of value is a systematic
development of its more objective and structural aspects. The concepts of
beauty, excellence, and goodness function at the center of his thought because each of them has received at his hands a formulation that is objective,
structural, and relational as well as subjective and evaluative. It is by giving
these concepts such a formulation that Edwards shapes them for the task of
articulating his essentially objectivist ontological-moral-theological vision of
reality. That vision is characteristically aesthetic, for it is from what is commonly called the aesthetic realm that he takes the primary models, beauty
and sensibility, in terms of which he articulates his vision and construes the
order of things. But the key aesthetic concept is beauty rather than sensibility;
and, within the concept of beauty, it is the objective definition according to
relations of consent and dissent among beings rather than the more subjective definition according to pleasantness to perceiving being that is fundamental. The concepts of excellence and goodness and holiness are all given
comparable development, informed by the governing models of beauty and
sensibility. But the concept of value is given no such objectivist development
and therefore remains on the periphery of Edwards' systematic vocabulary
regarding the perfection of being and is of relative insignificance as a clue to
the characteristic quality of his thought and vision. An essentially objectivist
program could be adequately served only by a more structurally developed
concept of value.

31. The reason for this may simply be that Edwards' already richly developed concepts
of beauty, excellence, and goodness served his purposes adequately and that he did not
therefore see himself as standing in any need of giving fuller development to yet one more
closely related concept.

BEAUTY: THE KEY TO ORDER AND UNITY IN THE SYSTEM OF BEING

The triangulation of Edwards' concept of beauty is now complete, at least in broad terms. That is, I have located its place in his thought by relating it to at least two other things with which it is connected and to which, in fact, it has been found to be the key. I have shown that beauty is for Edwards the first principle of both being and of the perfection of being. I shall now consider the significance of his finding in beauty the principle of both being and the perfection of being and therefore the unity of being and perfection or of being and good. This will be largely a matter of making explicit what has been so far at least implicit. In attending now to the unity of being and good that Edwards finds in their beauty and in attending therefore also to the primacy of beauty as the model of order throughout his whole system of being, I shall be drawing together some of the philosophical evidence so far examined regarding the formative place of beauty in his thought and vision.

BEAUTY: THE UNITY OF BEING AND GOOD

Edwards' philosophy is a philosophy of being. Nothing, not even God, is beyond being, for nothing has a higher ontological status than being-itself. But other concepts must be added to that of being if the system is to be given philosophical articulation. The first move in any such development is critical, for it will exercise a formative influence upon the manner in which the whole system is articulated. The concept of beauty is the one with which Edwards makes the first decisive move; it is the first concept he joins to that of being for the development of his philosophy of being. Since beauty has its own peculiar manner of articulation, the manner in which the whole system of being is articulated bears the mark of this priority of beauty among the characteristics of being. Accordingly, beauty is for Edwards not simply an important concept and reality, but, as the first principle of being, it functions in his thought as the primary category of being and the principal category of interpretation for understanding the whole articulated system of being as it is manifest to and encountered by intelligent perceiving beings.

As a category of being beauty is the objective, structural, and relational principle by virtue of which everything that is participates in being; it is the power of being, in the absence of which there is "nothing"—the boundary concept with which Edwards designates that condition of absolute contradiction toward which dissenting being moves. As such, beauty has priority over the other categories of being, such as those summed up by scholastic philosophy under the aspects of unity, truth, and goodness. These three characteristics of being remain essential for Edwards, but the unity, truth, and goodness of being are conceived by him in a manner decisively shaped by his concept of beauty.

As a category of interpretation beauty is again an objective, structural, and relational principle for measuring the ontological weight of any particular being. It is the principal clue to the location of determinate beings in relation to the whole system. Determinate, particular, finite beings participate in the fullness of being according to the measure of beauty in them. In the case of natural being the measure consists in the secondary beauty of harmony and proportion. In the case of moral or spiritual being the measure consists in the primary beauty of being's cordial consent to being-in-general. The relation between primary and secondary beauty as forms of the one rule of consent is Edwards' assurance that the natural and moral or spiritual orders are ultimately one. Intelligent, perceiving, willing beings—including God—participate in both the natural and the moral or spiritual orders, and are located in the economy of the universal system of being according to the range and quality of being and beauty to which they are related in consent or dissent or both. Any partiality of consent (to state it subjectively) or consent to partial being (to state it objectively) constitutes a loss of beauty and a corresponding impoverishment or deprivation of being in any particular consenting-dissenting being.

As the internal, structural principle of being-itself, beauty shapes the manner in which being is manifest to and encountered by intelligent perceiving being. For beauty, though its primary definition is objective, structural, and relational, must *appear* to intelligent perceiving being in order to *be*. Appearance to perceiving, enjoying being is essential to the very being of beauty. To conceive of beauty as the first principle and primary category of being is, therefore, a way of systematically construing being-itself as inclined to disclose and communicate itself. This is one way in which the characteristics of beauty inform the manner in which Edwards' whole system of being is articulated. And this aesthetic qualification of being-itself at its very center is perhaps the distinctive mark of his philosophical theology. Douglas Elwood notes that "the unity of being and goodness is an axiom of the Augustinian mystical-realist strain," with which he rightly associates Edwards. But he indicates only in an oblique fashion that Edwards' structural concept of beauty is the key to his peculiar way of representing and articulating the unity of being and goodness. Edwards gives the axiomatic unity of being and goodness a distinctive formulation in terms of his concept of beauty. Elwood concludes that for Edwards "goodness is inherent in Being-itself and determines its structure."[1] The evidence we have examined permits a further refinement of Elwood's conclusion; it permits us to say even more precisely that for Edwards beauty is inherent in being-itself and determines its structure.

Edwards' formulation is structural rather than evaluative. It consists not merely in affirming that being and goodness are one or that whatever is, is good, but goes on to offer a structural and ontological formulation of how this is so by finding in a primarily objective, structural, and relational concept of beauty at once the first principle of being-itself and the measure and objective foundation of goodness or the perfection of being. With respect to the perfection of being, we have seen that the virtual identity of beauty and excellence, as compared with the more dialectical relation between the concepts of beauty and goodness, and the more ambiguous and peripheral relation between Edwards' conceptions of beauty and value establishes beauty as fundamentally more a structural than an evaluative category for interpreting the order of the perfection of being. The same has been shown to be the case with respect to the order of being itself. In both cases beauty is a structural principle. And this is true whether the beauty in question is the primary beauty of objective relations of consent among beings or the secondary beauty of proportion and harmony. It is this structural principle of beauty that gives substance as well as both descriptive and normative validity to the primal trust expressed in the faith that being is good.

Since it has beauty as its formative, structural inner principle, being-itself is, according to Edwards, inherently inclined to appear, to manifest and communicate itself. But being-itself is never manifest to or encountered as such by intelligent perceiving being; it is encountered always in the form of the two coordinate modes of the articulated system of being. These two modes are always given and encountered jointly and are variously designated by Edwards in terms of one or another of the several pairs of coordinate concepts—being and good, existence and excellence, greatness and goodness—each pair of which is a form of the pair of concepts that constitute his model

---

1. Elwood, *The Philosophical Theology of Jonathan Edwards*, pp. 29, 30.

of order in the whole system, namely, secondary and primary beauty or proportion and consent. It is this relation between being-itself, in which beauty is resolved into being, and the articulated system of being as manifest to and encountered by intelligent perceiving being, in which beauty-as-excellence has a higher ontological status or greater ontological weight than does its coordinate mode of being-as-existence, that finds expression in Edwards' identification of God with being-itself in his vision of God, so conceived, as one who is

> not only infinitely *greater* and more *excellent* than all other being, but he is the head of the universal system of existence; the foundation and fountain of all *being* and all *beauty;* from whom all is perfectly derived, and on whom all is most absolutely and perfectly dependent; of whom, and through whom, and to whom is all *being* and all *perfection;* and whose *being* and *beauty* are, as it were, the sum and comprehension of all existence and excellence. [TV 15, italics added]

The emphasized pairs of concepts are some of the ways in which he designates the two coordinate orders of the articulated system of being, of being-itself as it is manifest to and encountered by intelligent perceiving being.

The conception of being-itself as having beauty for its formative, structural inner principle is the philosophical counterpart of Edwards' vision of the universal system of being as created and governed by God towards its redemption in the fullness of His own glory. God is the Creator: being-itself is creative, bestowing both being and beauty, manifesting and communicating itself in the modes of existence and excellence, secondary and primary beauty, etc. Being-itself bestows being as it bestows beauty, in a manner alternatively conceivable as *ad extra,* out of the fullness of being, or as *ex nihilo,* out of nothing, that is, out of complete contradiction and dissent from being into some measure of consent to being or at least of a secondary image of this in the beauty of harmony or proportion. God is also the Governor: being-itself governs the entire articulated system of being according to the inner structural principle of its own nature. Any and every portion of the system is sustained in being by the governing, sustaining presence in it of the first principle of being-itself, the principle of beauty. This principle of beauty is the law through which being-itself exercises governance over the articulated system of being according to the rule of proportion in the order of existence, greatness, natural being, etc., and according to the rule of consent in the order of excellence, goodness, moral or spiritual being, etc. Finally, God is a Redeemer: being-itself is redemptive; it articulates itself as harmony and consent rather than as discord and dissent among determinate beings, building up by the creative and attractive power of its own beauty both union (the secondary beauty of harmony and proportion) and communion (the primary beauty of cordial consent) among beings. In its consummation this redemption would fulfill in remanation what had been created in effulgent emanation—the beauty and joy of universal consent among beings.

In Edwards' thought beauty is a creative rather than a static aesthetic principle of the unity of being and goodness. It is self-giving rather than self-sufficient, and it finds appropriate expression in images of the universal system of being that emphasize the effulgence rather than the self-sufficiency of being-itself. Beauty is an abiding principle of being, tending not only to sustain itself in being but also to nourish and enrich the universal system of being by bestowing being and beauty. Whereas deformity and dissent with respect to being-itself or being-in-general are privative, tending to destruction, a movement toward nothing, proportion and consent to being-in-general are inclusive and creative. Beauty is a creative, even a recreative principle of being and goodness, for not only does beauty add to the ontological weight of consenting being while dissent and deformity impoverish beings, but also delight in primary beauty—and even in secondary beauty—transforms and renews the vitality of moral, spiritual beings. As we have seen, not only does goodness consist in "an inclination to show goodness" or to "exert goodness" [Misc. 87], but being-itself also has as its inner principle just such an inclination, since that inner principle is conceived by Edwards as beauty, the very being of which involves its appearing or showing and communicating itself. If the goodness of a being is defined as its inclination to communicate itself, then the ground of goodness must coincide with the ground of being, for otherwise there would be some being communicated that would not itself be good. Finally, beauty is more fully exemplified in the beautifying than in the beautified and consists more fundamentally in the creative power to bestow being and beauty than in the enjoyment of them.

But the enjoyment is nonetheless important. The point needs to be emphasized and developed, for it is essential to an understanding of Edwards' system of thought, and it brings us back to the rationale for the manner in which I have represented the structure of his vision of reality. The enjoyment of beauty is essential. His concept of beauty provides him with a model for the unity of being and goodness in which the enjoyment, delight, and appreciation that find things to be good are internally and necessarily involved in the very apprehension of the existence of things as being. As we have seen, the correspondence in intelligent perceiving being between the objective order of excellence and the subjective order of enjoyment is so thorough that Edwards is reluctant to press beyond an "is as" equation of the two and hesitates to give priority to either one. The priority he does grant is ontological rather than temporal or causal. So also with the correspondence between being and goodness in reality as encountered and apprehended by such intelligent and perceiving being. The articulated system of being is encountered by intelligent perceiving being as always at once both being and good, rather than first one and then the other, first fact and then value, or first existence and then excellence. He is unwilling to grant unequivocally "that things must be known really to exist before they can be known to exist excellent[ly] or really to exist with such and such a beauty," if by this is meant that "things must be known to have a real existence before the person has a clear understanding, idea, or apprehension of the thing . . . as it is in its qualities either odious or beautiful," for ordinarily "we first have some understanding or view of the thing in its qualities before we know its existence" [Misc. 1090]. If any priority is given here it is to the apprehension of beauty as excellence over that of being as existence. If a choice must be made, that is the one that, at the level of the articulated system of being, must follow if Edwards is consistent. For, as we have seen, of the two coordinate orders of the articulated system of being, the order of being as excellence has a greater ontological weight than the order of being as existence, since the one represents forms of primary beauty while the other represents forms of secondary beauty. But Edwards would rather not press for such a choice with respect to the system as it is encountered by intelligent perceiving being. What is there encountered is not being-itself or being-in-general in some undifferentiated simplicity but rather being-itself articulated and manifest as being and good. In fact, as we have seen, by conceiving of primary beauty as the principal category of both being and the perfection of being, Edwards has expressly rejected the notion of an undifferentiated unity even in God or in being-itself, since, as he says, without diversity in being there could be no consent and therefore no excellence. The beauty of being-itself is therefore a condition as well as a guarantee of the unity of being and goodness.

Although in ontology beauty is ultimately resolved into being and although in ethics complacence (delight in beauty) is properly resolved into and subordinate to benevolence (love of being), neither being nor beauty, neither benevolence nor complacence, ever appears in the articulated system of being—including both subjects and objects—in such a resolved state. They are manifest rather in the two coordinate orders of being as existence (secondary beauty) and being as excellence (primary beauty).

The relation between benevolence and complacence may be taken as illustrative of the indissoluble unity of being and goodness in Edwards' vision of reality. We have seen that he finds in the love of beauty the subjective link between the love of being and delight in beauty, for benevolence to beauty is necessarily involved in and comes to the same thing as benevolence to being, and benevolence necessarily carries with it a corresponding complacence. Benevolence can, in fact, reach no further than the range and quality (i.e. the perfection or the beauty) of being in which delight is taken. Since an apprehension of and delight in spiritual beauty is at once a function of and a declaration of the self-disposition (i.e. the inclination and sensibility) of intelligent perceiving being, the encounter with things as being or existing is never divorced from the encounter with them as beauty or excellence. It is therefore a function of both the objective, structural nature of being-itself as manifest and articulated to intelligent perceiving being and the affectional-aesthetic unity of understanding and will ("the enjoying faculty") in intelligent perceiving subjects that reality is encountered always as jointly being and good.

This may be expressed in terms other than those employed by Edwards, such as the view that there are "no facts without values," or that we do not apprehend reality as quantitative apart from an apprehension of it in qualitative terms also. H. Richard Niebuhr, employing the language of value theory, takes essentially the same position in explicating the significance for Christian ethics of the affirmation that whatever is is good, which is so central to his and to Edwards' understanding of the Christian faith.

> The fundamental ethical act is the act of appreciation or depreciation. We don't first know and then appreciate or depreciate. We acknowledge the *presence* and the *value* of things at once. When we know things we know them in appreciation; when we ignore them we do so in depreciation. This is the first ethical act, not chronologically, but originally.[2]

In Edwards' terms the presence of being is not given apart from its beauty; nor is it apprehended as being apart from an apprehension of its beauty (or deformity). And beauty is only apprehended if it is enjoyed.

2. H. Richard Niebuhr, class lectures in Christian ethics, as transcribed in my notes for 26 March 1954.

Beauty, it would seem, is a peculiarly appropriate first principle and measure of being and goodness for the philosophical articulation of a Christian vision such as Edwards', in which joy and delight as well as beauty and excellence are conceived as internal qualities of the Divine Being, of being-itself, and as central and definitive ends for creatures called to glorify God (to celebrate His Being) and enjoy Him forever (delight in His beauty).

BEAUTY: THE PRIMARY MODEL OF ORDER

An important aspect of any religious faith and of any philosophical-theological program that radically affirms the sovereignty of God will be the primary model in terms of which it conceives of order. For such a faith and reflective program is informed by confidence in the reality and presence of order even where men do not discern it, and by confidence that the order of things is sustained by the continuing immediate presence of One without whom there would be no order, One by whom all things are ordered—and ordered toward fulfillment in an ultimate eternal order. The reality of order is close to the center of such a position.

The primary model in terms of which order is conceived will have a decisive and formative influence on the way in which such a faith and program is articulated. Many possible models of order are available through which to construe the patterns of unity amid all the diversity of things in the world, to relate the One to the Many. Among these possibilities are organic, mechanical, mathematical, logical, dramatic, moral, and aesthetic models of order. In a variety of forms these and other diverse possibilities have provided the primary models of order that have informed the vision and the developed thought of men through the ages.

Edwards is among those, like Whitehead in our own century, whose vision and reflection are informed by a primary model of order that is essentially aesthetic in character. With Whitehead, who "finds the foundations of the world in the aesthetic experience" and for whom "the most individual actual entity is a definite act of perceptivity," Edwards would agree that:

> All order is . . . aesthetic order, and the moral order is merely certain aspects of aesthetic order. The actual world is the outcome of the aesthetic order, and the aesthetic order is derived from the immanence of God.[3]

Accordingly, Edwards' aesthetic model of order in terms of beauty and sensibility exercises a formative influence upon the articulation of what H. Rich-

3. A. N. Whitehead, *Religion in the Making,* pp. 101, 105.

ard Niebuhr would call his "radical monotheism." Beauty is not the only order; but beauty provides Edwards with the model in terms of which all other forms of order in the articulated system of being are to be understood.

Edwards' aesthetic conception of order in terms of beauty and sensibility has certain advantages. Some we have already had occasion to observe; others will appear later. Beauty provides him with a model of order for that which cannot be known without or apart from being enjoyed. Beauty is an appropriate model for designating the order of things if we want to say, as Edwards does, that the ultimate order of things cannot be known or apprehended apart from a disposition to enjoy that order and to find in its informing principle the model for order in one's own life also. Edwards' conception of beauty is a model of order that is at once ontological and moral; that is, it is at once objective and structural, on the one hand, and appropriate to an affectional-aesthetic conception of the moral self, on the other. It is a model of order in terms of which to hold objectivity and subjectivity together—to insist upon the importance of the passions, emotions, and affections in the moral life without surrendering the vision of structured order in the moral and natural world. Edwards' structural concept of beauty provides him with a model of order appropriate to his vision of reality as consisting of internally related things and events rather than of discrete and disconnected or only externally related items. According to such a model of order excellence consists not in the perfection of (pristine) being independent of other being(s) but in the manner in which being embraces being. The reach of the embrace that defines the identity of any being—especially of moral beings— is aesthetically measured by the secondary beauty of proportion and harmony and by the primary beauty of cordial consent. Proportion, as Edwards tries to show in *Images or Shadows of Divine Things* and in *The Nature of True Virtue* is a clue to the larger order of things but is itself always subject to transformation and reevaluation in the light of a higher order of (spiritual) beauty, which is not merely an extension of itself, that is, not merely an extension of the principle of secondary beauty. Accordingly, holiness, for example, measures rather than is measured by goodness, and validity is the measure of value rather than a projection of it. Order and disorder in the natural world are seen in terms of harmony and discord, of proportion and deformity. Order and disorder in the moral world are seen in terms of consent to being and dissent from being rather than primarily in terms of obedience and disobedience. For example, the difference between obedience to command and consent to being and beauty defines the difference between legal and evangelical faith and morality.[4]

His concept of beauty offers Edwards a model of order for a world in which responsible moral agents are called upon to act freely into a future they do not control but that is not without order. It is one of the merits of beauty as a primary model of order that it carries within itself the suggestion that it serves not as a fixed standard to be applied, a standard or norm the content of which will be clear before approaching the situation and experience in question, but rather as a pattern of discernment and a clue to the manner in which the spiritual condition or self-disposition of the moral agent is crucial to the determination of the patterns in terms of which the situation and the experience will be apprehended by him. Beauty provides Edwards with a model of the structure and dynamics of the moral life and of its proper objective foundation, which yet makes the categories of vision and perception, of imagination and discernment, fundamental to the moral and religious life.

If men's ideas of beauty ascend no higher than what Edwards regards as merely secondary beauty, they will be blind to primary beauty, and their vision can be restored only by providing a new foundation for their apprehension of being and beauty. Edwards is confident that God can be relied upon to do so by confounding and breaking through man's limited capacity to imagine and respond to real beauty—man's capacity for a narrowness of vision and a poverty of sensibility, which finds spiritual satisfaction in partial or false beauty while blind to larger beauties and which recoils in horror at minor deformities and vulgarity while remaining insensitive to the terror of darker spiritual deformities and more exquisite vulgarities.

No concept of beauty will itself restore the requisite vision. But if beauty is a fundamental clue to the nature of reality, then the very least that men can

---

4. In Edwards' analysis of the sixth sign of gracious affections—that they "are attended with evangelical humiliation" [RA 311]—the perception of beauty and participation in beauty are frequently invoked as distinguishing evangelical from merely legal humiliation. For example:

There is a distinction to be made between a *legal* and *evangelical* humiliation . . . in the former a sense of the awful greatness, and natural perfections of God, and of the strictness of his law, convinces men that they are exceeding sinful . . . but they don't see their own odiousness on the account of sin; they don't see the hateful nature of sin; a sense of this is given in evangelical humiliation, by a discovery of the beauty of God's holiness and moral perfections . . . Legal humiliation has in it no spiritual good, nothing of the nature of true virtue; whereas evangelical humiliation is that wherein the excellent beauty of Christian grace does very much consist. [RA 311–12]

do is to be guided in their perception of reality by the richest possible conception of the beauties it may contain. For while perception is not determined by the patterns of our anticipation and expectation, it is certainly informed and shaped—both limited and enlarged—by these patterns. The range of models in terms of which men are prepared to acknowledge order in experience and reality will set both limits and possibilities to their capacity for spiritual and moral discernment. Their arsenal of models might properly include, therefore, the capacity to perceive order in terms of beauty as well as in terms of some of the other possible models of order. Edwards' thought may be seen as offering an exploration of at least one such aesthetic model of order in terms of beauty and sensibility. His systematic thought may be taken as part of an effort to explore and articulate the significance of his own discovery that in the perception of beauty he found the most reliable and penetrating clue to the nature of reality. As such, his thought also offers a critique, that is, a probing after the true and the false, of men's conceptions and perceptions of beauty.

We have now seen how this primary model of order informs Edwards' philosophy of being, of the perfection of being, and of the relation of unity between being and perfection. We turn now more explicitly and systematically to the ways in which beauty and sensibility inform his theological program and the vision of man and the world that follows from it. For Edwards it is only by reference to God that the order of things can rightly be discerned. All being proceeds from the Divine Being, and insofar as it is articulated at all, that is, insofar as being has any order at all, the primary model and principle of that order is the very beauty of the Divine Being Himself.

PART II

BEAUTY AND THE DIVINE BEING

6

BEAUTY AMONG THE DIVINE PERFECTIONS

"God is God, and distinguished from all other beings, and exalted above 'em, chiefly by his divine beauty, which is infinitely diverse from all other beauty" [RA 298]. This proposition should be placed at the center of our thinking if we want to understand Edwards' conception of God. For he does not confine his claim regarding the divine beauty to the relatively simple idea that along with and along side of several other things, God is also beautiful. Many poets, saints, and theologians have said as much. Edwards says much more. He is, to be sure, much affected with the beauty of God and of "divine things." But when in his preaching and writing he invokes that divine beauty, it is not so much in order to sing God's praises as it is to speak as truly as he can about the nature of God and the relation of the triune God to His creation. For Edwards the divine beauty is not simply one along side the other attributes or perfections of God. He goes further and says that of all God's perfections it is by His beauty that He is primarily distinguished as God. God is not only beautiful but is beauty itself and the foundation and fountain of all beauty [TV 15].

The three chapters of Part II deal with various aspects of this priority of beauty in the Divine Being. They will show that beauty is first among the divine perfections, that Edwards' concept of beauty provides the framework for—if not indeed the platform upon which he erects—his doctrine of the Trinity, and that beauty is central to Edwards' view of the relation between transcendence and immanence in God and of the relation of God to the world in His creation, governance, and redemption of it. What is essential in all this is that for Edwards the divine beauty is "that . . . wherein the truest idea of divinity does consist" [RA 298].

Certainly one of the distinguishing marks—if it is not indeed *the* distinctive feature—of Edwards' theology, when looked at in relation to the whole history of Christian thought, is his radical elevation of beauty to preeminence among the divine perfections. To be sure, the beauty of God and of divine things has long been a recurrent theme of religious piety all around the world, including Christendom.[1] But the concept of beauty has rarely found an important—not to speak of a secure—place in Christian theology, especially within the main line of Christian orthodoxy and even more especially within Protestant Reformed orthodoxy.

Despite its appearance in a marginal way in the thought of such theologians as Thomas Aquinas and its more important appearance in the tradition of Christian Platonism from Augustine through pseudo-Dionysius to the Cambridge Platonists and their British heirs—to carry the story no further than Edwards' own day—the concept of beauty has had at most a very insecure position among theological concepts in Christian thought. Aquinas' use of the concept deserves to be better known than it is, though it is not central to his thought. But the concept of beauty as a divine perfection is more important to the tradition of Christian Platonism, to which Edwards is partly and quite consciously heir. Augustine may be said to have introduced the idea of beauty into what we now regard as Christian orthodoxy, but he made very little systematic use of it. Beauty was in his mind too closely wed to the concept of the good to receive independent development at his hands. Pseudo-Dionysius may have taken his lead partly from Augustine, but his more thorough development of the concept of beauty as a divine perfection was so radical as to be passed on to later ages as one of the identifying marks of his heterodoxy—or, as some have charged, his heresy. In fact, the extent to which the concept of beauty was given theological development as a perfection of God by any theologian before Edwards can be taken as a fairly accurate measure of the heterodoxy of his thought, at least in the eyes of the mainstream of Christian orthodoxy.[2] With the attenuated exception of Horace

1. The predisposition of Christian piety to associate beauty with things holy has been well served since the seventeenth century by the phrase "beauty of holiness"—that "magnificent mistranslation" (H. R. Niebuhr's phrase) of the Old Testament phrases now more accurately translated as "holy array." See, e.g. Psalms 29:2, 96:9, and 110:3. Edwards' theological appropriation of the concept of beauty in no way hangs on that phrase, though he does make occasional reference to it. Indicative of the fact that he does not rely upon it is the fact that of all his more than a thousand known sermons, none takes these "beauty of holiness" passages for their text. Edwards' use of the phrase is not unrelated to his study of Scripture but is based more on an appeal to his own religious experience and to his study of religious experience in others.

2. Anders Nygren's judgment on this matter is expressed rather more forcefully than is customary, but it is not untypical of orthodoxy's suspicion regarding beauty as a divine perfection: "Eros is of a markedly aesthetic character. It is the beauty of the divine that attracts the eye of the soul and sets its love in motion . . . To speak of the 'beauty' of God in the context of Agape, however, sounds very like blasphemy" (*Agape and Eros* [London, S.P.C.K., 1953], pp. 223–24).

Bushnell, who is more properly to be counted as a liberal than as an orthodox theologian, the same can be said for theology since Edwards as well, because not even his closest disciples can be said to have fully shared his vision of the divine beauty.[3] Finally, we may, with one exception, agree with Karl Barth, who finds, regarding the theological appropriation of the concept of beauty, that "Reformation and Protestant orthodoxy, so far as I can see, completely ignored it."[4] Obviously Barth did not see across the Atlantic and back into eighteenth-century New England, for it appears that he is not acquainted with Edwards.

Not until Karl Barth has any theologian of Reformed orthodoxy besides Edwards made significant theological use of the concept of beauty. It is a mark of Edwards' theological boldness and imagination that European Protestantism should have had to wait two hundred years longer than New England for the subject to be even broached seriously by a major orthodox theologian. That it should take a theologian as daring as Barth to do so is not surprising. As Barth himself notes:

3. Beauty and sensibility have an important place in the thought of Horace Bushnell, but his conception of them is less objectivist and reflects a more romantic and subjective spirit than does Edwards' thought. Also, unlike Edwards', he feels the need to introduce such aesthetic notions with the usual apologies. He says, for example, in his address on the "Atonement" at Harvard in July 1848:

> Were it not for the air it might give to my representations, in the view of many, I should like, in common with Paul (Phil. 1:9, 10), to use the word *esthetic,* and represent Christianity as a power moving upon man, through this department of his nature, both to regenerate his degraded perception of excellence, and also to communicate, in that way, the fullness and beauty of God" (*God in Christ* [Hartford, 1849], p. 204).

In language that continues to reverberate with echoes of Edwards, he says, in the same address, that "to renovate man now . . . requires a new motivity, one that will subdue him to love, and unite him to the good as good, not as profitable—to God's own beauty, truth, loveliness, and glory . . . and to regenerate the liberty of his fallen affections (p. 240). And lecturing on "Dogma and Spirit" at Andover two months later, Bushnell argues that:

> a right sensibility is as truly perceptive as reason, and there are many truths, of the highest moment, that can never find us save as we offer a congenial sensibility to them. What is loftiest and most transcendent in the character of God, his purity, goodness, beauty, and gentleness, can never be sufficiently apprehended by mere intellect, or by any other power than a heart configured to these divine qualities (*God in Christ,* pp. 301–02).

4. Karl Barth, *Church Dogmatics,* II/1 (Edinburgh, T. & T. Clark, 1957), p. 651. "Even Schleiermacher," Barth continues, "in whom we might have expected something of this kind, did not achieve anything very striking in this direction" (p. 651).

owing to its connexion with the ideas of pleasure, desire and enjoyment (quite apart from its historical connexion with Greek
thought), the concept of the beautiful seems to be a particularly
secular one, not at all adapted for introduction into the language of
theology, and indeed extremely dangerous.

Despite these and other considerations, he refuses to be put off. Dangers there
surely are, but "the aestheticism which threatens here is no worse than the
other 'isms' or any 'ism'. They are all dangerous." Barth asks, "Does biblical
truth itself and as such permit us to stop at this point because of the danger,
and not to say that God is beautiful?"[5] No, he answers, it does not.

In his development of beauty as a divine perfection Edwards, unlike
Barth, did not feel himself to be involved with an especially dangerous concept. As a latter-day Puritan he was nurtured in a tradition rich in resources
for just such a development. One reason he was more free to give theological
development to the concept of beauty without thereby jeopardizing his orthodoxy is that Puritanism had long been influenced by and sympathetically
involved with Platonism, overt and covert. Emmanuel College, Cambridge,
had been in the early seventeenth century both the breeding ground for the
first generation of Puritan preachers and theologians and the stronghold of
Cambridge Platonism at its height. More important than any influence traceable to sources outside of Puritanism itself is a deeper reason why Puritanism
and religious Platonism could associate so readily: the affinity between the
intuitionism of the latter and the unprecedented stress on immediate experience of the former.

It must also be remembered that the Puritans' simplicity of worship and
life was a function of their opposition to idolatry, pride, and self-indulgence
and is not to be attributed to any supposed opposition to beauty. On the
contrary, their sense of life as a pilgrimage of spiritual training and discipline
for a more lovely world to be opened up to the saints was tempered by a
sometimes mystical sense of the beauty of things natural as well as divine. In
matters aesthetic, the Puritan canons of beauty and taste compare favorably
with those of many movements and periods that are frequently regarded (or
regard themselves) as aesthetically more cultivated—a judgment that would
probably find wider acceptance if we did not tend to accept as definitive of
Puritanism what had become of it by the early nineteenth century rather
than what it had been at its zenith.

These and other related factors helped prepare the way for Edwards' theo-

5. Ibid., pp. 651, 652.

logical development of beauty as a divine perfection. But they do not in themselves account for it, since, after all, he is the only theologian who may be denominated Puritan who has done anything significant with the concept of beauty as a divine perfection.

Elwood finds that Edwards' qualification of Calvin (his neo-Calvinism) "appears most prominently in his fundamental conception of God in terms of absolute beauty and not merely absolute power, and in his appeal to immediate experience in our knowledge of God."[6] The greater stress upon immediate experience was already a major contribution of Puritanism before Edwards' time; in this respect he was less of a pioneer and more of a perfector. But in the manner in which he places beauty at the center of his conception of God he was indeed a pioneer, moving into terrain scouted but never systematically settled by earlier Puritan divines. Elwood's way of drawing attention to this matter is not, however, quite fair to Calvin. For the clear implication of the passage just quoted from Elwood is that Calvin's fundamental conception of God was in terms of "merely absolute power." That is neither fair to nor accurate of Calvin himself, whatever merit it might have if applied to the followers of Calvin in their more defensive and doctrinaire phases. But Elwood does thereby draw our attention to the relationship between beauty and power in the divine being, a relationship that was a matter of concern to Edwards and one that is also of concern to that eminent contemporary Calvinist, Karl Barth.

In Barth's discussion of the divine glory as the sum of the divine perfections, it is to the concept of beauty that he turns for what he finds lacking in the concept of power. "We speak of God's beauty only in explanation of His glory," says Barth. Regarding the idea of beauty, he continues:

> With the help of it we are able to dissipate even the suggestion that God's glory is a mere fact, or a fact which is effective merely through God's power, a formless and shapeless fact. It is not this. It is effective because and as it is beautiful. This explanation as such is not merely legitimate. It is essential.

Barth introduces the concept of beauty into his consideration of the divine glory:

> We have seen that when we speak of God's glory we do emphatically mean God's 'power.' Yet the idea of 'glory' contains some-

6. Elwood, *Philosophical Theology*, p. 9.

thing which is not covered by that of 'power' . . . The concept
which lies ready to our hand here, and which may serve legiti-
mately to describe the element in the idea of glory that we still
lack, is that of beauty.[7]

For Edwards too the idea of beauty as a divine perfection involves consideration of the relationship between beauty and power. But for him beauty takes
priority over power in the divine glory.

The relationship between power and beauty in God is a good point of entry
into Edwards' doctrine of the divine perfections and of the place of beauty
among them, for an understanding of their relationship requires a refinement
of the major division he makes among the divine perfections—the division
between God's natural and His moral perfections. Power is a natural perfection of God, and beauty might be taken simply as a moral perfection. But
actually the place of beauty among the divine perfections is a little more complicated than is suggested by a simple juxtaposition of power and beauty as
instances, respectively, of natural and moral perfections in God.

Beauty has such a unique place among the divine perfections that it will
be helpful to think of it as a third kind of divine perfection rather than as
simply one among either the natural or the moral perfections. God's beauty,
like that of all intelligent spiritual beings, consists primarily in his moral
perfection or holiness. But not all of even the divine beauty is a moral perfection. The natural perfections of God also have a kind of beauty, natural
rather than spiritual, consisting in proportion and harmony rather than in
being's cordial consent to being. We shall, accordingly, have to distinguish
(as Edwards himself explicitly does) not only between God's natural and
moral perfections, but also (as Edwards clearly but not so explicitly does)
between both of those and God's beauty, which is His distinguishing perfection and the perfection of all His natural and moral perfections.

Edwards distinguishes two kinds of perfections or attributes in God: "his
moral attributes, which are summed up in his holiness, and his natural attributes of strength, knowledge, etc. that constitute the greatness of God"
[RA 256]. He finds this to be a special case of the distinction between moral
and natural good commonly made by divines. Just as:

there is a distinction to be made between the natural good that men
are possessed of, and their moral good . . .

7. Barth, *Church Dogmatics,* II/1, pp. 653, 650.

So divines make a distinction between the natural and moral perfections of God: by the *moral perfections* of God, they mean those
attributes which God exercises as a moral agent, or whereby the
heart and will of God are good, right, and infinitely becoming, and
lovely; such as his righteousness, truth, faithfulness, and goodness;
or, in other words, his holiness.

By God's *natural attributes* or perfections, they mean those attributes, wherein, according to our way of conceiving of God, consists, not the holiness or moral goodness of God, but his greatness;
such as his power, his knowledge whereby he knows all things,
and his being eternal, from everlasting to everlasting, his omni-
presence, and his awful and terrible majesty. [RA 255, italics
added]

All the divine perfections, as Edwards conceives them, are to be referred to
one or the other of these two comprehensive classes—all, that is, except
the beauty and the glory of God. The divine glory will be considered presently. First I must show the priority of beauty with respect to the natural and
the moral perfections of God.

To know all the natural and moral perfections of God is no small thing,
of course. But in Edwards' view it is not yet to know what is most peculiar
and distinguishing about God, most essential and central to His divinity. It is
not yet to know that "wherein the truest idea of divinity does consist" [RA
298], namely, the divine beauty. "God is God, and distinguished from all
other beings, and exalted above 'em, chiefly by his divine beauty" [RA
298]. This divine beauty is not itself either a natural or a moral perfection of
God. But it does manifest itself and is articulated in and through God's
natural and moral perfections, most especially in and through the divine
attribute that is the sum of God's moral perfections, his holiness or moral
excellence.

Early in his discussion of the important third sign of true religious affections[8] Edwards sums up a good deal of what is essential about the relation
between the beauty of God and his natural and moral perfections:

The true beauty and loveliness of all intelligent beings does primarily and most essentially consist in their moral excellency or

8. "III. Those affections that are truly holy, are primarily founded on the loveliness of
the moral excellency of divine things. Or (to express it otherwise), a love to divine things
for the beauty and sweetness of their moral excellency, is the first beginning and spring of
all holy affections" [RA 253–54].

holiness . . . 'Tis moral excellency alone that is in itself, and on its
own account, the excellency of intelligent beings: 'tis this that gives
beauty to, or rather is the beauty of their natural perfections and
qualifications. Moral excellency is the excellency of natural excellencies. Natural qualifications are either excellent or otherwise,
according as they are joined with moral excellency or not. Strength
and knowledge don't render any being lovely, without holiness; but
more hateful: though they render them more lovely, when joined
with holiness . . . *The holiness of an intelligent creature, is the
beauty of all his natural perfections. And so it is in God,* according
to our way of conceiving of the divine Being: *holiness is in a peculiar manner the beauty of the divine nature.* Hence we often read
of the beauty of holiness (Ps. 29:2, Ps. 96:9, and 110:3). This
renders all his other attributes glorious and lovely. [RA 257, italics added]

Much of the case to be made for the distinctive status of beauty among the
divine perfections hangs on the difference between his moral perfections
themselves and the beauty of those moral perfections—or, to put it more
accurately, the difference between the moral perfections of God and the
beauty of God manifest in those moral perfections. This difference is one
that pertains to the being of God rather than to any change in view on the
part of the perceiver—though the latter difference or change is so important that the former can easily be missed. But to miss it is to risk missing the
objectivist character of Edwards' understanding of both beauty and sensibility.

Edwards argues that "spiritual understanding consists primarily in a sense
of the heart . . . of the supreme beauty and sweetness of the holiness or moral
perfection of divine things" and goes on to point out that this "sense of the
heart, wherein the mind don't only speculate and behold, but relishes and
feels," must be distinguished from "a mere notional understanding" [RA
272]. He insists, however, that no "clear distinction can be made between
the two faculties of understanding and will, as acting distinctly and separately, in this matter" and that therefore, while "the heart is the proper subject of" this sense of the heart, "yet there is the nature of instruction in it; as
he that has perceived the sweet taste of honey, knows more about it, than he
who has only looked upon it" [RA 272].

To apprehend the beauty of the holiness or moral perfection of God is not simply a subjective matter of being affected and pleased with God or of being inclined to him as holy and beautiful. It is to apprehend something about God himself, to be instructed about the being of God in such a fashion as to not only open up and unfold to view a whole new dimension of the divine being but also open up to view a whole new world [RA 273]. To come to an apprehension or a sense of the beauty of God is not simply to change one's attitude toward God, even though a transformation of inclination and self-disposition toward God is an essential part of such an apprehension.[9] It is also, and more importantly, to apprehend something about God himself. More importantly, I say, because if the beauty of God is in the eye of the perceiver and not in God himself, then the perception of beauty can provide no foundation for any part of what Edwards insists, in passages such as the following, rests ultimately upon it.

> Spiritual understanding primarily consists in this sense, or taste of the moral beauty of divine things; so that no knowledge can be called spiritual, any further than it arises from this, and has this in it. But secondarily, it includes all that discerning and knowledge of things of religion, which depends upon and flows from such a sense.
>
> When the true beauty, and amiableness of the holiness or true moral good that is in divine things, is discovered to the soul, it as it were opens a new world to its view. [RA 273]

Edwards goes on to specify some of what is opened up to view when the beauty of God's moral perfection or holiness is seen, some of which should be noted insofar as it pertains to the divine perfections or attributes. In the first place, this "shows the glory of all the perfections of God, and of everything appertaining to the divine being: for . . . the beauty of all arises from God's moral perfection" [RA 273].

> By this sense of the moral beauty of divine things, is understood the sufficiency of Christ as a mediator: for *'tis only by the discovery of the beauty* of the moral perfection of Christ, that the believer is let into the knowledge of the excellency of his person, so as to know anything more of it than the devils do: and 'tis only by the knowl-

9. "When a person has this sense and knowledge given him, he will view nothing as he did before" [RA 275].

edge of the excellency of Christ's person, that any know his sufficiency as a mediator. [RA 273, italics added]

After enumerating a variety of other things that are brought into view in this
way, Edwards is carried to the heights of eloquence in a passage of special importance to this essay.

> He that sees *the beauty of holiness,* or true moral good, sees *the
> greatest and most important thing in the world,* which is the full-
> ness of all things, without which all the world is empty, no better
> than nothing, yea, worse than nothing. Unless this is seen, nothing
> is seen, that is worth the seeing: for there is no other true excellency
> or beauty. Unless this be understood, nothing is understood, that is
> worthy of the exercise of the noble faculty of understanding. *This
> is the beauty of the Godhead, and the divinity of Divinity* (if I may
> so speak), the good of the infinite Fountain of Good; without
> which God himself (if that were possible to be) would be an in-
> finite evil: without which, we ourselves had better never have
> been; and without which there had better have been no being. He
> therefore in effect knows nothing, that knows not this: his knowl-
> edge is but the shadow of knowledge. [RA 274, italics added]

"He that sees not the beauty of holiness . . . in effect is ignorant of the whole
spiritual world," for from this sense of spiritual beauty arises "all true experimental knowledge of religion" [RA 275].

The significance of this sense of spiritual beauty has not been missed by
students of Edwards' thought. But insufficient attention has been given to
the object of that sense—to the beauty itself, as it is understood by Edwards.
To focus attention on the beauty rather than on the sense of beauty requires
some deliberation, because much of what he has to say on the matter is em-
bedded in works such as the *Religious Affections,* where his primary concern is with sensibility rather than beauty. But even there his objectivism is
clear: religious affections are to be tested by their object—"a holy love has a
holy object" [RA 260]—and by the nature of that object as it is in itself.

Edwards does not permit his emphasis on spiritual understanding as
grounded in a sense or taste to open the door to antinomianism. In *The Nature of True Virtue* he argues that such a taste is not "given arbitrarily" but is
grounded in "the nature of things" [TV 99]; and in the *Religious Affections*
he develops the point more thoroughly.

A holy person is led by the Spirit, as he is instructed and led by his holy taste, and disposition of heart . . . and judges what is right, as it were spontaneously, and of himself, without a particular deduction, by any other arguments than the beauty that is seen, and goodness that is tasted. [RA 282]

A holy disposition and spiritual taste, where grace is strong and lively, will enable a soul to determine what actions are right and becoming Christians, not only more speedily, but far more exactly, than the greatest abilities without it. [RA 283]

Just as "there is such a thing as good taste of natural beauty" [RA 282], "so there is likewise such a thing as a divine taste . . . in discerning and distinguishing the true spiritual and holy beauty of actions" [RA 283]. However, this "divine supernatural sense and relish of the heart" is to be strictly distinguished from many of the "falsely supposed leading of the Spirit" with which Edwards was well acquainted. He exerted himself to show:

the difference between spiritual understanding, and all kinds and forms of enthusiasm, all imaginary sights of God and Christ and heaven, all supposed witnessing of the Spirit, and testimonies of the love of God by immediate inward suggestion; and all impressions of future events, and immediate revelations of any secret facts whatsoever; all enthusiastical impressions and applications of words of Scripture, as though they were words not immediately spoken by God to a particular person, in a new meaning, and carrying something more in them, than the words contain as they lie in the Bible; and all interpretations of the mystical meaning of the Scripture, by supposed immediate revelation. None of these things consists in a divine sense and relish of the heart, of the holy beauty and excellency of divine things; nor have they anything to do with such a sense; but all consist in impressions in the head; all are to be referred to the head [i.e. under the heading] of impressions on the imagination, and consist in the exciting external ideas in the mind. [RA 285f]

Because many such manifestations were falsely taken for "leadings of the Spirit," Edwards wrote and preached with increasing discrimination to the task of discerning between true and false or "bastard religion" [RA 287]. "As a man of a rectified palate judges of particular morsels by his taste: but yet his palate itself must be judged of, whether it be right or no, by certain rules and reasons" [RA 284f], so also the "spiritual taste" of the saints is "subject to the rule of God's Word, and must be tried by that, and a right reasoning upon it" [RA 284]. It must also be tested by attending to the nature of its object. The second sign of gracious affections begins: "The first *objective* ground of gracious affections is the transcendently excellent and amiable nature of divine things, as they are *in themselves*" [RA 240, italics added].

It is important to note that this thing that is "the greatest and most important thing in the world . . . the beauty of the Godhead, and the divinity of Divinity" is not simply the holiness or the moral perfection of God but is rather the beauty of that holiness and of the moral perfections summed up in His holiness. If it is felt that this is a distinction without a difference, let the following evidence be carefully considered.

If, as Edwards says, "the beauty of the divine nature does primarily consist in God's holiness" [RA 258], which is the sum of His moral perfections, then it is to them that men must attend if they would apprehend the divine beauty. But there is a difference between the moral perfections of God and His beauty, for His moral perfections may be apprehended and known and still the beauty of God not be seen. To see and have a sense of the one is not necessarily to see and have a sense of the other. To see and have a sense of God's natural perfections, such as His greatness, power and knowledge, is not yet to see His true beauty; it is at best to apprehend His natural beauty, that secondary beauty that is defined by proportion rather than consent. Nor does an apprehension of God's true beauty necessarily follow from seeing or having a sense of His moral perfections or attributes, such as His justice, righteousness, goodness and holiness, as can be seen from passages such as the following ones; their meaning for the point now under consideration is clear, although their own immediate concern is rather with the significance of the sense than with the status of the beauty.

> If persons have a great sense of the natural perfections of God, and are greatly affected with them, or have any other sight or sense of God, than that which consists in, or implies a sense of the beauty of his moral perfections, it is no certain sign of grace: as particularly, men's having a great sense of the awful greatness, and terrible majesty of God; for this is only God's natural perfection, and what men may see, and yet be entirely blind to the beauty of his moral perfections. [RA 263]

Wicked men and devils will see, and have a great sense of *every-thing* that appertains to the glory of God, but only [i.e., *except for*] *the beauty of his moral perfection.* They will see his infinite greatness and majesty, his infinite power, and will be fully convinced of his omniscience, and his eternity and immutability; and *they will see and know everything appertaining to his moral attributes themselves, but only [i.e. except for] the beauty and amiableness of them:* they will see and know that he is perfectly just and righteous and true; and that he is a holy God . . . and they will see the wonderful manifestations of his infinite goodness and free grace to the saints; and there is nothing will be hid from their eyes, but only [i.e. except for] the beauty of these moral attributes, and that beauty of the other attributes, which arises from it. And so natural men in this world are capable of having a very affecting sense of everything else that appertains to God, but this only. [RA 264, italics added]

It is clear from this that there is something very special about beauty as a divine attribute or perfection. There is nothing very remarkable about the view that God's natural perfections may be apprehended without having a sense of the divine beauty, although Edwards finds there is in those natural perfections a derivative and secondary or natural beauty defined by proportion and harmony rather than by cordial consent. But the idea that God's infinite goodness and grace and His other moral attributes, even His holiness, may be known while yet the divine beauty remains hidden to view is what is remarkable in Edwards' scheme. If even the holiness of God may, according to this passage, be apprehended while one is still blind to the divine beauty, and if, as is the case in Edwards' scheme, beauty is actually a perfection of God and not simply a name for a form of human response to God (or to the vision of God), then surely the divine beauty must be seen as having a peculiar or unique place among the divine perfections.

Edwards sees this focus on God's beauty and his moral perfections as standing in sharp contrast with a major prevailing tendency of his day to stress instead what he regards as merely natural perfections in God. " 'Tis beyond doubt," he writes in the course of his maturest analysis of the Great Awakening, "that too much weight has been laid, by many persons of late, on discoveries of God's greatness, *awful* majesty, and natural perfection . . . without any real view of the holy, *lovely* majesty of God" [RA 265, italics added].

Although some of Edwards' impact on his own age and—even more so—much of his reputation in ages since his own rested upon his capacity to make the terrors of hell and separation from God real and apparent to his hearers, it was the divine beauty and the real good in God rather than the horrors following upon sin that he tried most passionately to make apparent to those in his spiritual care. It was the beauty of God and of all things in God rather than the fires of hell that most moved his mind to dialectics and his tongue to eloquence. In fact, it was one of the central and recurring themes of his whole work as a moralist, preacher, and theologian that he who is moved in what he does by fear rather than by love, by a fear, for example, of God's awful power rather than by a sense of His even more awesome beauty, is precisely to that extent already alienated from God and, but for the grace of God, separated from his holiness and redeeming presence.[10]

If the Divine Being is rightly to be discerned, he felt, more must be made of God's goodness than of His greatness, more made of His "holy, lovely majesty" and moral perfection than of His "awful majesty and natural perfection" [RA 265]. To this end it is not enough to attend from the natural to the moral perfections of God. A further requirement is that the beauty of those moral perfections must be seen, for "if the moral beauty of God be hid," not only will "the enmity of the heart . . . remain in its full strength" [RA 264] whatever else is known of God's greatness and goodness, but also that "wherein the truest idea of divinity does consist" [RA 298] and by

10. Both A. N. Whitehead and H. R. Niebuhr place near the center of their understanding of the religious life a root option with respect to the perception and interpretation of reality as governed by either Friend or Enemy. And for both of them the transition from one perception to the other constitutes the decisive moment in the life of faith. For Whitehead there is an earlier "transition from God the void to God the enemy," but the critical passage is from the perception of "God the enemy" to a perception of "God the companion" (*Religion in the Making*, p. 16). For Niebuhr the primal options are trust or distrust of being: "Between these two there seems to be no middle term. The inscrutable power by which we are is either for us or against us" (*The Responsible Self* [New York, Harper and Row, 1963], p. 119). And the decisive transition is from a "deep distrust of the One in all the many," a perception of the self as "surrounded by animosity" (pp. 142, 140) and in bondage to an Enemy to "the liberty to interpret in trust all that happens" (p. 142) and to affirm that the principle of being and the principle of good are one.

Edwards offers an aesthetic model for construing the same root option of the life of faith. For him the critical transition is from the knowledge of God's awful power to the knowledge of his beauty and a participation in the joy and glory of God by cordial consent to being-in-general. Man's vision of order is related to his aesthetic-affectional response to reality, whether in delight and trust and consent to being or in fear and distrust and dissent from being.

which God is most distinguished from and exalted above all other beings will remain unknown. That is, Edwards' conception of the divine beauty provides the most critical measure not only of our existential response to God but also of our philosophical and theological conception of God. This would not be so if Edwards' definition of beauty were subjective, emotional, and relativist rather than objective, structural, and relational, for in that case the attribution or predication of beauty to God would be only an expression of our existential response to the divine reality and would involve no cognitive claim about the Divine Being itself. But Edwards sees beauty as the central clue not only to the appropriate human response to God, as in a right inclination of the will, true religious affections, and true virtue but also to the divine object (subject) of that response—as a clue to the inner nature of the Divine Being itself.

The relation between beauty and holiness presents a problem here. The problem arises from the fact that while for Edwards holiness is the sum of the moral perfections of God, it is also more than a moral concept. Holiness follows beauty in reaching beyond its identification with the moral perfection of God to designate also the most objective and essential portion of the fullness of the divine glory. The divine beauty, which consists principally in God's holiness or the sum of his moral perfections, then, consists even more fully in God's glory. If this distinction can be sustained, then it might be said that to apprehend the holiness of God as the sum of his moral perfections apart from any vision of its place in the full glory of God would involve no more than an apprehension *that* God is holy; but to apprehend the beauty of God's holiness would, in addition, involve a sensible knowledge of wherein that holiness consists, namely, its share or portion in the fullness of good in God, which is His glory or beauty.

This—in addition to his own rather clear language on the matter—warrants the conclusion that for Edwards there is a greater increment of knowledge of the Divine Being involved in having a sense of the beauty of God's holiness than there is in simply an apprehension of that holiness itself understood as the sum of the moral perfections of God. To know the primary beauty of something is to know not simply that the object is beautiful, as may well be the case with respect to secondary beauty but to know also wherein the beauty consists. That is, the knowledge of primary beauty involves an essential increment that is not necessarily a part of the knowledge of secondary beauty. It is not essential to the enjoyment of the beauty of a piece of music that one know wherein the beauty consists—the laws of harmony, for example. It is, however, ingredient to the apprehension of primary beauty that there be an apprehension not only of the beauty but also of that wherein the beauty consists.

This has two consequences, the second of which is especially relevant to the present discussion. First, the knowledge of secondary beauty implies nothing about the knower himself. One does not have to know anything about the principles of proportion and harmony in order to apprehend secondary beauty. The knowledge of primary beauty, on the other hand, does imply something necessarily about the knower. One cannot apprehend primary beauty unless one does not merely enjoy the beauty but also is disposed to know and enjoy the principle by which such beauty is constituted, that is, unless one knows and delights in the cordial consent of being to being. It is certainly possible to enjoy music without being devoted to a knowledge of the laws of harmony. It is also possible to delight in virtue without being devoted to the laws of virtue. But in that case virtue is apprehended only for its secondary beauty and not for its primary beauty. To enjoy virtue on those terms is to enjoy it only because of its relation to self and not for what it is objectively and in itself, while to delight in virtue in the latter fashion is to delight in it for the primary beauty that is in it. A second consequence is that the secondary beauty of something may be known and enjoyed without knowing anything about the object itself; it may involve knowing nothing more than how one feels about the object aesthetically. To know the primary beauty of something, on the other hand, necessarily involves knowing not only how one feels about the object but also—and primarily—something about that object itself. Therefore, if God's beauty consists principally in the spiritual beauty of His moral perfections, to know the beauty of God must involve not simply knowing something about one's response to the divine being as encountered but must also involve the knowledge of something about the divine being itself.

It is the genius of Edwards' settling upon beauty as the most distinguishing perfection or attribute of God that he has thereby a concept in terms of which to insist at once upon the objectivity of God and upon his view that God can be fully known only to the extent that he is genuinely enjoyed. When placed at the center of his conception of God, beauty has the peculiar merit of offering at once a way of conceiving of the nature of God in structural and ontological terms and of so conceiving of that divine object as to make it not only dogmatically but also philosophically clear that (and why) God can be fully known only if he is the direct object of enjoyment. Beauty provides

Edwards with a perfectly flexible category, at the very heart of the Divine Being itself, which also constitutes a definition or specification of the relation between the creature and the Creator.

The divine beauty is hidden from all but the saint. Beauty of whatever sort can be apprehended or seen only if it is enjoyed—to enjoy it is to apprehend it—so that an apprehension of the divine beauty is reserved to those who delight in His being (and in being-in-general or in the good of being-in-general). However, even if an apprehension and direct experience of the divine beauty is open only to the saints, to conceive of God primarily in terms of the concept of beauty is open to all. Therefore, such a conception of the Divine Being is not essentially private and does not constitute a sort of aesthetic gnosticism. Quite the contrary. To conceive of God primarily in terms of beauty offers a way of giving discursive formulation to a particular vision of God in which all real knowledge of God must be grounded in direct experience of the Divine Being. But such a conception of God is not itself dependent, at least for its conception and articulation, upon the perception and direct experience or enjoyment of that divine beauty. This conception of God is open to examination and consideration, even to adoption, by men who cannot themselves lay claim to a saving acquaintance with the divine beauty so central to this conception of His being and nature.

There are, then, three stages or moments in our knowledge of God, each of which corresponds to and designates at once something about the Divine Being and something about the manner of our relation to him: the knowledge of God's natural perfections, the knowledge of His moral perfections, and finally the knowledge of His beauty. Since the divine beauty consists primarily in the beauty of His moral perfections, it is their beauty that must first be apprehended if the fullness of God's beauty is to be known, for the beauty of all His other attributes is derived from the beauty of His moral perfections, most especially his holiness. "A sight of God's loveliness must begin here . . . with a delight in his holiness . . . for no other attribute is truly lovely without this" [RA 257]. What is here affirmed about the place of beauty among the divine perfections in the order of knowing is confirmed by what has been shown to be its place among them in the order of being.

This may be further confirmed by attending to the relation between beauty, goodness, and power among the perfections of God. Power may, for the present purpose, be taken as representative of the natural perfections of God. And goodness may, in the same manner, be taken as representative of the moral perfections of God—goodness rather than holiness since holiness, though it is the sum of the moral perfections of God, also has a wider than moral significance. Beauty, goodness, and power may be taken as representative of the three kinds of divine perfections into which all of them may be resolved. And their rank order among the divine perfections is first beauty, then goodness, then power, in descending order.

What needs to be said here about the relation between beauty and goodness in God may be put in the form of commentary on what we have already seen to be Edwards' view of the relations between beauty and goodness generally. The divine beauty is the measure of God's goodness; His goodness is related to His beauty as part to whole. God's goodness is a "part of the beauty of his nature" [RA 248], just as in man virtue or moral goodness is a "kind of beauty" [TV 1]. To Edwards it makes sense to ask, what moved God to exercise his power? Such a question can be answered in terms of something other than power. But to the parallel question—what moved God to exercise His goodness—there can be no such answer but only an infinite regress within the terms of the question itself. Since Edwards understands goodness to consist in a disposition to communicate good, the only answer must be God's goodness itself. One can, in other words, try to get behind God's power but not behind His goodness. However, if God's goodness is a part of His beauty, then at least the divine beauty can be said to stand behind His goodness; or rather, beauty alone carries us closer to the center of the mystery of the Divine Being.

The divine beauty is the most objective portion of the divine goodness and the foundation of all that is good in God. Beauty is so central to Edwards' conception of the Divine Being that a knowledge of that beauty constitutes for him the critical measure of the objectivity of our knowledge of God and of our judgments respecting the Divine Being. For him, no real good is fully known until its beauty is known and enjoyed. Since God is man's real good, a knowledge of the divine beauty is for him the key to a knowledge of God as He is in Himself or objectively. To know His beauty is to know Him as intrinsically and essentially good, as distinguished from the knowledge of God as good to me or to some other particular being. Beauty is Edwards' measure of the disinterestedness of such knowledge and of the objectivity of the judgment "God is good."

Something more than goodness is required if God is to be God; goodness must be united with power. The divine beauty designates and constitutes the attractive and creative power of His goodness; it expresses the identity of power and goodness in God. The above rank-ordering of beauty, goodness, and power among the divine perfections ought not to be read as setting power and beauty against each other. It would be more accurate to say that power is conceived and defined by Edwards in terms of beauty. Beauty provides him with his model of spiritual power, of transforming and creative power, and of the very power of being. It is the divine beauty that constitutes the foundation of God's sovereignty and the pattern for its exercise. God exercises his sovereignty not by brute force but by placing before men their real good as their apparent good and by giving them that divine sense of the heart that finds in this real good the apparent good in which it delights.

> A sight of the awful greatness of God, may overpower man's strength, and be more than they can endure; but if the moral beauty of God be hid, the enmity of the heart will remain in its full strength, no love will be enkindled, all will not be effectual to gain the will, but that will remain inflexible; whereas the first glimpse of the moral and spiritual glory of God shining into the heart, produces all these effects, as it were with omnipotent power, which nothing can withstand. [RA 264f]

God's beauty, then, is his power unto salvation. And of these three representative divine perfections—power, goodness, and beauty—it is a knowledge of God's beauty that is the knowledge unto salvation. Not the knowledge of God's power, as is supposed, or at least suggested by the more defensive moments in Calvinist orthodoxy, including some to which Edwards addressed himself, nor the knowledge of God's goodness, as in moralistic liberalism or Arminianism, but the knowledge of the divine beauty, in which power and goodness are one.

The preeminence of beauty among the divine perfections will further appear from a consideration of the relation between the divine beauty and the divine glory as Edwards understands them. The relation would certainly have to be a close one for anyone who makes significant theological use of the concept of beauty. Karl Barth, for example, finds the concept of beauty essential to the clarification of the divine glory, and it is only at this point in his systematic program—in explanation of the divine glory—that Barth introduces the concept of beauty. Edwards sees the relation between beauty and glory in God to be even closer than it is for Barth, who wants to keep beauty in a clearly "subordinate and auxiliary" relation to glory as a divine perfection.[11]

For Edwards the relation between beauty and glory in God is one of virtual identity—an identity between the divine glory and the primary, spiritual, and moral beauty of God understood as a beauty distinct from and yet embracing also as a shadow and image of itself the secondary or natural beauty of proportion and harmony manifest in God's natural perfections. Edwards' identification of the divine beauty with the divine glory appears all the more important when it is remembered that it is precisely the divine glory that constitutes the unity of all the otherwise diverse ends for which God created the world. The creation of the world and the whole course of its history is a manifestation and communication and shining forth of the divine beauty.

To speak of the divine glory is another way of speaking of the divine beauty; the terms are largely synonymous, so Edwards can contrast the situation in which "the moral beauty of God" is hidden from the situation in which "the moral and spiritual glory of God" shines forth into the heart [RA 264f]. Or again, Edwards can speak interchangeably of beauty and glory in arguing that a solid conviction of the truth of the gospel is given only "by a sight of its glory" [RA 303] or by imparting a "spiritual taste of divine beauty" [RA 302]. The divine glory and beauty are so identified as to be frequently spoken of in tandem where the intention is clearly to reinforce or emphasize rather than to qualify or supplement the meaning already carried by the use of only one of the concepts. So, for example, the good of the creature is said to consist in part in a "knowledge or view of God's glory and beauty" [TV 25].

The divine beauty is identified most especially with what is highest in and most peculiar to the divine glory. The divine beauty designates God's "moral or spiritual glory, which is much more distinguishing" than his "natural glory" [RA 306]. Therefore, "wicked men and devils, who are perfectly destitute of any sense or relish of that kind of beauty," may yet have "a very great knowledge of the natural glory of God (if I may so speak)"—the parentheses are Edwards'—"and have a great sense of everything that appertains to the glory of God but only [i.e. except for] the beauty of his moral perfections" [RA 263f]. The natural glory they may know, but not that greater glory, "the glory of God consisting in the beauty of his holiness" [RA 264].

11. Barth, *Church Dogmatics,* II/1, p. 653.

For it is, Edwards says—again parenthetically, for emphasis and clarification —"the moral and spiritual glory of the divine Being (which is the proper beauty of the Divinity)" [RA 299].

The beauty of God's moral perfections, which is in turn also the beauty of all his other perfections, is His glory—a more comprehensive term and a more embracing reality than God's holiness. For God's holiness refers especially to His moral perfections, while God's glory includes all the good in Him, all the good manifested and communicated, both natural and moral [EC 206]. The glory of God comprises a fullness of good both internal to the Divine Being and exhibited, manifested, and communicated to the creature. When this real good is perceived as the apparent good defining the will of the creature, it is loved and enjoyed or delighted in as the fullness of good, the *summum bonum*—a *bonum formosum* or beautiful good—rather than a *bonum utile*. The fullness of Glod's glory and the fullness of the creature's good are one, rather than diverse, so that in having a regard to the former in all that He does, God also has a regard to the good of the creature. The good of the creature is included in and is inseparable from the glory or beauty of God and in fact consists in a participation in that very beauty in such a way as to bear the mark of the divine beauty in the form of the spiritual image of God in men [EC 256].

Glory is one of those concepts that, more than most, cannot easily be contained and readily overflows every definition. Edwards is sensitive to this and explores thoroughly the many ways in which the concept is employed in the Scriptures. Even as he concludes that exploration in an attempt to define the relation between "God's internal glory" and that "glory of God" that he finds to be God's ultimate end in the creation of the world, he adds that:

> It is confessed that there is a degree of obscurity in these definitions; but perhaps an obscurity which is unavoidable, through the imperfection of language, and words being less fitted to express things of so sublime a nature. And therefore the thing may possibly be better understood, by using many words and a variety of expressions, by a particular consideration of it, as it were by parts, than by any short definition. [EC 253]

Edwards himself employs the concept of glory with the same freedom he finds in the Scriptures, so that in his thought too its meaning can better be exhibited and explored than defined. One constant, however, is that for Edwards especially and, as he shows, for Scripture also the concept of glory is always closely identified with, if not identical to, those of excellency, highest good, holiness, perfection, and beauty. It is, for example, "the divine excellency and glory of God" [RA 240] or again "a beauty, glory, and supreme good, in God's nature, as it is in itself" [RA 241] that is "the first objective ground" of truly gracious affections. It is common for Edwards to use glory and excellency, beauty, and even holiness interchangeably, apparently understanding by them very much the same thing.

> He that sees the *glory* of God, in his measure beholds that of which there is no end. The understanding . . . may discover more and more of the *beauty* and loveliness of God, but it never will exhaust the fountain. [Nor can man] extend his faculties to the utmost of God's *excellency*.[12]

In arguing, for example, that "God in seeking his glory therein seeks the good his creatures" [EC 218], Edwards employs his characteristic formula for summing up the moral perfections of God and, since the content is the same, the moral good communicated to the creatures—the formula "excellency and happiness"—shifting freely from one to another of the concepts glory, excellency, perfection, beauty, and holiness without any shift in meaning. Speaking of the creature's good, he says:

> Their *excellency and happiness* is nothing but the emanation and expression of God's glory. God, in seeking their *glory and happiness,* seeks himself, and in seeking himself, i.e. himself diffused and expressed (which he delights in, as he delights in his own beauty and fulness), he seeks their glory and happiness. [EC 219, italics added]

Elsewhere in the same treatise he is as likely to change the formula to "holiness and happiness" [EC 212f, 218, 234]. The same formula becomes on occasion "perfection and happiness," as in another summary statement of these same two branches of God's "one supream end" in all his works, namely, "God's glorifying himself or causing his glory and perfection to shine forth, and his communicating himself or communicating his fulness and happiness" [Misc. 1066]. "God's being glorified," then, consists at once in "God's infinite perfection being exerted and so manifested" and in "his infinite happiness being communicated" [Misc. 1066]. This same formula becomes at yet other places "virtue and happiness" [EC 254]. Finally, the formula

12. *Works,* ed. S. E. Dwight (New York, 1829–30), *8,* 292, italics added.

sometimes appears as "beauty and happiness," such as where "the infinite fulness of good in God" is summarized by Edwards as "a fulness of every perfection, of all excellency and beauty, and of infinite happiness" [EC 206] or where he represents God, "the fountain of both being and beauty," as so inclined to the good of the creature as to give both actual and possible beings "beauty and happiness" [TV 6]. Most of the relations summarized here are brought together in the course of a sermon: "Holiness is the very beauty and loveliness of Jehovah himself. 'Tis the excellency of his excellencies, the beauty of his beauties, the perfection of his infinite perfections, and the glory of his attributes."[13]

But the wide variety of meanings given to the concept of glory is not without some order. Insofar as the concept refers to the being of God this order can be designated by distinguishing the internal and external glory of God. These are two modes or moments in the fullness of the Divine Being and of the good in God. The external glory of God, which is the glory He seeks as His end in the creation of the world and which men are to seek in all they do, living to the greater glory of God, is simply the emanation and communication of his internal glory. It is characteristic of Edwards that he should resolve problems respecting the many always by referring to the One beyond the many in whom all variety has its origin. Any variety found in the communicated glory of God must be traceable to a corresponding variety in the internal glory of God, for

> though we suppose all these things, which seem to be so various
> are signified by that glory which the Scriptures speaks of as the last
> end of all God's works; yet it is manifest there is no greater, and no
> other variety in it, than in the internal and essential glory of God
> itself. [EC 254]

The variety of manifestations of this internal glory "at first view may appear to be entirely distinct things; but if we more closely consider the matter, they will all appear to be one thing, in a variety of views and relations. They are all but the emanation of God's glory" [EC 253]. "The emanation or communication is of the internal glory or fulness of God as it is" [EC 253].

The relation of the divine beauty to the fullness of glory and good in God and to the other divine perfections, especially His holiness and happiness, will be further clarified if we follow Edwards in his specification of the variety he finds essential and intrinsic to the internal glory of God. That variety derives

---

13. Sermon on Psalm 89:6, Yale University Manuscript Collection.

from the distinction in God between His understanding and His will. "God's internal glory is partly in his understanding, and partly in his will" [EC 254].

> Now God's internal glory, as it is in God, is either in his understanding or will. The glory or fulness of his understanding is his knowledge. The internal glory and fulness of God which we must conceive of as having its special seat in his will is his holiness and happiness. [EC 253]

This formulation of the internal glory of God introduces a second major way Edwards has of conceiving of the order among the principal perfections of God.

Knowledge, holiness, and happiness are the three summary perfections of God according to a second formulation of them that Edwards sometimes employs, an alternative formulation to the one I have so far been considering based on the division between natural and moral perfections in God and yet one that is closely related to and compatible with that formulation. Employing this second formulation, Edwards sometimes finds, as he does in his treatise on *The End For Which God Created the World,* that the divine perfections may be reduced to three perfections or attributes: knowledge, holiness, and happiness. This trinity of perfections is basic to his anthropology as well as to his theology. The last passage I quoted continues:

> The whole of God's internal good or glory, is in these three things, viz., his infinite knowledge, his infinite virtue or holiness, and his infinite joy or happiness. Indeed there are a great many attributes in God, according to our way of conceiving or talking of them, but all may be reduced to these, or to the degree, circumstances and relations of these. [EC 253]

He proceeds to specify how it is that he conceives several of the divine attributes—power, infinity, eternity, and immutability, for example—to be reducible to these three. His treatment of power will illustrate his procedure. "We have no conception of God's power," he says, "different from the degree of these [three] things, with a certain relation of them to effects" [EC 253]. In sum, "the fullness of the Godhead is the fullness of his understanding, consisting in his knowledge, and the fullness of his will, consisting in his virtue and happiness" [EC 254].

It is in the manifestation and communication of this fullness of good in

God that the divine glory consists. Not something about God or even merely some relation to God but rather something of the very being of God himself is herein communicated or diffused to the creature. Of the summary perfections of God, the first (knowledge or understanding) is a natural perfection of God, while the second (holiness, excellency, virtue, or love) and the third (happiness, joy, or delight) are seen by Edwards as among—even preeminent among—God's moral perfections. Certainly "his moral attributes can't be without his natural attributes" [RA 256f]; indeed they presuppose them, for "all the attributes of God do as it were imply one another" [RA 257]. But it is in the moral perfections of God that the divine beauty, once again, is most especially and primarily manifest.

It should be noted carefully in this connection that the knowledge, holiness, and happiness here spoken of as divine perfections are quite particular rather than general or abstract. Their particularity is defined by their object; beauty and excellence are in this sense always defined objectively by Edwards. The object that defines these three divine perfections is God Himself, the only object properly worthy of being the motive or end aimed at in the exercise of any of the divine perfections. That is, these three divine perfections are not knowledge, holiness, and happiness in general but specifically the knowledge of God, the love of God, and joy in God. Edwards is worth quoting at length on this point; the critical passage is the one that culminates in his vision of a vast "emanation and remanation" of the divine fullness or glory.

> The emanation or communication of the divine fulness, consisting in the knowledge of God, love to God, and joy in God, has relation indeed both to God, and the creature; but it has relation to God as its fountain, as it is an emanation from God; and as the communication itself, or thing communicated, is something divine, something of God, something of his internal fulness, as the water in the stream is something of the fountain, and as the beams of the sun, are something of the sun. And again, they have relation to God as they have respect to him as their object; for the knowledge communicated is the knowledge of God; and so God is the object of the knowledge; and the love communicated is the love of God, so God is the object of that love; and the happiness communicated is joy in God, and so he is the object of the joy communicated. In the creature's knowing, esteeming, loving, rejoicing in, and praising God, the glory of God is both exhibited and acknowledged; his fulness is

received and returned. Here is both an emanation and remanation.
The refulgence shines upon and into the creature, and is reflected
back to the luminary. The beams of glory come from God, and are
something of God, and are refunded back again to their original.
So that the whole is *of* God, and *in* God, and *to* God, and God is
the beginning, middle and end in this affair. [EC 255]

God is the object of the knowledge, the love, and the joy. These three summary perfections of God comprise the fullness of good in God, the glory and
beauty of God shown forth and communicated to the creature. To receive any
of them from God is, then, more than to receive something from God; it is to
receive something of God himself; it is to participate in God's own perfect
knowledge of Himself, His own perfect love of Himself, and His own perfect
joy in Himself, since "these things are but the emanation of God's own
knowledge, holiness and joy" [EC 206]. "What is communicated is divine,
or something of God" [EC 210]. And it is communicated out of "an infinite fulness of all possible good in God, a fulness of every perfection, of all
excellency and beauty, and of infinite happiness" [EC 206].

The preeminence of beauty in the Divine Being may be further shown by
examining its relation to these three summary perfections. In his discussion
of the "second distinguishing sign" of true religious affections—that their first
objective ground be the transcendent excellency of divine things in themselves
—Edwards argues that the first foundation of true love of God must be "that
whereby he is himself lovely . . . or the supreme loveliness of his nature."

> What chiefly makes a man, or any creature lovely, is his excel-
> lency; and so what chiefly renders God lovely, and must undoubt-
> edly be the chief ground of true love, is his excellency. God's na-
> ture, or the divinity, is infinitely excellent; yea 'tis infinite beauty,
> brightness and glory itself. But how can that be true love of this
> excellent and lovely nature, which is not built on the foundation of
> its true loveliness? How can that be true love of beauty and bright-
> ness, which is not for beauty and brightness' sake? . . . This infinite
> excellency of the divine nature, as it is in itself, is the true ground
> of all that is good in God in any respect. [RA 242f]

God's beauty or excellency is the ground of all that is good in God. And the
fullness of that good consists summarily in His knowledge, holiness, and joy,
so that of these three perfections it is God's holiness that is the proper beauty

and excellency of the divine nature and that therefore has a kind of objective priority among the divine perfections because it is itself the ground of the other components of the fullness of good in God—his knowledge and joy.

Such priority as holiness has among the divine perfections derives from its special identification with the divine beauty. But it is also true of the divine perfections of knowledge and joy that they qualify to stand among the three summary perfections of God by virtue of their relation to the divine beauty.

The divine knowledge, as a perfection of God and as a good communicated to the creature, has as its object the perfection, glory, excellency, and beauty of God. "God's perfections, or his glory, is the object of this knowledge, or the thing known; so that God is glorified in it, as his excellency is seen" [EC 210]. In fact, it is Edwards' view that what is most peculiar and distinctive about this divine knowledge is that "the immediate object of it is the supreme beauty and excellency of the nature of divine things, as they are in themselves" [RA 271]. He calls this divine knowledge a "spiritual understanding" that "consists primarily in a sense of the heart of that spiritual beauty" [RA 272], including also "all that discerning and knowledge of things of religion, which depends upon, and flows from such a sense" [RA 273]. Having the divine beauty or some emanation of that beauty as its object marks this knowledge as a perfection in God and, when communicated as a good to the creature, as "the highest excellency and perfection of a rational creature."[14]

Edwards is not prepared to settle for designating such spiritual understanding in the creature as only the communication or emanation of the fullness of knowledge in God; its divinity or its divine origin is even more firmly attested by its being "a kind of emanation of God's beauty." In his important sermon on "A Divine and Supernatural Light" Edwards argues that while lesser gifts of God may be left by him to "second causes," this spiritual knowledge is of such transcendent importance as to be bestowed only "immediately by himself," for

> there is no gift or benefit that is in itself so nearly related to the divine nature, there is nothing the creature receives that is so much of God, of his nature, so much a participation of the deity: it is a kind of emanation of God's beauty, and is related to God as the light is to the sun.[15]

14. "A Divine and Supernatural Light," *Works, 4*, 448.
15. Ibid., italics added.

This divine knowledge is "so nearly related to the divine nature" that it is "a kind of emanation of God's beauty!" That is, the divine beauty is what is most intimately related to the divine nature, or the divine beauty is that "wherein the truest idea of divinity does consist" [RA 298]. The unique and distinctive place among the divine perfections here being ascribed to the divine beauty is shown in part, then, by its being the one perfection or attribute of God that is the peculiar object of that "sense of the heart" in which spiritual understanding consists.

The divine happiness or joy, like the divine knowledge and holiness, also qualifies as a perfection of God by virtue of its relation to the divine beauty and especially by virtue of its being grounded in and, as it were, being one with the holiness of God, which is most properly the beauty of the divine nature. As a perfection of God his happiness consists in his "enjoying and rejoicing in himself" and more particularly "in his own beauty" [EC 210], which consists principally in his holiness. And as a good communicated to the creature, this happiness "arises from that which is an image and participation of God's own beauty," that is, it arises from holiness in the creature "and consists in the creature's exercising a supreme regard to God, and complacence in him" [EC 255].

This dependence of joy upon holiness in the Divine Being rests, furthermore, upon Edwards' conviction that complacence (delight in beauty) is not virtuous unless it is based upon benevolence (love of being). Holiness consists essentially in such benevolence, while happiness or joy is a form of complacence. The perfection of joy in God, accordingly, consists in his delight in the beauty of holiness, whether it is in himself as a part of his internal glory or whether it is "diffused, overflowing, and as it were, enlarged, or in one word, existing *ad extra*" [EC 253] and therefore also communicated to the creatures as a part of his external glory and beauty.

Although logically distinct, in God holiness and joy or benevolence and complacence are one, as they are also in the creature insofar as he is conformed to God.[16]

> If universal benevolence in the highest sense, be the same thing
> with benevolence to the Divine Being, who is in effect universal

16. "Man's true happiness is his perfection and true excellency. When any reasonable creature finds that his excellency and his joy are the same thing, then he is come to right and real happiness, and not before" (*Works*, ed. S. E. Dwight, 9, 288).

being, it will follow, that love to virtue itself is no otherwise virtuous, than as it is implied in or arises from love to the Divine
Being. Consequently God's own love to virtue is implied in love to
himself. [EC 217]

Benevolence is a love directed essentially to being rather than to beauty, while
complacence is a love directed to benevolent being or to a being for its beauty,
holiness, or virtue. In God these two are one. In Him "the love of virtue
cannot be a distinct thing from the love of Himself" [EC 217]; complacence (the love of His own beauty) is identical with benevolence (the love
of His own being, or of being-in-general). Beauty and being are one in God,
"the foundation and fountain of all being and all beauty . . . of whom, and
through whom, and to whom is all being and all perfection; and whose being
and beauty are, as it were, the sum and comprehension of all existence and
excellence" [TV 15].

This second summary formulation of the divine perfections as reducible to
knowledge, holiness, and joy is remarkable for several reasons, not the least
of which is its elevation of joy or happiness or delight to such prominence
among the perfections of God and the conjunction of joy with holiness as together constituting a summary of the moral perfections of God. It should be
emphasized that in this view joy stands together with holiness at the heart of
the Divine Being; for Edwards they are together the sum of God's moral perfections. In their interdependence they carry into the heart of divinity itself
the unity of beauty and sensibility that is such an important element in Edwards' understanding of the whole realm of what he calls "intelligent being."

The experience of the beauty of divine things constituted for Edwards the
most intimate and fullest communion with God. This is clear and now even
notorious from his own accounts of his youthful "awakening" to a "new sense
of things" and from his early "Notes" and "Miscellanies." And as Douglas
Elwood has rightly observed, "In maturer years Edwards found increasing
satisfaction in the view that God is known most surely and most convincingly
by an immediate awareness of His creative beauty in and through all the
things He has made."[17] There is no escaping our manner of conceiving things,
including our manner of conceiving God. But there are many ways of conceiving of reality and of construing the shape of things. Edwards, taking his
clue from his experience of the beauty of divine things, came to regard the

17. Elwood, *Philosophical Theology*, p. 16.

concept of beauty as affording the deepest possible penetration into the inexhaustible mystery of the Divine Being. According to his way of conceiving God, beauty is first among the divine perfections. God's perfection is precisely His beauty. Beauty is not only *a* major divine perfection but is *the* distinguishing perfection of God and the perfection in turn of all His other perfections.

It is interesting, in this connection, to take note of an alternative aesthetic possibility to the one taken by Edwards in the development of his thought. The possibility I have in mind is that of the sublime. The contrast between the beautiful and the sublime is not one that Edwards is known to have entertained, but it may help to suggest and underline some of what is involved in his placing the concept of beauty at the center of his systematic thought.[18] I have employed the term "articulation" in considering the formative influence of the concept of beauty upon the manner in which Edwards' thought develops. The term is not one employed by Edwards himself. But it is peculiarly appropriate to the examination of an ontological and theological system in which beauty is so decisive. For beauty is always an articulated reality, even if it leaves the beholder verbally inarticulate in its presence—as perhaps it ought to do. In this respect beauty differs from the sublime, an aesthetic category that was only coming into currency in Edwards' day and that would in any event have been less to his purpose than the concept of beauty. Edwards was more suspicious of the natural and less charmed by chaos than were those who were later to make much of the sublime. The sublime is an aesthetic category appropriate to the awesome and even awful, while Edwards was very much concerned with recovering a sense of the "lovely majesty" of God, as opposed to the "awful majesty" of God so much emphasized by many of his contemporaries among evangelical Christians. He did not propose, of course, to make of God a ready comforter of complacent men much taken with their own fabrication of a gentle and lovely Jesus walking peacefully in the garden hand in hand with all who would follow the Golden Rule. Divine majesty remained as important to him as to Calvin. But the divine majesty was for him a lovely rather than an awful or awesome majesty. Beauty and light and joy rather than terror and darkness are what he found at the heart of God and of being-in-general, whereas the sublime, unlike beauty, has about it always at least a touch of terror. Furthermore, proportion and harmony were too important to his vision of reality to permit any elevation of

18. For an authoritative study of the sublime see Samuel H. Monk, *The Sublime* (Ann Arbor, University of Michigan Press, 1960).

the sublime into prominence in the Divine Being or to a normative status in the divine scheme of things. For while proportion is but a secondary form of beauty, it is yet to be found in God Himself and is a distinguishing mark of all his works: "There is symmetry and beauty in God's workmanship" [RA 365]. The sublime, on the other hand, has in it no symmetry or proportion.

7

BEAUTY AND THE TRINITY

Jonathan Edwards' conviction that "God is God, and distinguished from all other beings, and exalted above 'em, chiefly by his divine beauty" [RA 298] nowhere reveals itself more clearly central to his conception of God than when that conception is approached through his doctrine of the Trinity. Although during his own lifetime he published nothing systematic on the subject, he did preach on it, and when he died he left substantial manuscripts on it;[1] and his private notebooks reveal a continuing interest in the subject. He was not afraid to address himself to it and repudiated as unwarranted timidity the view of those who "cry of late against saying one word, particularly about the Trinity, but what the Scripture has said, judging it impossible but that, if we did, we should err in a question so much above us" [Misc. 94]. Though he felt that "the joining of reason and Scripture" need not lead to a departure from Scripture and made bold to cope with the subject of the Trinity out of a conviction that "the Almighty's knowledge is not so different from ours, but that ours is the image of [it]" [Misc. 94], he certainly did not suppose that his speculations had cracked wide open the eternal mysteries: "I would not be understood to pretend to give a full explication of the Trinity; for I think," he said, in concluding another of his many explications of the Trinity, "it still remains an incomprehensible mystery, the greatest and most glorious of all mysteries" [Misc. 308].

One of his earlier "Miscellanies" on the Trinity shows in a preliminary but unmistakable way how his concept of spiritual beauty provides the platform upon which he erects his doctrine of the Trinity.

---

1. Some of these manuscripts appear to have been ready, or nearly ready, for the printer. When, over a century after his death, considerable portions of the manuscripts were published, their appearance (and earlier rumors about their contents) stirred up a small storm of controversy among the quarrelsome company of New England divines who still felt that something was at stake in either attacking or defending the orthodoxy of Edwards' theology. The purpose of the present essay would not be materially advanced by entering into that controversy. See *An Unpublished Essay of Edwards on the Trinity,* ed. G. P. Fisher (New York, 1903).

Love is certainly the perfection as well as the happiness of a spirit. God doubtless, as He is infinitely perfect and happy, has infinite love. I cannot doubt but that God loves infinitely . . . Then, there must have been an object from all eternity which God infinitely loves. But we have showed that all love arises from the perception, either of consent to being in general or a consent to that being that perceives. [He is probably referring especially to No. 45 of his "Notes on the Mind."] Infinite loveliness to God, therefore, must consist either in infinite consent to entity in general or infinite consent to God. But we have shown that consent to entity and consent to God are the same, because God is the general and proper entity of all things. So that 'tis necessary that that object which God infinitely loves must be infinitely and perfectly consenting and agreeable to Him. But that which infinitely and perfectly agrees is the very same essence; for if it be different, it don't infinitely consent.

Again, we have shown that one alone cannot be excellent, inasmuch as, in such case, there can be no consent. Therefore, if God is excellent, there must be a plurality in God; otherwise there can be no consent in Him. [Misc. 117]

That "object from all eternity which God infinitely loves" for the beauty of its "infinite consent to entity in general or infinite consent to God" is, of course, the Second Person of the Trinity. And that infinite and perfect mutual consenting action between the Father and the Son is itself the Third Person of the Trinity. "The Holy Spirit is the act of God between the Father and the Son, infinitely loving and delighting in each other" [Misc. 94], an action that "is properly a substance" since "the perfect act of God must be a substantial act" [Misc. 94]. Edwards has an interesting way of putting this, by analogy with delight among men.

I believe it will be plain to anyone that thinks intensely, that the perfect act of God must be a substantial act. We say that the perfect delights of reasonable creatures are substantial delights: but the delight of God is [much more] properly a substance, yea, an infinitely perfect substance, even the essence. [Misc. 94]

God's being the Triune God of Christian faith, then, depends upon the substantial and not merely ideal reality of this infinite consent or primary spiritual beauty.

Edwards' most common summary formulation of the composition of the Trinity is "that there are no more than these three really distinct in God— God, and His idea, and His love and delight. We can't conceive of any further real distinctions" [Misc. 259]. The Son, as the object of the love that is both the perfection and the happiness of God, is "the express and perfect image of God" or "His idea of Himself"; they come to the same thing, image, or idea because for Edwards "ideas are images of things, and there are no other images of things in the most proper sense but ideas" [Misc. 259]. The Holy Spirit is Himself God's love of and delight in His Son. There are, then, these three: God the Father; His idea, the Son; and His love and delight, the Holy Spirit.

This summary formulation of the Trinity is related to the three summary perfections of God[2]—knowledge, holiness, and joy—into which, Edwards argues, all other attributes and supposed distinctions in God can be resolved. Of the three summary perfections, the first (His knowledge or understanding) is identified with the Second Person of the Trinity, while the second (His love, holiness, or virtue) and the third (His joy, delight, or happiness) are the "love and delight" here identified as the Third Person of the Trinity.

The relation between the three summary perfections of God and the second two persons of the Trinity is established for Edwards by his model of intelligent perceiving being or of the structure of the self. That structure is one of a willing and understanding person whose relation to things in knowledge is designated as his reason or understanding—not a faculty but a mode of relation to reality for the whole self—and whose relation to things by way of love and delight is designated as his will—again, not a faculty, properly speaking, but a manner of speaking about this aspect of the relation of the whole aesthetic-affectional self to reality.

Edwards' speculations about the internal structure and life of God are, in fact, generally tied to his efforts to understand the meaning and structure of moral selfhood, to understand the character and quality of particular goods communicated by God to his creatures, and to understand the ends God must have in view in that communication and in that manner of constituting moral beings. This practical motive must account at least in part for his conceiving of the essay on *The End For Which God Created the World,* in which his speculations about the self-communication of God *ad intra* and *ad extra* appear, as a companion piece to his essay on *The Nature of True Virtue.*

---

2. For a discussion of these see Ch. 6, pp. 140–45.

The relation of Edwards' conception of the structure of selfhood and his conception of the nature of the fullness of good communicated by God to the creature to his conception of the Trinity is exhibited most economically in one of his "Miscellanies" on "the end of God's creating the world." Commenting on God's "communication of Himself *ad extra,* which is what is called His glory," Edwards writes:

> This communication is of two sorts: the communication that consists in understanding an idea, which is summed up in the knowledge of God; and the other is in the will consisting in love and joy, which may be summed up in the love and enjoyment of God. Thus, that which proceeds from God *ad extra* is agreeable to the twofold subsistences which proceed from Him *ad intra,* which is the Son and the Holy Spirit—the Son being the idea of God, or the knowledge of God, and the Holy Ghost which is the love of God and joy in God. [Misc. 1218]

I will return to a consideration of that communication *ad extra* in the next chapter. Here I am concerned with the communication *ad intra* of which the other is an extension, for in this we have to do with the three persons of the Trinity.

The structure of selfhood Edwards finds in the person of God is developed by analogy from the structure of selfhood he finds in intelligent perceiving creatures, though the meaning of this analogy is expressed the other way around when he concludes that "there is, in resemblance to this threefold distinction in God, a threefold distinction in created spirit—namely, a spirit itself, and its understanding, and its will or inclination or love. And this indeed is all the real distinction there is in created spirits" [Misc. 259]. Since primary beauty involves not simply proportion or harmony but also cordial consent, the real beauty of both created spirits and of God is located especially in the will or the self as willing being; it consists in the love and delight that, whether in God or communicated to the creature, is the Holy Spirit.

The divine beauty, together with its corresponding sensibility, is therefore identified with and located by Edwards in the Holy Spirit. But the divine beauty, which *is* the Holy Spirit, also *appears* as the Son. Accordingly, it may be said that the divine beauty is given as man's inherent good in the indwelling of the Holy Spirit, which is the substantial beauty of God, and is offered as man's apparent good in the beauty of Jesus Christ. The one communication of beauty is a manifestation of the creative power of God's goodness, and the other is a manifestation of the attractive power of God's goodness. The unity of the one Triune God, the fountain of all being and beauty, in whom it has been shown that Edwards found beauty to be preeminent among the divine perfections, is his guarantee that this inherent and apparent good is also man's objective good.

BEAUTY AND SENSIBILITY IN THE HOLY SPIRIT

In a "Miscellany" on "Spirit creation" Edwards expresses most succinctly his radical identification of the divine beauty with the Holy Spirit.

> It was made especially the Holy Spirit's work to bring the world to its beauty and perfection out of the chaos; for the beauty of the world is a communication of God's beauty. *The Holy Spirit is the harmony and excellency and beauty of the deity.* Therefore, 'twas His work to communicate beauty and harmony to the world, and so we read that it was He that moved upon the face of the waters. [Misc. 293, italics added]

God's "infinite beauty," Edwards had written earlier in the important "Note" 45, "is his infinite mutual love of Himself." This mutual love is God's holiness, which is the substantial beauty of God. That is, God's holiness is not simply an idea or a quality of God but is something of the substantial reality of God's very being.

> 'Tis peculiar to God that He has beauty within Himself (consisting in being's consenting with His own being, or the love of Himself in His own Holy Spirit), whereas the excellence of others is in loving others, in loving God, and in the communications of His Spirit. [Mind 45, Part 12]

"The excellence of spirits," he says in the same "Note," "consists in their disposition and action." But God

> exerts Himself towards Himself no other way than in infinitely loving and delighting in Himself, in the mutual love of the Father and the Son. This makes the third—the personal Holy Spirit, or the holiness of God—which is His infinite beauty. And this is God's infinite consent to being in general. [Mind 45, Part 9]

As he says elsewhere, the "honor of the Father and the Son is that they are Infinitely Excellent, or that from them Infinite Excellency Proceeds; but the honour of the Holy Ghost is equal for he *is* that divine excellency and beauty itself" [Trinity, 118f, italics added].

Edwards' identification of the corresponding spiritual sensibility in God with the Holy Spirit is no less radical. In "Miscellany" 133, in which he meditates upon how the Holy Spirit, as the "personal energy, the divine love and delight, eternally and continually proceeds from both" the Father and the Son, Edwards tells himself:

> Remember to look, the next time I have the opportunity, to see, if spirit in Scripture phrase is not commonly put for affections, and never for understanding; and to show, that there is no affection in God, but love to himself. [Misc. 133]

In "Miscellany" 136 he fulfills that design and concludes:

> The word "spirit," most commonly in Scripture, is put for affections of the mind; but there is no other affection in God essentially, properly, and primarily, but love and delight—and that, in himself; for into this, is his love and delight in his creatures resolvable.
>
> I don't remember, that any other attributes are said to *be* God, and God to *be* them, but Logos and Agape, or reason and love.

In "Miscellany" 157 he adds that "the spirit of God is the same with the breath of God . . . Now what are so properly said to be the breathings of the soul as its affections[?]." His examination of "all the metaphorical representations of the Holy Ghost in the Scripture, such as water, fire, breath, wind, oil, wine, a spring, a river of living water" confirms him in his view that the Holy Spirit is "the perfectly active, flowing affection, holy love, and pleasure of God" [Misc. 336].

Because of the intimate internal relation and correspondence of beauty and sensibility in moral beings, when Edwards identifies the Holy Spirit as the substantial beauty, excellence, and perfection of God, that identification necessarily carries with it a corresponding identification of the Holy Spirit with the joy, delight, happiness, affection, and inclination of God.

As was shown in the last chapter, of the three summary perfections of God —His knowledge, holiness, and joy—Edwards regards the first as a natural perfection and the second and third as together summing up God's moral perfections. The latter two perfections are together identified with the Holy Spirit—not only the beauty of holiness, love, virtue, or moral excellence and goodness but also the sensibility of joy, delight, and happiness.[3] The formula

---

3. The relation between holiness and joy here is the same as that between benevolence and complacence discussed above, Ch. 6, pp. 144f.

or choice of terms varies—holiness and happiness, excellency and happiness, beauty and happiness, love and delight—but the meaning is the same.

The interdependence or correspondence of love and delight is so reliable for Edwards that he sometimes speaks of the Holy Spirit as simply "the delight in God" without explicit reference to the beauty, excellence, holiness, or love that constitutes the more objective aspect of the Holy Spirit. For example, in a "Miscellany" already frequently quoted above, he concludes a long discussion of the "substantial" reality of this "delight" in the Godhead:

> The Holy Ghost is Himself the delight and joyfulness of the Father
> in that idea [of Himself which He has in His Son], and of the idea
> in the Father . . . So that, if we turn in all the ways in the world, we
> shall never be able to make more than these three, God, the idea of
> God, and delight in God. [Misc. 94]

After showing how other possible attributes and distinctions in God, such as His power, wisdom, and goodness, may all be resolved into these three, he concludes: "And as to holiness, 'tis delight in excellency, 'tis God's sweet consent to Himself or, in other words, His perfect delight in Himself, which we have shown to be the Holy Spirit" [Misc. 94].

But isn't this resolving of holiness into delight an overstatement and even a reversal of priorities between what Edwards usually regards as primary and secondary whenever pressed to resolve one of them into the other? His normative position is to resolve the more subjective (e.g. delight or complacence) into the more objective (e.g. holiness or benevolence). This instance of apparent overstatement or reversal of priority may reflect one of those moments in the continuing debate he carries on with himself over the priority (if such there must be) between benevolence and complacence when he is prepared to grant priority to complacence—a position from which he ultimately retreats.

More likely, however, this instance reflects a radical "is as" correspondence between love and delight so intimate that either term may at times stand for the other (or for both) in Edwards' mind.[4] After all, he often uses the terms

---

4. What is here referred to as "love and delight" in God is elsewhere referred to as the "holiness and happiness" of God; and in *Freedom of the Will,* for example, it is only with the greatest reluctance that Edwards grants that there may be conceived to be in God a priority of holiness over happiness.

> Though we are obliged to conceive of some things in God as consequent and de-
> pendent on others, and of some things pertaining to the divine nature and will as

love and delight synonymously, as in his definition of the will as a man's love or as his "enjoying faculty" [Misc. 332], in his distinction between the love of benevolence as consent to being and the love of complacence as delight in beauty, and in another summary formulation of the Trinity in which he says that "there are no more than these really distinct in God, God and His Idea, and his Love or Delight" [Misc. 259]. He also lets enjoyment or delight stand for both love and delight, as in a "Miscellany" of somewhat later date than the one under discussion, which begins:

> God is glorified within Himself these two ways: 1. By appearing or being manifest to Himself in His own perfect idea, or in His Son who is the brightness of His glory. 2. By enjoying and delighting in Himself, by flowing forth in infinite love and delight towards Himself, or in his Holy Spirit. [Misc. 448]

To love God is to participate in this "excellency, beauty, and essential glory" [Misc. 448] of God communicated *ad extra.* To delight in Him is to participate in the fulfillment of the very end for which He created the world, which, Edwards notes, can be formulated as either that glory or as His own enjoyment—"all things" having been "created for God's pleasure" [Misc. 448]. To glorify God and enjoy Him forever is, therefore, an end for man that has its foundation laid in the very nature of God—in His primary beauty, His spiritual sensibility, and His perfect vision—and in the structure of selfhood in which the beauty and sensibility of the Holy Spirit may, by the grace of God, become articulated principles of being in a person.

---

the foundation of others, and so before others in the order of nature: as, [for example] we must conceive of the knowledge and holiness of God as prior in the order of nature to his happiness . . . Yet when we speak of cause and effect, antecedent and consequent, fundamental and dependent, determining and determined, in the first Being, who is self-existent, independent, of perfect and absolute simplicity and immutability, and the first cause of all things; doubtless there must be less propriety in such presentations, than when we speak of derived dependent beings, who are compounded, and liable to perpetual mutation and succession. [FW 376–77]

The obligation by which Edwards feels constrained is that of grounding the subjective order of pleasure in the objective order of excellence, the inherent good in the objective good, complacence in benevolence, happiness in holiness, sensibility in beauty, and the subjective definition of beauty in the objective, structural, and relational definition of beauty. But he also wants to insist upon the correspondence as well as the priorities to which these various sets of terms refer, as I tried to show above (pp. 83f.) in my discussion of the relation between benevolence and complacence in the light of his "is as" formula for the determination of the will.

Both love and delight, both holiness and joy, both perfection and happiness, that is, both beauty and sensibility, are together identified by Edwards with the Holy Spirit. What is essential about the Holy Spirit, religiously, is that it is at once an objective reality and an indwelling principle of life in the subject.

Primary beauty and spiritual sensibility, therefore, provide Edwards with a peculiarly appropriate model for the representation of the nature of the Holy Spirit. Although the primary definition of beauty is objective in terms of structural relations of consent among beings, it is also essential to the being or reality of beauty that it appear and be enjoyed, that is, that the objective principle of beauty also be a subjective principle engaging the delight of perceiving being. It is the communication of this beauty and sensibility to the creature that constitutes the spiritual image of God in man. What is important to note here is that in his doctrine of the Trinity and of the nature of the Holy Spirit and its place in the Godhead, Edwards carries the intimate correlation of beauty and sensibility in moral beings right to the center of the divine life itself, from which it derives its validity in the creature. He shows in this way that the place of beauty and sensibility in the moral life of creatures has an ontological basis in the very nature of things and especially in the nature of Him from Whom and in Whom and to Whom all things are. For Edwards ethics is grounded in an ontology and a theology informed at their center by the coordinate aesthetic concepts of beauty and sensibility. And it is especially in the reality of the Holy Spirit that primary beauty and spiritual sensibility have their substantial or substantive and ontological foundation.

BEAUTY IN JESUS CHRIST

The divine beauty that *is* the Holy Spirit *appears* especially in the Son. "Holiness is in a peculiar manner the beauty of the divine nature" [RA 257]. God is distinguished from other beings in that He has this beauty in Himself as His own Holy Spirit, which "is not only holy as the Father and Son are" but "*is* the holiness of God itself in the abstract" [Grace 48, italics added]; the "bond of perfectness" between Father and Son, the love, holiness and happiness of the Godhead stand forth as "a distinct personal subsistence" [Grace 47]. Communicated to and dwelling in the creature, this "Spirit of God" makes the soul "a partaker of God's beauty and Christ's joy, so that the saint has truly fellowship with the Father and with his Son Jesus Christ, in thus having the communion or participation of the Holy Ghost" [RA 201].

The saints are therein "made partakers of God's fullness, that is, of God's spiritual beauty and happiness, according to the measure and capacity of the creature" [RA 203]. But this divine beauty, as man's real objective and inherent good, is not given arbitrarily; it is offered as the apparent good in the beauty of all divine things and especially in the beauty and excellency of Jesus Christ.

> As the beauty of the divine nature does primarily consist in God's holiness, so does the beauty of all divine things . . . Herein does primarily consist the amiableness and beauty of the Lord Jesus, whereby he is . . . altogether lovely . . . All the spiritual beauty of his human nature, consisting in his meekness, lowliness, patience, heavenliness, love to God, love to men, condescension to the mean and vile, and compassion to the miserable, etc. all is summed up in his holiness. And the beauty of his divine nature, of which the beauty of his human nature is the image and reflection, does also primarily consist in his holiness. [RA 258–259]

The beauty and excellency of Christ consists in His being filled with the Spirit of this holiness, the Spirit that is this holiness. For

> the Holy Spirit is the *summum* of all good. 'Tis the fulness of God. The holiness and happiness of the Godhead consists in it; and in the communion or partaking of it consists all the true loveliness and happiness of the creature. [Grace 49]

The Holy Spirit is "the sum of the blessings Christ sought by what he did and suffered in the work of redemption" [HA 447].

The priority of emphasis given by Edwards to the Holy Spirit in the Godhead conforms well with the argument of this essay regarding the priority of beauty in his conception of God, for it is in the Holy Spirit Himself that he finds the substantial beauty of God, and the beauty of Christ consists in His being filled with that Spirit.

But the beauty of Christ is given another formulation by Edwards, not indirectly in terms of His being possessed and filled with the Holy Spirit but directly in terms of the beauty and excellency of His own person. A perception of the beauty of Christ is essential to a knowledge of his excellency, in part because beauty is the foundation and content of real excellency but also because here as elsewhere "he that sees not the beauty of holiness . . . in effect is ignorant of the whole spiritual world" [RA 275].

> By this sense of the moral beauty of divine things, is understood
> the sufficiency of Christ as a mediator: for 'tis only by the discov-
> ery of the beauty of the moral perfection of Christ, that the believer
> is let into the knowledge of the excellency of his person, so as to
> know anything more of it than the devils do: and 'tis only by the
> knowledge of the excellency of Christ's person, that any know his
> sufficiency as a mediator. [RA 273]

Edwards' most systematic analysis of "The Excellency of Christ" is contained in a 1734 sermon bearing that title. He begins with a review of the
"admirable conjunction of diverse excellencies" in Christ, emphasizing the
contrasts among the excellencies mentioned, both divine and human, that
meet and consent to each other in Him and, by their very diversity, enhance
His beauty and excellence. In Him meet the diverse excellencies of the Lion
and the Lamb, of strength and majesty, of meekness and patience, infinite
highness and infinite condescension, and so on, through a long catalogue of
further contrasting pairs of excellencies, culminating in the conjoining in
Christ of infinite greatness and infinite goodness, in which conjunction is
summarily expressed for Edwards the infinite beauty of Christ.

> His greatness is rendered lovely by his goodness. The greater any
> one is without goodness, so much the greater evil; but when infinite
> goodness is joined with greatness, it renders it a glorious and ador-
> able greatness. So, on the other hand, his infinite goodness receives
> lustre from his greatness. He that is of great understanding and
> ability, and is withal of a good and excellent disposition, is deserv-
> edly more esteemed than a lower and lesser being, with the same
> kind inclination and good will. Indeed, goodness is excellent in
> whatever subject it be found; it is beauty and excellency itself, and
> renders all excellent that are possessed of it; and yet more excel-
> lent when joined with greatness.[5]

Another aspect of the beauty of Christ that Edwards dwells upon in this
sermon is His presentation by God as the apparent good to the widest possible range of sensibility and perception, since, with such a diversity of human
and divine excellencies meeting in Him, "there is everything in him to render
him worthy of your love and choice, and to win and engage it." "One design
of God in the gospel," Edwards argues, "is to bring us to make God the object

5. "The Excellency of Christ," *Works, 4*, 180, 197.

of our undivided respect," so that he may be the center not only of our spiritual inclination but also of "whatever natural inclination there is in souls . . . to complacence in some one as a friend" in whom "to love and delight" as brother and companion. In his human excellencies Christ is presented as such an apparent good to natural as well as spiritual inclination. Though these "human excellencies . . . are no proper addition to his divine excellencies," yet they are

> additional manifestations of his glory and excellency to us, and are additional recommendations of him to our esteem and love, who are of finite comprehension. Though his human excellencies are but communications and reflections of his divine; and though this light, as reflected, falls infinitely short of the divine fountain of light in its immediate glory; yet the reflection shines not without its proper advantages, as presented to our view and affection. As the glory of Christ appears in the qualifications of his human nature, it appears to us in excellencies that are of our own kind, that are exercised in our own way and manner, and so, in some respects, are peculiarly fitted to invite our acquaintance and draw our affection.

The beauty or glory of Christ as it appears in His divine excellencies,

> though it be far brighter, yet doth it also more dazzle our eyes, and exceeds the strength or comprehension of our sight: but as it shines in the human excellencies of Christ, it is brought more to a level with our conceptions, and suitableness to our nature and manner, yet retaining a semblance of the same divine beauty, and a savor of the same divine sweetness. But as both divine and human excellencies meet together in Christ, they set off and recommend each other to us . . . [and] encourages us to look upon these divine perfections, however high and great, yet as what we have some near concern in, and more of a right to, and liberty freely to enjoy.[6]

Just as in his understanding of the operation of grace through the indwelling of the Holy Spirit it is a "sense of divine beauty" that "is the first thing in the actual change made in the soul in true conversion, and is the foundation of everything else,"[7] so also is it the beauty of Christ that is His attractive

6. Ibid., pp. 197, 198.
7. "True Grace," *Works, 4,* 468.

power. "It is this sight of the divine beauty of Christ that bows the wills and draws the hearts of men."[8] This primary beauty of Christ is also reflected in a secondary beauty of harmony and proportion, for, as Edwards observes in his *Thoughts on the Revival of Religion in New England,* "God, in the revelation that he has made of himself to the world by Jesus Christ, has taken care to give a proportionable manifestation of two kinds of excellencies or perfections of his nature"[9]—to which the appropriate response involves being "proportioned Christians" [CF 409]. It is in his beauty that the real, objective good in Jesus Christ is presented to men as their apparent good, engaging an "is as" consent and conformity of their will, inclination, or affection.

Once again we find here the correspondence in Edwards' thought between beauty and sensibility as the objective and subjective determinants of the moral and spiritual life. If what is presented as the beauty of the apparent good in Christ is to be viewed as such, there must be in the perceiving subject the corresponding inherent good of primary beauty and spiritual sensibility, which consists in the indwelling of the Holy Spirit. For although as pastor Edwards insists that "the excellency of Christ is an object adequate to the natural cravings of the soul,"[10] he is no less certain—and preaches accordingly—that only "he that has his eyes open" by the gift of "a new spiritual sense" will "behold the divine superlative beauty and loveliness of Jesus Christ."[11] It is in "a sight or sense of this that . . . does fundamentally consist . . . the saving grace of God's Spirit." Without this sense of beauty and disposition to consent to being-in-general "that wherein the beauty of the divine nature does most essentially consist, viz., his holiness or moral excellency" will appear as "furthest from beauty"; the "holy and infinite beauty and amiableness" of Christ, "which is all in all, and without which every other quality and property [of His] is nothing, and worse than nothing, they will see nothing of."[12] The communication of the divine beauty in Christ and of the divine beauty and sensibility in the Holy Spirit correspond to each other, for in each the beauty is the same—being's cordial consent to being-in-general.

God is for Edwards a "communicating being" [Misc. 332], giving out of His own fullness an infinite good to the creature, which is in sum Himself.

8. Ibid., pp. 469–70.

9. *Works, 3,* 384–85.

10. "Safety, Fullness, and Sweet Refreshment to be Found in Christ," *Works,* ed. S. E. Dwight, *8,* 367.

11. "True Grace," *Works, 4,* 469.

12. Ibid., pp. 469, 468f.

This self-communication of the creature's objective good may be interpreted in terms of the inherent good consisting in the indwelling of the Holy Spirit or in terms of the apparent good manifested in Christ. One might even attempt to penetrate behind this manifestation and communication of God *ad extra* to the internal life and structure of the Godhead *ad intra.* In any event, whichever of these alternatives is followed, it is always his concept of beauty that provides Edwards with the central clue to the Divine Being as it is in itself and as it is manifest and communicated to intelligent perceiving being. This brings me to a more explicit consideration of the place of his concept of beauty in his understanding of God's relation to the world as Creator, Governor, and Redeemer.

8

BEAUTY AND THE DIVINE

Because of the central and formative role of the concept of beauty in the thought of Jonathan Edwards, his interpretation of God's relation to the world can best be understood in terms of the model provided by his concept of beauty. It is out of God's own beauty that creation proceeds; it is by His beauty that the creation is ordered; it is according to His beauty that God governs the world, both natural and moral; it is by His beauty that God redeems. Beauty provides the model for Edwards' understanding of the structure and dynamics of the restored and redeemed life of God's people as a community of love and justice among free and responsible selves, a people in community with Himself and with the grand universal system of being-in-general, a cordially consenting community manifest in His Kingdom among men on earth and in the promised Kingdom in which the beauty and joy of all beings is to be fulfilled to the glory of God. Finally, in all this, it is the divine beauty that constitutes the model for Edwards' interpretation of the manner of God's transcendence and immanence with respect to the world.

To take the last of these points first, God is represented by Edwards as transcendent with respect to the world by virtue of His infinite and preeminent beauty, and He is represented as immanent with respect to His creation in the manner in which beauty is present. The beauty of God is the principal mark of both His transcendence and His immanence.

> God is God, and distinguished from all other beings, and exalted above 'em, chiefly by his divine beauty, which is infinitely diverse from all other beauty. They therefore that see the stamp of this glory in divine things, they see divinity in them, they see God in them, and so see 'em to be divine; because they see that in them wherein the truest idea of divinity does consist. [RA 298]

God is exalted above all other beings, that is, He is transcendent, chiefly by His beauty; and His immanence or presence in the world is chiefly to be discerned by seeing in it this same divine beauty.

Consider beauty first as the mark and measure of God's transcendence. In an early "Miscellany" Edwards expresses, in a manner that can most fairly be understood if quoted in full, his concern for an adequate model of divine transcendence—a model adequate also to the representation of what he wants to affirm about the divine immanence.

> That is a gross and unprofitable idea we have of God, as being something large and great as bodies are and infinitely extended throughout the immense space. For God is neither little nor great with that sort of greatness, even as the soul of man. It is not at all extended, no more than an idea, and is not present any where as bodies are present, as we have shewn else where. So 'tis with respect to the uncreated Spirit. The greatness of a soul consists not in any extension but its comprehensiveness of idea and extendedness of operation. So the infiniteness of God consists in his perfect comprehension of all things and the extendedness of his operation equally to all places. God is present no where any otherwise than the soul is in the body or brain, and he is present every where as the soul is in the body. We ought to conceive of God as being omnipotence, perfect knowledge, and perfect love, and not extended any otherwise than as power, knowledge, and love are extended, and not as if it was a sort of unknown thing that we call substance that is extended. [Misc. 194]

Citing Augustine's formulation of the view that God is "above us, not in place, but by His own awful and wonderful excellence,"[1] Douglas Elwood has rightly pointed out that Edwards rejects "the idea of interpreting the otherness of God as otherwordliness."[2] No spacial metaphor is adequate to express the transcendence of God—or His immanence. Edwards copies into his private notebooks, with apparent approval, the view that "We justly admire that Saying of the Philosopher, That God is a Being whose Center is every where and Circumference is no where, as one of the noblest and most exalted Flights of human Understanding," despite its absurdity and internal contradiction [Misc. 1234].[3] "The difference between the nature of the deity

1. St. Augustine, *An Augustine Synthesis,* ed. Erich Przywara, S.J. (New York, Harper and Brothers, Torchbook, 1958), p. 139.

2. Elwood, *Philosophical Theology,* p. 60.

3. The passage is copied from Philip Skelton's *Ophiomaches: or Deism Revealed* (2 vols. London, 1749), 2, 110–11. The "Philosopher" quoted is apparently Nicholas Cusanus. See Elwood, *Philosophical Theology,* p. 167, n. 46.

and created spirits," Edwards writes, "naturally results from His greatness
and nothing else . . . So that, if we should suppose the faculties of a created
spirit to be enlarged infinitely, there would be the deity to all intents and
purposes" [Misc. 150]. God is distinguished by His greatness, but His greatness is to be conceived in terms of His excellence; it "consists in his perfect
comprehension of all things and the extendedness of his operation equally to
all places"; and that extendedness "is not extended any otherwise than as
power, knowledge, and love are extended" [Misc. 194]. As we have seen,
the nature of beauty and the manner in which it is articulated is basic to Edwards' understanding of God's power, knowledge, and love. Beauty is the
model for his conception of the power of being or the power of God and (as
we shall now see) for the exercise of that power in Creation, Governance,
and Redemption of the world; it is the peculiar object of God's spiritual
knowledge or "sensible understanding"; and love is itself a form of beauty,
so the divine love is itself the substantial beauty of God bodied forth as the
Holy Spirit. Beauty is the essential mode of the divine transcendence. God is
distinguished from all other beings and transcendent with respect to them
"chiefly by his divine beauty, which is infinitely diverse from all other
beauty" [RA 298].

The divine transcendence may also be formulated in terms of God's beauty
by recalling that " 'tis peculiar to God that He has beauty within Himself" [Mind 45], consisting in His own Holy Spirit, which "is God's infinite
consent to being in general" [RA 298]. Only in God does love of being coincide necessarily with self-love. Only God is both infinitely consenting being
—He is "infinitely the most beautiful and excellent" [TV 14] being—and
the proper object of such infinite consent. He is "the Being of Beings," and
"has infinitely the greatest share of existence" such that "all other being, even
the whole universe, is as nothing in comparison of the divine Being" [TV
14]. "God himself is in effect being in general" [TV 100]. Only in God
do the coordinate orders of existence and excellence, of greatness and goodness, of secondary and primary beauty, of being and beauty, necessarily and
absolutely coincide. For God's being and beauty is, as it were, "the sum
and comprehension of all existence and excellence" [TV 15].

Consider beauty next as the mark of God's immanence, which involves at
least two dimensions. The divine beauty is present as the first principle and
structure and power of being by virtue of which all things are brought into
being, sustained in being, and ordered toward their natural and moral perfec-

tion of being. It is also present as the immediate encountered reality that is the first objective foundation of the creature's proper spiritual joy and delight. To know and delight in the divine beauty is to stand most assuredly in the presence of God.

The key to the knowledge of God's reality and presence is the perception of His beauty. It is chiefly the beauty of things that sets them apart as divine; with respect to the divinity of things "the argument is but one, and the evidence direct" [RA 298f].

> He that truly sees the divine, transcendent, supreme glory . . . and unparalleled beauty . . . of those things that are divine, does as it were know their divinity intuitively; he not only argues that they are divine, but he sees that they are divine; he sees that in them wherein divinity chiefly consists. [RA 298]

What he sees is the divine beauty, glory, or excellency, and it is in this that God chiefly manifests His reality and presence.

> Doubtless there is that glory and excellency in the divine being, by which he is so infinitely distinguished from all other beings, that if it were seen, he might be known by it. It would therefore be very unreasonable to deny that it is possible for God, to give manifestations of this distinguishing excellency, in things by which he is pleased to make himself known; and that this distinguishing excellency may be clearly seen in them. [RA 299]

God is present in the manner in which beauty is present. He is manifest and discloses His presence in the manner in which beauty is disclosed, that is, as the immediate or direct object of the sense, taste, or relish for primary beauty. The knowledge and enjoyment of God's beauty is the seal of validity and authenticity upon that knowledge of God in which He is acknowledged as God. For to find in God one's highest beauty, which is His anyway and which distinguishes him as God, is for Edwards precisely what it means to recognize God for Who He Is and to respond accordingly. Everything else about God may be known while the heart or will or self remains unreconciled, finding elsewhere its apparent good. But if God's beauty is known, it means that He has become one's apparent good and the object of greatest delight, since beauty can be seen only insofar as it is enjoyed. In this experience of the divine beauty the immanence and presence of God is manifest.

Beauty as the primary clue to the nature of the Divine Being is peculiarly consonant with the Biblical view of the nature of revelation not so much as a disclosure of something about God as the self-disclosure and self-communication of God; the divine presence is a living reality that lays its claim upon the cordial consent of the one to whom the event of divine self-disclosure comes as revelatory. There is in this view of revelation an essential intimacy and even identity between the event of revelation and its content, so that to apprehend the essential nature of God is precisely and therein to stand in His presence. Beauty is a peculiarly appropriate model for construing the nature of a Divine Being so conceived, for to apprehend beauty is to stand in its presence, to enjoy and respond to its claims, to be grasped by its power—or else it has simply not been apprehended as beauty.

Conversely, insensibility or blindness to the divine beauty is one way of defining Edwards' understanding of sin and alienation from God. Just as beauty is the measure of the presence of God—and of grace, holiness, and virtue— so deformity and dissent from being, together with a corresponding insensibility to true beauty, are the measure of sin and alienation from God. It is in fact only when measured against the beauty of God that the dimensions of human sin are fully disclosed: "The light of God's beauty, and that alone, truly shows the soul its own deformity, and effectually inclines it to exalt God and abase itself."[4] In a sermon on "The True Christian's Life" Edwards urges that "we should labor to be growing continually in the knowledge of God and Christ, and clear views of the glory of God, the beauty of Christ, and the excellency of divine things."[5] In view of the relations we have found among the divine glory, beauty, and excellency, it is fair to take beauty as standing for all three, as the measure of the spiritual distance (or the proximity and communion) between the Creator and His creatures. The location of created things in relation to God—and of God in relation to created beings —in terms of beauty is crucial to Edwards' conception of divine immanence.

As the first principle of being beauty is the basic principle in terms of which to locate particular beings in relation to other beings or to systems of being, whether to some limited and confined system or to the universal system of which God is the head and fountain, and whether the relations are natural or moral and spiritual. Edwards measures distance and location and ontological weight in the universal system of being in terms of relations of consent and dissent, of proportion and harmony, or of deformity and "contrarieties and jars in being" [Mind 45]. In a system of being conceived according to the

4. "True Grace," Works, 4, 471.
5. "The True Christian's Life," Works, 4, 576.

model of beauty, anything has a place only by virtue of the relations of consent and dissent in which it stands to other beings. Anything, that is, except God, for His "being and beauty is . . . the sum and comprehension of all existence and excellence" [TV 15]. God, whose transcendence consists chiefly in His having His beauty within Himself, is therefore also, by virtue of that beauty, immanent with respect to the whole system of being. He is immediately (rather than mediately, through a chain of being) related to everything that has being because finite beings have being only insofar as they are related to the being and beauty of God. To be totally unrelated to God, to be in a state of complete dissent from being, is for Edwards, to have passed beyond mere deformity into complete contradiction and contrariety of being and therefore to be in no state at all—to be, in sum, nothing. To be anything at all is to be related somehow to God, for to be is to consent to being and therefore involves some measure of participation in the Divine Being and beauty.

These relations of divine transcendence and immanence according to the model of order Edwards finds in beauty can perhaps best be understood by proceeding now to an examination of the relation of God to the world as Creator, Governor, and Redeemer.

Creation, governance, and redemption are distinguishable, but they are not distinct, and they are certainly not simply successive ways in which God is related to the world. Redemption, of course, presupposes creation and a fall. But if creation is understood as involving a movement through time toward some end sought in creation, then redemption is in a sense present in the work of creation in that it is the form taken since the fall of the divine work of fulfilling that intention and end in creation. In bringing things into being God seeks their perfection of being. Creation is governed, for Edwards, by some end in which the work of creation will reach fulfillment. Since the fall that fulfillment involves a work of redemption. And creation is not simply before the work of redemption; Edwards understands creation as continuous. "It's most agreeable to the Scripture to suppose creation to be performed every moment. The Scripture speaks of it as a present, remaining, continual act" [Misc. 346]. God governs not by secondary causes but by His own immediate creative presence, and every moment is to be understood as created anew rather than following out of some independent necessity from a previous state of the world.

Perhaps it could be said of Edwards, as of Calvin, that the divine governance is the most widely applicable of these three relations of God to the world. But if that is true, it is because the world stands between the times, between creation and fulfillment or redemption. Though God is essentially gracious and is therefore most fully known as a redeemer, He is most widely known and discernible as governor. As Edwards tries to discern the pattern of God's redemptive work, he therefore looks primarily to the manner in which God the Redeemer discloses Himself in His actual governance of the world. Also, when he tries to understand God's work of creation, he finds the explanation contained in the end sought. But that end or vision of fulfillment is also to be discerned by attending primarily to the manner and pattern of the actual governance of the world by God. The work of creation is manifest for Edwards in the creative presence of God as actual governor. He sees the work of redemption as a greater one than that of creation; hence it is even more blasphemous and incredible to him that men should suppose they can redeem themselves than it would be for them to pretend to have created themselves in the first place [WR 419]. It is toward fulfillment or redemption—the perfection and beauty of being—of the creation that God's governance is exercised. But Edwards' actualism leads him to interpret both creation and redemption primarily in the light of what can be discerned about the manner of God's actual governance of the world as it exhibits itself to the experience and understanding of intelligent perceiving being. For it is by attending to the particularities of the articulated system of being that men may come to participate in or share a measure of the divine vision in which all things are ordered according to their beauty. To come to a knowledge of God is identical for Edwards with coming to see things as they are.

Distinctions, then, can and must be made between creation, governance, and redemption. But the distinctions are not neat, and one can easily get lost by insisting too much upon them or by seeking clear priorities among them, whether in logic, in time, or in importance. Each is understood by Edwards to be present in the others.

As a matter of convenience I shall first treat beauty in the creative being of God and then treat jointly the place of beauty in the divine governance and redemption.

BEAUTY AND THE CREATIVE BEING OF GOD

From what has already been shown it is only to be expected that the concept of beauty will be important to Edwards' understanding of the creative being of God. For his conception of beauty is such that it is more fully exemplified by the dynamic notion of the beautifying than by the more static notion of the beautified; it is more a formative principle of being than a principle of well-formed being; it is more fully exhibited in bestowing beauty than in receiving it; and it is more properly exhibited in creative spiritual relations of consent than in created material relations of proportion.

The relation of beauty to the creative being of God can be illuminated by attending to the relation between self-sufficiency and effulgence in the Divine Being. It is by virtue of God's beauty that effulgence has priority over self-sufficiency in Edwards' conception of God. God's beauty consists in the first instance, of course, not in His seeking, receiving, or loving beauty but in His exhibiting, communicating, and bestowing beauty by His love of being—His consent to being-in-general. For in addition to what has already been said about its being a creative principle of being, beauty is communicative in that it is not self-contained.

In the first place, beauty is not grounded in itself but in being and consists more properly or fundamentally in the love of being than in the love of beauty, even though, as we have seen, the love of being necessarily carries with it a love of consenting being because consenting being both agrees with the love of being and, by the beauty of its consent to being, enlarges its own being or increases its own ontological weight in a system of being of which beauty is the first principle. In the second place, beauty is not self-contained in that it does not terminate in itself. However objectively defined by relations of consent and proportion among beings, it is also essential to the very being of beauty that it appear, shine forth, manifest, and communicate itself to intelligent perceiving being. Beauty is neither grounded in itself nor does it terminate in itself, but it is grounded in being and terminates in communicating itself to being.

With beauty as his primary model of order in the Divine Being or as his central clue to the nature of God, Edwards sees that God's communicative being or effulgence has priority over His self-sufficiency. As Thomas Schafer has shown,[6] the love of complacence in God corresponds to His self-sufficiency, while His love of benevolence corresponds to His creative being—His communicative effulgence. Self-sufficiency in God, then, bears the same relation to effulgence as complacence does to benevolence. The relation is ordinarily conceived by Edwards as one of correspondence, but if pressed for priority of one over the other, the former is (in each case) resolved into the latter, since the objective foundation of complacence in (or enjoyment of) beauty is to be found in benevolence to being rather than the reverse. This

6. Thomas A. Schaefer, "The Concept of Being," esp. Ch. X.

leads to the position that because of His beauty God's identity as God is established not by reference to His independent self-sufficiency but rather by reference to the manner in which He is related to other beings and to being-in-general. Self-sufficiency is understood as sufficiency or self-determination rather than as independence.

Self-sufficiency in God is interpreted by Edwards in terms of His communicative and creative effulgence. His doctrine of the Trinity may be seen as an effort to do just this. "God is a communicating being" [Misc. 332], and even His self-sufficiency consists in His infinite delight in communicating rather than withholding Himself. "It is God's essence to incline to communicate Himself" [Misc. 107]. Hence God must be conceived as Triune, as having diversity within himself—God, His idea of Himself, and His love and delight in Himself—in order to be able adequately to represent God as communicative and creative even in His self-sufficiency, even in His internal life, and hence as not dependent upon anything outside Himself for His own being as (and Who) He is. The divine presence communicated *ad extra* is, through the doctrine of the Trinity, shown to be essentially what already has its transcendent being *ad intra*.

Interpreted in terms of God's effulgence, Edwards' understanding of God's self-sufficiency might be better represented by using the term sufficiency rather than self-sufficiency. That is, in fact, Edwards' own practice.

> There is such a thing in the divine nature as a tendency or propensity to communicate of Himself and of His own happiness not from any want or deficiency in God that he should stand in need of any other, but from his infinite fulness, and which doth as it were overflow to the creature. Goodness or an inclination to communicate happiness argues a *sufficiency* and not a *deficiency,* for a deficiency rather inclines to receive than communicate.[7]

As Elwood has shown in his discussion of "the Self-Giving Nature of God," for Edwards it is precisely out of His "infinite sufficiency"[8] that God creates. Sufficiency, then, may be added to fullness, effulgence, glory, goodness, and beauty as the principal terms of discourse into which Edwards' interpretation of God's creative being resolves itself.

We have seen that if beauty is taken seriously as the formative, structural, inner first principle of being-itself, then it is essentially the same thing to

---

7. Sermon on Luke 2:14, Yale University Manuscript Collection, quoted in Elwood, *Philosophical Theology,* p. 97.
8. Elwood, p. 97.

represent creation as either *ex nihilo* (out of nothing) or *ad extra* (out of the fullness of the Divine Being). In bestowing or communicating beauty God at once takes out of nothing and gives being. Edwards' preferred way of representing that out of which the world is brought by the divine act of creation is in terms of the formula *ad extra* rather than *ex nihilo*. (Perhaps this preference is in part because he would rather think about something than about nothing; to him absolute nothing is unthinkable anyway because not until we can "think of the same that the sleeping rocks dream of . . . shall we get a complete idea of nothing.")[9] Associated with this preference is a similar one for the image of the universal system of being as a graded system ranging from the fullness of being and beauty in God and descending asymptotically toward the boundary of nothing or else flowing back in remanation toward its source in the fullness of God.

Edwards' manner of representing the creative being of God in relation to the world, and especially to intelligent perceiving creatures, consists of innumerable variations upon the summary schematized in Diagram E.

DIAGRAM E

Just as (1) (a) in *Jesus Christ* God is *manifest* to the creature *as* his *apparent good*, and

(b) in the *Holy Spirit* God is *communicated* to the creature *as* his *inherent good;*

so also, (2) there is in the creation of the world, and in the relation of God's creative being to the world,

(a) a *manifestation* of His *glory*, *beauty*, and *excellency*, and

(b) a corresponding *communication* of His *happiness*, *joy* and *delight*,

consisting in (3) (a) God's *shining* forth as *light* to the *understanding*, and

(b) His *going* forth as *love* to the *heart* or *will*,

such that (4) (a) the *fullness* of God's glory is *seen*, and

(b) the *fullness* of the *creature's good* is *enjoyed*.

9. "Of Being," in H. G. Townsend, ed., *The Philosophy of Jonathan Edwards*, p. 9.

This summary formulation should be read first as a single sentence expressing four related points of two parts each, (a) and (b). The schematic arrangement of the sentence is designed to call attention to several systematic relationships in Edwards' thought. Most particularly, it is arranged to suggest how several aspects of his thought can be seen as systematically related to his concept of beauty and to his understanding of the relation between beauty and sensibility.

Some of these relations can be seen by noting the correspondence between each italicized term appearing in the (a) portion on the left and the coordinate italicized term appearing opposite it in the (b) portion. Others among these relations may be seen if this summary formulation is next read not as one continuous sentence, but as two parallel and coordinate formulations consisting of the four (a) portions taken together and of the four (b) portions taken together. The key coordinate terms in such a reading of this formulation are:

(a) Jesus Christ / apparent good / manifest   /
(b) Holy Spirit / inherent good / communicated /

(a) glory, beauty, excellency / shining forth / as light /
(b) happiness, joy, delight   / going forth   / as love /

(a) to the understanding / as God's glory   / seen.
(b) to the heart or will   / as the creature's good / enjoyed.

In all this can be seen how several important aspects of Edwards' thought are related systematically to his conception of the creation of the world as proceeding out of the being and beauty of God—as a manifestation and communication of that very "excellency, beauty, and essential glory, *ad extra*" [Misc. 448].

This formulation brings together, in relation to Edwards' conception of the creative self-manifestation and self-communication of God out of the overflowing sufficiency of His own being and beauty, Edwards' trinitarian model of the being of God in terms of the beauty in Jesus Christ and the beauty that is the Holy Spirit. It relates the creative being of God to Edwards' understanding of the apparent good, which is defined for him by the attractive beauty of the objective good, and of the inherent good, which is defined for him jointly by the beauty and sensibility of the subjective good, and relates both of them to the being of God, the *summum bonum,* the *bonum formosum* or beautiful good, which is itself (or Who is Himself) the good manifest and communicated in the creation of the world. It also relates Edwards' understanding of the creative being of God to his conception of beauty as the first principle of being, by virtue of which the communication of being is internally and essentially related to the appearance or manifestation of being to some intelligent perceiving being. The formulation relates the creative being of God, understood here in terms of His self-manifestation and self-communication, to the distinction drawn between being-in-general and "being as manifest and encountered". Thus it contributes to an adequate representation of transcendence and immanence in Edwards' understanding of God's relation to the world. It relates to the creative being of God the internal relation between beauty and sensibility in God and the same internal relation between beauty and sensibility in the creature. Finally, it relates to each other and to the creative being of God Edwards' conceptions of glory, fullness, and the beauty of God; and it relates to the creative being of God the relation between understanding and will in the intelligent perceiving creature, which Edwards construes in terms of an aesthetic-affectional model of the self for which the concepts of beauty and sensibility are definitive.

In regard to the Second and Third Persons of the Trinity, Edwards' theology is clearly one of the Holy Spirit. This calls for one simple but important qualification of this schematic formulation, for the division of labor between Christ and the Holy Spirit cannot be so neatly or so sharply drawn as this formulation may suggest. On the one hand, as the inherent good, the Holy Spirit embraces both sides of the last three parts of the formulation. On the other hand, although Jesus Christ, as the apparent good, is primarily related to the more objective terms comprising the left-hand or (a) portions of the formulation, He nevertheless—both as theological Christ and as historical Jesus—is not, for Edwards, unrelated to the love and joy of God communicated to the creature. Though his is a theology of the Spirit, Edwards understands both Jesus Christ and the Holy Spirit to be related to both sides of the last three parts of the formulation.

Some illustrations will show that this formulation is not arbitrary and that it does in fact correctly represent the structure and pattern of Edwards' thought about creation as at once a manifestation and a communication of God's beauty. The beginning of "Miscellany" 448, which has already been quoted in connection with other issues, is worth quoting here at some length because it illustrates in a relatively brief compass so much of what has been distilled into my summary formulation.

God is glorified within Himself these two ways: 1. By appearing or being manifested to Himself in His own perfect idea, or in His Son who is the brightness of His glory. 2. By enjoying and delighting in Himself, by flowing forth in infinite love and delight towards Himself, or in his Holy Spirit.

So God glorifies Himself towards the creatures also two ways: 1. By appearing to them, being manifested to their understanding. 2. In communicating Himself to their hearts, and in their rejoicing and delighting in, and enjoying, the manifestations which He makes of Himself. They both of them may be called His glory in the more extensive sense of the word, viz., His shining forth or the going forth of His excellency, beauty, and essential glory, *ad extra*. By one way it goes forth towards their understandings, by the other it goes forth towards their wills or hearts. God is glorified not only by His glory's being seen, but by its being rejoiced in. When those that see it delight in it, God is more glorified than if they only see it. His glory is then received by the whole soul, both by the understanding and by the heart. God made the world that He might communicate, and the creature receive, His glory; and that it might [be] received both by the mind and heart. He that testifies his idea of God's glory don't glorify God so much as he that testifies also his approbation of it and his delight in it. Both these ways of God's glorifying Himself come from the same cause, viz., the overflowing of God's internal glory, or an inclination in God to cause His internal glory to flow out *ad extra*. What God has in view in either of them, either in His manifestating His glory to the understanding or His communication of it to the heart, is not that He may receive but that He go forth. The main end of His shining forth is not that He may have His rays reflected back to Himself, but that the rays may go forth. And this is very consistent with what we are taught of God's being the alpha and omega, the first and the last. God made all things; and the end for which all things are made, and for which they are disposed, and for which they work continually, is that God's glory may shine forth and be received. From Him all creatures come, and in Him their well being consists. God is all their beginning, and God, received, is all their end. From Him and to Him are all things. [Misc. 448]

It will be noticed that the wider and narrower meanings of the term glory examined earlier,[10] which are closely related to the wider and narrower meanings of the term fullness, also examined earlier,[11] play a significant role in Edwards' understanding of divine creation. The beauty and excellency of God is identified with the divine glory and with the objective portion and foundation of the inherent good or the fullness of good in God. In the formulation now under discussion glory appears only in the (a) portions, that is, in its narrower meaning as that which is manifest or shown forth as distinguished from that which (in creation) is communicated and enjoyed. But the divine glory (and beauty) also has a wider meaning that embraces both the (a) and the (b) portions of this formulation. The divine glory, beauty, and excellency, as the alpha and omega of creation, is therefore really one rather than double, though it is articulated in terms of the two coordinate formulations.

The problem is in part one of language, as Edwards observes in "Miscellany" 1066, which also illustrates further the pattern formulated above.

> Language seems to be defective and to want a proper general word to express the supreme end of the creation and of all God's works, including both these two as branches of it, viz., [1] God's glorifying Himself or causing His glory and perfection to shine forth, and [2] His communicating himself or communicating His fullness and happiness. The one supreme end of all things is the infinite good, as it were flowing out, or the infinite fountain of light, as it were shining forth. We need some other words more properly and fully to express what I mean. This one supreme end consists in two things, viz., in God's infinite perfection being exerted and so manifested, that is, in God's glorifying Himself; and second, His infinite happiness being communicated and so making the creature happy. Both are sometimes in Scripture included in one word, namely, God's being glorified. [Misc. 1066]

The end in view in the divine creation of the world is single rather than double, then, in a second sense also. First, the term glory has both a wider and a narrower meaning, and, second, the glory of God (both beauty and joy) and the creature's good are one rather than diverse. The latter is in-

10. See Ch. 6, pp. 134–41.
11. See Ch. 4, pp. 80–83.

cluded in the former, so that in seeking His own glory God therein seeks precisely the creature's good; "his respect to himself and to the creature in this matter are not properly to be looked upon as a double and divided respect in God's heart" [EC 255]. Or, to express it otherwise, the good of the creature consists in a participation in the glory, fullness, and beauty of God.

> It can't be properly said that the end of God's creating of the world is twofold, or that there are two parallel coordinate ends of God's creating the world: one, to exercise His perfections *ad extra,* another to make His creatures happy. But all is included in one, viz., God's exhibiting His perfections or causing His essential glory to be exercised, expressed, and communicated *ad extra.* [Misc. 1218]

Yet, in the same "Miscellany" that begins with these words, Edwards later notes that "the things which God inclines to and aims at are in some respects two" [Misc. 1218]. They may, however, and ultimately ought to be, "reduced to one, i.e., God's exerting Himself in order to the effect. The exertion and the effect ought not to be separated as though they were two ends" [Misc. 1218].

> Both these dispositions of exerting Himself and communicating Himself may be reduced to one, viz., a disposition effectually to exert Himself, and to exert Himself in order to an effect. That effect is the communication of Himself *ad extra,* which is what is called His glory. This communication is of two sorts: the communication that consists in understanding an idea, which is summed up in the knowledge of God; and the other is in the will consisting in love and joy, which may be summed up in the love and enjoyment of God. Thus, that which proceeds from God *ad extra* is agreeable to the twofold subsistences which proceed from Him *ad intra,* which is the Son and the Holy Spirit—the Son being the idea of God, or the knowledge of God, and the Holy Ghost which is the love of God and joy in God. [Misc. 1218]

The two ends that are ultimately one and that are therein identical with the divine glory in the wider meaning of the term can be, and are, spoken of as two coordinate ends or two coordinate articulations of the same single end —the communication of God's happiness to the creature and the manifestation of his glory. "Miscellany" 1151 illustrates this aspect of my formulation.

It is true that God delights in communicating his happiness to the creature, as therein he exercises a perfection of his nature and does that which is condecent, amiable, and beautiful, and so enjoys himself and his perfection in it, as his perfection is exercised in it. So in like manner he delights in glorifying himself as it is in itself condecent and beautiful that infinite brightness and glory should shine forth, and it is a part of the perfection of God to seek it. [Misc. 1151]

Edwards finds it "beautiful" that the divine perfections are thus exercised and that it is in conformity with their own beautiful nature. "The glory of God is the shining forth [or manifestation] of His perfections. The world was created that they might shine forth—that is, that they might be communicated" [Misc. 247]. Note also how the coordinate and internal relation between the communication of happiness and the manifestation of God's glory corresponds to the internal relation between the orders of beauty and sensibility that I have argued runs through Edwards' whole system of intelligent perceiving being.

Even where the language is not precisely the same as in my summary formulation, the meaning and the pattern illustrated in the above examples is the same. For example, in the concluding summary section of *The End for Which God Created the World* Edwards writes that:

The things signified by that name, *the glory of God,* when spoken of as the supreme and ultimate end of the work of creation, and of all God's works, is the emanation and true external expression of God's internal glory and fulness; meaning by his fulness, what has already been explained.[12] Or, in other words, God's internal glory extant, in a true and just exhibition, or external existence of it. [EC 253]

What is formulated elsewhere as a manifestation of God's glory is here called an "expression" and an "exhibition" of it, while what is formulated elsewhere as a communication of God's glory is here called an "emanation" and an "external existence" of it.

The divine excellency and beauty and joy in themselves and the divine excellency and beauty and joy manifest and communicated to the creature are one and not diverse. In both the latter coordinate articulations of the creative

12. For the explanation here referred to, see Ch. 4, pp. 80–83.

being of God it is God Himself Who is both alpha and omega. "The end, or the thing which God attains" in the creation of the world "is Himself in two respects. He Himself flows forth, and He Himself is pleased and glorified. For God's pleasure all things are and were created" [Misc. 1218].

God creates out of His own fullness and according to His own pleasure. This correspondence between excellency and pleasure in the divine being is reflected in the correspondence between excellency and pleasure, between the orders of beauty and sensibility, throughout the system of intelligent perceiving being. That God finds pleasure in and through the creation of the world in no way diminishes His self-sufficiency. "Many," Edwards argues, "have wrong notions of God's happiness, as resulting from his absolute self-sufficiency, independence, and immutability" [EC 212]. These notions lead them to suppose that because "man cannot be profitable to God" [EC 213], God's pleasure cannot possibly be increased either by the being or by the perfection of the world or of anything in the world. Against such views Edwards argues:

> Though it be true, that God's glory and happiness are in and of himself, are infinite and cannot be added to, unchangeable, for the whole and every part of which he is perfectly independent of the creature; yet it does not hence follow, nor is it true, that God has no real and proper delight, pleasure or happiness, in any of his acts or communications relative to the creature; or effects he produces in them; or in any thing he sees in the creature's qualifications, dispositions, actions and state. God may have a real and proper pleasure or happiness in seeing the happy state of the creature; yet this may not be different from his delight in himself; being a delight in his own infinite goodness; or the exercise of that glorious propensity of his nature to diffuse and communicate himself, and so gratifying this inclination of his own heart. This delight which God has in his creature's happiness, cannot properly be said to be what God receives from the creature. For it is only the effect of his own work in, and communications to the creature, in making it, and admitting it to a participation of his fulness. As the sun receives nothing from the jewel that receives its light, and shines only by a participation of its brightness. [EC 212]

Such pleasure in God, far from grounding the divine pleasure objectively outside Himself, is rather a pleasure in diffusing and communicating to the creature, than in receiving from the creature. Surely, it is no argument of indigence in God, that he is inclined to communicate of his infinite fulness. It is no argument of the emptiness or deficiency of a fountain, that it is inclined to overflow. [EC 213]

With respect to the creature's holiness, for example:

God may have a proper delight and joy in imparting this to the creature, as gratifying hereby his inclination to communicate of his own excellent fulness. God may delight with true and great pleasure in beholding that beauty which is an image and communication of his own beauty, an expression and manifestation of his own loveliness. And this is so far from being an instance of his happiness not being in and from himself, that it is an evidence that he is happy in himself, or delights and has pleasure in his own beauty. If he did not take pleasure in the expression of his own beauty, it would rather be an evidence that he does not delight in his own beauty; that he hath not his happiness and enjoyment in his own beauty and perfection. So that if we suppose God has real pleasure and happiness in the holy love and praise of his saints, as the image and communication of his own holiness, it is not properly any pleasure distinct from the pleasure he has in himself; but is truly an instance of it. [EC 212]

Edwards is quick to point out that his location of the creature's good within the divine glory and beauty involves no dissolution of the real being of the creature or of the actuality of his determinate and particular good into the shadows of figure and metaphor. On the one hand,

these communications of God, these exercises, operations, effects and expressions of his glorious perfections, which God rejoices in, are in time; yet his joy in them is without beginning or change. They were always equally present in the divine mind. [EC 213]

But on the other hand, Edwards refuses simply to appeal away from time and into eternity, for

if God had any last end in creating the world, then there was something, in some respect future, that he aimed at, and designed to bring to pass by creating the world: something that was agreeable to his inclination or will; let that be his own glory, or the happiness of his creatures, or what it will. Now if there be something that God seeks as agreeable, or grateful to him, then in the accomplishment of it he is gratified. [EC 213]

"To suppose," he concludes, "that God has pleasure in things, that are brought to pass in time, only figuratively and metaphorically, is to suppose that he exercises will about these things, and makes them his and only metaphorically" [EC 214].

This view of the relation of God—in His self-manifestation and self-communication, in His excellency and pleasure, in His beauty and delight—to the temporal structure of concrete events comports well with the interpretation of Edwards' system of being offered in this essay: that beauty is the first principle of being according to which the whole system of being is articulated and that primary beauty is defined objectively by determinate relations of consent and dissent among beings. The conception of the creative being of God in such a relation to the divine pleasure as well as to God's effulgent, overflowing fullness of being and beauty brings determinate, historical creatures into significant relation with the transcendent Creator and His design in the creation. The possession and enjoyment by the creature of the good thus manifest and communicated is identical with the experience of the creative presence of God and with a participation in the fullness, glory, and beauty of His being. The creation of the world according to the sovereign pleasure of the Creator, whose pleasure is moved only by "what appears in His eyes beautiful and fit" [Misc. 1182], is reflected in the life of His intelligent perceiving creature, whose only real and abiding pleasure or happiness "arises from that which is an image and participation of God's own beauty" [EC 256]. Creation, then, proceeds out of the fullness of the Divine Being and beauty and consists in the manifestation and communication of God's fullness, glory, and beauty.

Creation is a communication of beauty, and both the Holy Spirit and Jesus Christ are seen by Edwards as communicating the divine beauty to the world. He does not assign the work of creation to any One alone of the Persons of the Trinity. He sometimes speaks of the communication of the divine beauty to the world as a work of the Holy Spirit, Who is Himself the substantial beauty of God, and sometimes as a work of Jesus Christ, Whose beauty is displayed and reflected in the world.

Consider first how Jesus Christ is portrayed as communicating divine beauty in the creation of the world. In an alternative formulation of his view that the glory or beauty of God is the end for which He created the world, Edwards says that "the Son of God created the world for this very end, to communicate himself in an image of his own excellency" [Misc. 108]. This excellency or beauty is communicated most fully to spiritual beings, while "the beauty of the corporeal world consists chiefly in its imaging forth spiritual beauties" [Misc. 186], so that "we see far the most proper image of the beauty of Christ when we see beauty in the human soul" [Misc. 108]. And yet the whole created order is seen as also bodying forth the beauty of Christ, Who is portrayed as not only the efficient cause of the beauties of the world but also as the very substance of the primary beauty communicated to spiritual beings and of the secondary beauty communicated to material or corporeal beings. For not only do "all beauties of the universe . . . immediately result from the efficiency of Christ" [Misc. 185], but "the beauties of nature are really emanations or shadows of the excellencies of the Son of God" [Misc. 108]. In a "Miscellany" on the "Excellency of Christ" these convictions are set forth in a manner typical of several better-known passages:[13]

> The Son of God created the world for this very end to communicate himself in an image of his own excellency. He communicates himself properly only to spirits, and they only are capable of being proper images of his excellency for they only are properly beings as we have shown. Yet he communicates a sort of shadow or glimpse of his excellencies to bodies which as we have shewn are but the shadows of being and not real beings. He who by his immediate influence gives being every moment, and by his spirit actuates the world, because he inclines to communicate himself and his excellencies, doth doubtless communicate his excellency to bodies as far as there is any consent or analogy. And the beauty of face, and sweet airs in men are not always the effect of the corresponding

---

13. See e.g. the "Personal Narrative," in Clarence H. Faust and Thomas H. Johnson, eds., *Jonathan Edwards: Selections* (rev. ed. New York, Hill and Wang, 1962), pp. 57–72. See also the manuscript fragment on "The Beauty of the World," in Jonathan Edwards, *Images or Shadows of Divine Things,* ed. Perry Miller (New Haven, Yale University Press, 1948), pp. 135–37.

excellencies of mind yet the beauties of nature are really emanations or shadows or the excellencies of the Son of God.

So that when we are delighted with flowery meadows and gentle
breezes of wind we may consider that we only see the emanations
of the sweet benevolence of Jesus Christ. When we behold the fra-
grant rose and lily, we see his love, and purity. So the green trees
and fields, and singing birds are the emanations of his infinite joy
and benignity. The easiness and naturalness of trees and vines shadows of his infinite beauty and loveliness. The christal rivers and
murmuring streams, have the footsteps of his sweet grace and
beauty. When we behold the light and brightness of the sun, the
golden edges of an evening cloud, or the beauteous bow we behold
the adumbrations of his glory and goodness, and the blue skies of
his mildness and gentleness. There are also many things wherein
we may behold his awful majesty. In the sun in his strength, in
comets, in thunder, in the hovering thunder clouds in ragged rocks,
and the brows of mountains. That beauteous light with which the
world is filled in a clear day is a lively shadow of his spotless holiness and happiness and delight in communicating himself and
doubtless this is a reason that Christ is compared so often to these
things and called by their names, as the Sun of Righteousness the
morning star the Rose of Sharon and lily of the valley, the apple
tree amongst the trees of the wood a bundle of myrrhe, a Roe, or a
young hart. By this we may discover the beauty of many of those
metaphores and similes which to an unphilosophical person do
seem so uncouth.

In like manner when we behold the beauty of man's body in its
perfection we still see like emanations of Christ's divine perfections, although they do not always flow from the mental excellencies of the person that has them. But we see far the most proper
image of the beauty of Christ when we see beauty in the human
soul. [Misc. 108]

It is a mark of Edward's actualism and of his identification of creation
with the communication of beauty that he is as prepared to argue to the
beauty of Christ from the beauty of the world as he is to derive the latter
from the former. Another "Miscellany" on the "Excellence of Christ" reads
in its entirety:

When we see beautiful airs of look and gesture we naturally think the mind that resides within is beautiful. We have all the same and more reason to conclude the spiritual beauty of Christ from beauty of the world, for all the beauties of the universe do as immediately result from the efficiency of Christ as a cast of an eye or a smile of the countenance depends on the efficiency of the human soul. [Misc. 185]

He does not suppose that the natural tendency to find in the beauty of human "airs of countenance and gesture" a clue to the spiritual beauty of mind and disposition is a reliable guide to the spiritual beauty, virtue, or holiness of men, for "they do not always flow from the mental excellencies of the person that has them" [Misc. 108]. But the beauties of the natural order are taken as a reliable guide to the creative presence of God in the world. Spiritual beauties are "much the greatest, and corporeal beauties but the shadows of them" [Misc. 187]. But natural beauties are no less immediately from God; they are "so immediately derived from God that they are but emanations of his beauty" [Misc. 187].

Edwards' view of the beauty of the world as not only a manifestation of God's beauty but also a substantial communication of that beauty finds even sharper formulation in his manner of attributing to the Holy Spirit the work of communicating beauty to the world in its creation. "Whose office," he asks, "can it be so Properly to give all things their sweetness and beauty as he who is himself the beauty and Joy of the Creator?" This is why "we read that the Sp. of G. moved upon the face of the waters or the Chaos to bring it out of its Confusion into harmony & beauty."[14]

It was more especially the Holy Spirit's work to bring the world to its beauty and perfection out of the chaos; for the beauty of the the world is a communication of God's beauty. The Holy Spirit is the harmony and excellency and beauty of the Deity, as we have shown. Therefore, 'twas his work to communicate beauty and harmony to the world, and so we read that it was he that moved upon the face of the waters. [Misc. 293]

A later "Miscellany" portrays this work of creation as a step toward the even fuller communication of divine beauty that constitutes the redemption of the world.

14. "An Essay on the Trinity," in C. H. Faust and T. H. Johnson, eds., *Jonathan Edwards: Selections*, p. 378.

The proper work of the Spirit of God is to sanctify. . . . But yet the Spirit of God does other things besides this. He also works those works that have a relation to it and are in order to it. . . . So the Spirit of G. in the first creation brought things into their order and beauty and gave them their excellency and perfection. [Misc. 675]

That "primitive beauty" of the world, in which "God, when he created the world, showed his own perfections and beauties forth most charmingly and clearly" [Misc. 186], has been marred by the Fall. And if it is to be re-stored again, "it will undoubtedly be by way of immediate emanation from his beauty" [Misc. 187].

THE PLACE OF BEAUTY IN GOD'S GOVERNANCE AND REDEMPTION

Although "the work of redemption is a new creation" [EC 234], Edwards regards it as decidedly a greater work, to which even the work of creation is subordinate—as is the whole of the divine providential governance of the world. "If it be inquired which of the two works, the work of creation or the work of providence, is the greatest; it must be answered, the work of provi-dence; but the work of redemption is the greatest of the works of providence" [WR 391]. Hence he warns his congregation that "to take on yourself to work out redemption, is a greater thing than if you had taken it upon you to create a world" [WR 419]. Just as creation is understood as a communication of beauty, so also the "new creation" of redemption is understood as a com-munication of beauty. And beauty provides also the central model for under-standing the manner of the divine governance of the world toward its con-summation in the divine glory or beauty.

Beauty is so central to Edwards' understanding of order that it is identical for him with the reality of order, and in construing the order of things as created by God the concepts of order and beauty are regarded as synonymous. Thus, in distributing and ranking things into their several species or sorts, it is in the "disposition of parts" and the "inward conformation" by which one thing is in "agreement" or consent with another that Edwards finds "the real essence of the thing" [Mind 47]. "If the world had been created without any order, or design, or beauty, indeed all species would be merely arbitrary" [Mind 47]. And if we "in distributing things" into various sorts and species "differ from that design we don't know the true essence of things" [Mind 47].

The place of beauty in Edwards' understanding of God's governance and redemption of the world can be examined in detail by explicating six propositions: (1) secondary beauty is the law of the natural world; (2) the beauty that is the law of the natural world is but the shadow of the beauty by which the spiritual world is governed; (3) God governs the world according to his pleasure, and he is pleased only with the perception of true beauty in being; (4) beauty is the law of the moral or spiritual world; (5) beauty is both the end or goal of redemption and the principal means for the redemption of the moral or spiritual world; and (6) beauty is the constitution of genuine community among men. These propositions focus our attention first upon secondary beauty and then upon primary beauty; and they carry us from a consideration of the divine governance toward a consideration of the place of beauty in God's redemptive scheme.

The secondary beauty of proportion and harmony governing the natural world is an expression of "God's love of order and hatred of confusion" [Misc. 712]. It constitutes both the rule for God's ordering of the natural world and an expression of the instrumental and dependent relation of the natural to the moral world, according to which the beauty of the former consists in its shadowing forth the beauty of the latter. "The moral world is the end of the natural world" [FW 251], and "the beauty of the corporeal world consists chiefly in its imaging forth spiritual beauties" [Misc. 186]. Both these aspects of secondary beauty as the law governing the natural world are expressed in one of Edwards' notes on *Images and Shadows of Divine Things,* which may serve as a text for further explicating these two points.

> The whole material universe is preserved by gravity or attraction, or the mutual tendency of all bodies to each other. One part of the universe is hereby made beneficial to another; the beauty, harmony, and order, regular progress, life, and motion, and in short all the well-being of the whole frame depends on it. This is a type of love or charity in the spiritual world. [Images 79]

Secondary beauty is the law of the natural world. This is put most succinctly in the very first of Edwards' "Notes on the Mind": "Being, examined narrowly, is nothing but proportion" [Mind 1].[15] As I have shown, being, "ex-

---

15. The same point is made in other language when in the same "Note," speaking of intelligent beings insofar as they participate in the natural world, Edwards argues that self-love (which is a form of secondary beauty, of consent to limited being) is "only the entity of the thing, or his being what he is."

amined narrowly," must be understood as referring to the articulated system
of being and not to being-itself, of which the definitive and constitutive principle is not the secondary beauty of proportion but the primary beauty of
consent. Within that system of "being as manifest and encountered," "being-
as-proportion" is coordinate with but ontologically inferior to "being-as-
excellence." And yet that secondary beauty of the natural world is no less real
and no less immediately from God.

In a "Miscellany" on "God's Moral Government" Edwards finds that there
is

> much evidence of the most perfect exactness of proportion harmony
> equity & beauty in the mechanical laws of nature & other methods
> of providence which belong to the course of nature which are
> means by which God shews his regard to harmony fitness and
> beauty in what he does as the Governour of the natural world.
> [Misc. 1196]

The mutual tendency or attraction of gravity governing the material universe is real and substantial. It is typically or typologically rather than
metaphorically related to the even more substantial beauty of the spiritual
world. Not only the being but also "the well-being of the whole frame" of
the universe "depends on it" [Images 79]. And the beauty therein exhibited
—as it is also in so many other places and ways—is not only real but over-
whelming and impressive. Reflecting on these beauties, Edwards concludes:

> Hence the reason why almost all men, and [even] those that
> seem to be very miserable, love life, because they cannot bear to
> lose sight of such a beautiful and lovely world. The ideas, that
> every moment whilst we live have a beauty that we take not dis-
> tinct notice of, brings a pleasure that, when we come to the trial,
> we had rather live in much pain and misery than lose. [Images,
> p. 137]

However, the manuscript fragment that ends on this note begins:

> The beauty of the world consists wholly of sweet mutual con-
> sents, either within itself or with the supreme being. As to the cor-
> poreal world, though there are many other sorts of consents, yet the
> sweetest and most charming beauty of it is its resemblance of spir-
> itual beauties. The reason is that spiritual beauties are infinitely the
> greatest, and bodies being but the shadows of beings, they must be

so much the more charming as they shadow forth spiritual beauties. This beauty is peculiar to natural things, it surpassing the art
of man. [Images, p. 135]

*The beauty that is the law of the natural world is but the shadow of the
beauty by which the spiritual world is governed.* Although Edwards understands consent to apply strictly only to spiritual relations, since "there is no
proper consent but that of minds" [Mind 45], he does employ it on occasion
more loosely and by analogy in speaking of natural and material beauty, as
in the passage just quoted. The many forms of secondary beauty governing
the material universe are, in Edwards' terms, pleasing to God—Who governs
according to His pleasure and Whose pleasure is moved only by real beauty
—because the proportion and harmony in them have "an appearance of consent" [Mind 63] or of spiritual beauty. "The immense magnificence of the
visible world in inconceivable vastness, the incomprehensible height of the
heavens, etc., is but a type of the infinite magnificence, height, and glory of
God's work in the spiritual world" [Images 212].

As bodies, the objects of our external senses, are but the shadows
of beings, that harmony wherein consists sensible excellency and
beauty is but the shadow of excellency. That is, it is pleasant to the
mind because it is a shadow of love. When one thing sweetly har-
monizes with another, as the notes in music, the notes are so conformed and have such proportion one to another that they seem to
have respect one to another as if they loved one another . . .

There is no other way that sensible things can consent one to
another but by equality or by likeness or by proportion. Therefore
the lowest or most simple kind of beauty is equality or likeness,
because by equality or likeness one part consents with but one part.
But by proportion one part may sweetly consent with all the rest
and, not only so, but the parts taken singly may consent with the
whole taken together. [Mind 62]

If God governs according to his sovereign pleasure and pleasure is objectively rather than subjectively determined, that is, defined primarily by the
character of the beauty in the object of pleasure rather than by the intensity
of pleasure in the subject,[16] then there is a single rule of beauty according to
which God exercises his sovereign pleasure in the governance (as well as the

16. See Ch. 4, pp. 60–63.

creation and redemption) of the world. "Pleasedness to perceiving being always arises either from a perception of consent to being in general or of consent to that being that perceives" [Mind 1]. Only in God do these two determinants of beauty necessarily coincide. Therefore, only by God's perfect vision is natural beauty perceived in determinate beings and relations only where it is in fact, and not only apparently, in conformity with the primary beauty of cordial consent to the universal system of being.

In these terms Edwards did achieve what Perry Miller says he was striving to express: "a new vision of the world in which the conflict of the spirit and the flesh, of the divine and the rational . . . could be resolved into a single perception of beauty."[17] To the objectively determined divine vision the natural and moral orders are governed by a single rule of beauty, expressed most substantially in the governance of the moral world but expressed no less impressively in the complexity of the proportion and consent that constitute the central principle of order in the natural world. By finding in the perception of spiritual beauty the central clue to the nature of reality, Edwards provides both philosophical and theological support for such a conception of the divine governance of the world. For only if beauty is the formative inner principle of being-itself, only if the principle of beauty is identical with the principle of being, can even the divine vision of beauty offer a reliable guide to the order of the universal system of being.

God governs the world according to his pleasure, and he is pleased only with the perception of true beauty in being. There is one problem related to this formulation of the principle of divine governance according to the rule of beauty. It has to do with the sufficiency and freedom of God. The problem is whether God's governing according to His pleasure and His pleasure being moved by beauty in its object is not an infringement upon the sufficiency and the freedom of God. The problem is illustrated by the following passage from a "Miscellany" on "Free Grace." The complexities in which Edwards gets himself involved in this passage reflect the difficulty he has when he attempts to distinguish too sharply between beauty and being in the object and between complacence and benevolence in the subject, that is, in God. He is driven to offer an image of God pulling a sleight-of-hand trick on Himself in order that He may do what He wants to do, i.e. act according to his pleasure, and still do what is fitting and right according to the order and nature of things.

17. Perry Miller, Intro. to Edwards, *Images or Shadows of Divine Things,* p. 40.

[God] wills absolutely . . . all the happiness that he ever confers on the elect, and his wisdom determines the degree of happiness antecedent to any consideration of the degree of goodness [or beauty] in them.

But because *God does everything beautifully,* he brings about this their happiness which he determined, in an excellent manner; but it would be a grating, dissonant, and deformed thing for a sinful creature to be happy in God's love. He therefore gives them holiness, which holiness he really delights in—*he has really complacence in them after he has given them beauty and not before*— and so the beauty that he gives, when given, induces God in a certain secondary manner to give them happiness. That is, he wills their happiness antecedently, of himself, and he gives them holiness that he may be induced to confer it; and when it is given by him, then he is induced by another consideration besides his mere propensity to goodness. For there are these two propensities in the divine nature: to communicate goodness to that which now is nothing, and to communicate goodness to that which is beautiful and holy, and which he has complacence in. He has a propensity to reward holiness, but he gives it on purpose that he may reward it; because he loves the creature, and loves to reward, and therefore gives it something that he may reward. [Misc. 314, italics added]

The necessity for imputing such sleight-of-hand maneuvers to God could follow only from Edwards' neglect at this point of his own best insights into the relation between beauty and being in the object of God's vision and action and the relation between benevolence and complacence in God as subject.[18]

It is precisely the measure of God's freedom that He acts only in conformity with a will or pleasure disposed to find the largest beauty in nothing less than being's cordial consent to the universal system of being. His freedom consists in the fact that the beauty with which He is pleased and according to which He governs the world is itself the inner structural principle of being-itself. God's delight in beauty is identical with His love of being; and therein consists His freedom and the beauty of His own Being. The freedom of God's creation, governance, and gracious redemption of the world is confirmed

18. I have already examined these insights in considering the relation in Edwards' thought between virtuous complacence (delight in beauty) and benevolence (love of being and beauty) and the relation within benevolence between being and beauty as the primary and secondary objects of virtuous benevolence.

rather than put into question by Edwards' view that the divine will and pleasure is moved by beauty in its object.

Furthermore, the beauty of that object—of any possible object—of God's moral governance is itself

> an image and communication of his own beauty, an expression and manifestation of his own loveliness. And this is so far from being an instance of his happiness not being in and from himself, that it is an evidence that he is happy in himself, or delights and has pleasure in his own beauty. If he did not take pleasure in the expression of his own beauty, it would rather be an evidence that he does not delight in his own beauty; that he hath not his happiness and enjoyment in his own beauty and perfection. [EC 212]

God's own spiritual beauty is so extensive as to bestow as well as delight in beauty; His "virtue is so extended as to include a propensity not only to being actually existing, and actually beautiful, but to possible being, so as to incline him to give a being beauty and happiness" [TV 6]. This pleasure God takes in the beauty of his creatures

> is rather a pleasure in diffusing and communicating to the creature, than in receiving from the creature. Surely, it is no argument of indigence in God, that he is inclined to communicate of his infinite fulness. It is no argument of the emptiness or deficiency of a fountain, that it is inclined to overflow. [EC 213]

The delight of God in the beauty of His creatures is not distinct from, but is rather contained within and is an overflowing manifestation and communication of, the delight He takes in His own beauty. This divine beauty, whether in Himself or communicated *ad extra,* is the only proper object of God's unqualified pleasure, for "if God esteems, values, and has respect to things according to their nature and proportions, he must necessarily have the greatest respect to himself" [EC 200]. Accordingly, the divine beauty or the "glory of God is the last end in his government of the world . . . and particularly in the work of redemption, the chief of all his dispensations in his moral government of the world" [EC 234]. The sufficiency as well as the freedom of God is therefore also confirmed by His governance of the world according to the pleasure He takes in beauty.

Beauty is the law of the moral or spiritual world. Two formulations of this rule feature prominently in Edwards' analysis of the structure and dynamics of the moral life. In *The Nature of True Virtue* he finds the varieties of virtue to be forms of secondary and primary beauty; and he distributes holiness and sin, virtue and vice, love and self-love, and love and hatred into forms of beauty and deformity. In *Freedom of the Will* he formulates a descriptive "is as" definition of the will—"The will always is as the greatest apparent good is" [FW 142]—according to which beauty is determinative for both sides of the "is as" equation. Furthermore, each of these formulations emerges out of an analysis of what he regards as itself a form of beauty.

> Excellence in and among spirits is, in its prime and proper sense, being's consent to being. There is no proper consent but that of minds, even of their will; which, when it is of minds towards minds, it is love, and when of minds towards other things, it is choice. [Mind 45]

Love and the will are essentially identical insofar as the structure of the self and the dynamics of the moral life are concerned. Whether the focus is upon love or the will—or upon the religious affections—Edwards' analysis yields beauty, first primary and then secondary, as the model for the structure and the law of the dynamics of the moral or spiritual life.

Among the most impressive features of Edwards' treatise on *The Nature of True Virtue* is that he employs—I may even say deploys—beauty as a structural analytic concept for the interpretation of the full range of the moral life rather than simply as a term of praise for only the highest form of virtue. He does not simply argue that true virtue is really a thing of beauty. He offers an analysis, universal in its comprehensiveness, of the full range of the moral life, from the true virtue or holiness of the saints through the limited but real virtue of the natural man (what Augustine called "splendid vices") to the deformity of sin—an analysis in which all these are resolved into forms of beauty and deformity and of primary and secondary beauty.

Only "true virtue . . . is beautiful by a general beauty, or beautiful in a comprehensive view, as it is in itself, and as related to every thing with which it stands connected" [TV 3]. By defining true virtue as "benevolence to being in general" or as "that consent, propensity and union of heart to being in general, which is immediately exercised in a general good will" [TV 3], Edwards defines moral perfection by locating it with respect to the universal system of being, identifying it with nothing less than the first principle and law of being-itself. The foundation of true virtue, therefore, is not laid in the first instance upon a deontological order of imperatives nor upon a projected ideal moral order that ought to be (and that if actualized would surely be most beautiful!). Instead, the foundation of true virtue is found in the law of the things that are.

> If every intelligent being is some way related to being in general, and is a part of the universal system of existence; and so stands in connection with the whole; what can its general and true beauty be, but its union and consent with the great whole? [TV 4]

Practically speaking, such conformity with the things that are, with the universal system of being, amounts to the same thing as conformity with He Who Is, with God, "the head of the universal system of existence; the foundation and fountain of all being and beauty" [TV 15].

To this primary beauty, which is "the proper and peculiar beauty of spiritual and moral beings, which are the highest and first part of the universal system, for whose sake all the rest has existence" [TV 27], there is related a secondary beauty that is a subordinate law by which God governs both the spiritual and the material worlds, both the moral and the natural orders, in order to support the dominion of primary beauty.

> There is another, inferior, secondary beauty, which is some image of this, and which is not peculiar to spiritual beings, but is found even in inanimate things; which consists in a mutual consent and agreement of different things, in form, manner, quantity, and visible end or design; called by the various names of regularity, order, uniformity, symmetry, proportion, harmony, etc. [TV 27–28]

This rule of secondary beauty is a sort of natural law of the moral world as well as the model of order in the physical world. Edwards even calls this secondary beauty of proportion or harmony a law of nature.

> It pleases God to observe analogy in his works . . . And so he has constituted the external world in analogy to the spiritual world . . . He makes an agreement of different things, in their form, manner, measure, etc. to appear beautiful, because here is some image of an higher kind of agreement and consent of spiritual beings. It has pleased him to establish a law of nature, by virtue of which the uniformity and mutual correspondences of a beautiful plant, and the respect which the various parts of a regular building seem to have one to another, and their agreement and union, and the con-

sent or concord of the various notes of a melodious tune, should appear beautiful; because therein is some image of the consent of mind, of the different members of a society or system of intelligent beings, sweetly united in a benevolent agreement of heart. [TV 30–31]

The natural law of secondary beauty has force in God's governance of intelligent perceiving beings because there is in them a corresponding sensibility such that the law of nature is in them as well as in the external world. Edwards finds that the presence in men of the natural law of secondary beauty takes several forms. One he calls instinct.

The cause why secondary beauty is grateful to men, is only a law of nature which God has fixed, or an instinct he has given to mankind . . . it is not any reflection upon, or perception of, such a resemblance [to the cordial agreement in primary beauty] . . . but [rather] their sensation of pleasure, on a view of this secondary beauty, is immediately owing to the law God has established, or the instinct he has given. [TV 32–33]

But there are other more morally significant forms of the law by which intelligent perceiving beings are governed, because:

This secondary kind of beauty, consisting in uniformity and proportion, not only takes place in material and external things, but also in things immaterial; and is, in very many things, plain and sensible in the latter, as well as the former . . . If uniformity and proportion be the things that affect and appear agreeable to this sense of beauty, then why should not uniformity and proportion affect the same sense in immaterial things as well as material, if there be equal capacity of discerning it in both? and indeed more in spiritual things (*coeteris paribus*) as these are more important than things merely external and material?

This is not only reasonable to be supposed, but is evident in fact, in numberless instances. [TV 34–35]

There is, for example, "a beauty of order in society" that is "of a secondary kind" not different in kind from "the regularity of a beautiful building" and additional to the primary beauty, which there is in the cordial consent among men in society [TV 35]. There is "the same kind of beauty in what is

called wisdom" [TV 36] and "in the virtue called justice, which consists
in the agreement of different things, that have relation to one another, in
nature, manner, and measure" [TV 36]. For example:

> Things are in natural regularity and mutual agreement, in a literal
> sense, when he whose heart opposes the general system, should
> have the hearts of that system, or the heart of the ruler of the sys-
> tem, against him; and, in consequence should receive evil, in pro-
> portion to the evil tendency of the opposition of his heart. [TV 36]

So also there is a secondary beauty in the justice of mutual love and in gratitude being proportioned to good received [TV 36] and in "most of the duties
incumbent on us" [TV 37].

Edwards devotes several chapters in *The Nature of True Virtue*[19] to showing how several influences operate according to the laws of secondary beauty,
at best, and of positive deformity and contrariety to being, at worst. Among
these are the influence of self-love, of "a man's love to those who love him"
[TV 48], of gratitude and anger, of natural conscience and the "moral
sense" (Hutcheson), and of a variety of "particular instincts" such as "natural
appetites and aversions" [TV 75], "mutual inclinations between the sexes"
[TV 75], the natural affection or "love of parents to their children" [TV
76], and "natural pity" [TV 80–83].

They may at times "have something of the general nature of virtue" [TV
85] in them and may thus "be beautiful within their own private sphere"
[TV 86]. Even a "natural conscience," if awakened, is better than one stupe-
fied and rendered insensible by pride and sensuality; at least it "tends to re-
strain" sin [TV 95]. And, "even self-love often restrains from acts of true
wickedness; and not only so, but puts men upon seeking true virtue" [TV
95], though it is itself not only distinct from true virtue "but is the source of
all the wickedness that is in the world" [TV 95]. Given the present state of
the world, Edwards finds that "these natural principles, for the most part,
tend to the good of mankind" and therein "agree with the tendency of general benevolence" [TV 94]. In fact, "many of these natural principles resem-

---

19. The following chapter headings are uncommonly descriptive: Ch. III, "Concerning
the Secondary and Inferior Kind of Beauty"; Ch. IV, "Of-Self-Love, and its Various Influence, to Cause Love to Others, or the Contrary"; Ch. V, "Of Natural Conscience, and the
Moral Sense"; Ch. VI, "Of Particular Instincts of Nature, Which in Some Respects Resemble Virtue"; and Ch. VII, "The Reasons Why Those Things That Have Been Mentioned,
Which Have Not the Essence of Virtue, Have Yet by Many Been Mistaken for True
Virtue."

ble [true] virtue in its primary operation, which is benevolence," and also "in its secondary operation, which is its approbation of and complacence in virtue itself" [TV 89]. But they should not therefore be taken as truly virtuous or as having in them any primary beauty. At best they exhibit only a secondary and private, not a general and public, beauty. "What they are essentially defective in is, that they are private in their nature; they do not arise from any temper of benevolence to being in general" [TV 86].

The authority of the natural law of secondary beauty appears ambiguous and precarious because this essential defect stands always ready to distort even the secondary beauty of the natural man into the deformity of splendid vices. Conformity to the natural law of harmony or proportion and "natural agreement" [TV 32] may, on the one hand, tend to agreement with the higher law of cordial consent to being-in-general. Properly harnessed to "the principle of disinterested general benevolence," the principle of secondary beauty operates beautifully to produce virtuous and beautiful (as distinguished by Edwards from merely natural) gratitude, love of justice, sense of desert, conscience, and bonds of affection for members of one's family, for members of the opposite sex, or for members of one's own community or nation [TV 96]. But conformity to the same principle of "natural agreement" and proportion may, on the other hand, set honor among thieves or love of country against the universal system of being, creating discord, deformity, and contrariety to being. So it is that men set up their private kingdoms against each other and against the universal system and against God, its one head. "All sin has its source from selfishness, or from self-love not subordinate to a regard to being in general" [TV 92]. "Though self-love is far from being useless in the world, yea, it is exceedingly necessary to society; yet . . . it may make a man a common enemy to the general system" [TV 89].

Certainly the perception of beauty in material things has no necessary connection with virtue, neither supporting nor producing it.

> Who will affirm, that a disposition to approve of the harmony of good music, or the beauty of a square or equilateral triangle, is the same with true holiness, or a truly virtuous disposition of mind? It is a relish of uniformity and proportion that determines the mind to approve these things. [TV 40]

Why should it be otherwise with respect to the perception of beauty in spiritual or immaterial things if the nature of the beauty is essentially the same, namely, the secondary beauty of harmony or proportion? Although

there is an analogy between secondary and primary beauty, men do not
delight in secondary beauty because they perceive such an analogy.

> Not only reason but experience plainly shows, that men's appro-
> bation of this sort of beauty does not spring from any virtuous tem-
> per, and has no connection with virtue. For otherwise their delight
> in the beauty of squares, and cubes, and regular polygons, in the
> regularity of buildings, and the beautiful figures in a piece of em-
> broidery, would increase in proportion to men's virtue; and would
> be raised to a great height in some eminently virtuous or holy men;
> but would be almost wholly lost in some others that are very vi-
> cious and lewd. It is evident in fact, that a relish of these things
> does not depend on general benevolence, or any benevolence at all
> to any being whatsoever, any more than a man's loving the taste of
> honey, or his being pleased with the smell of a rose. [TV 41]

Edwards parts company with moralists such as Shaftesbury and Hutcheson,
who identify virtue with a moral sense or taste for a beauty defined in terms
of harmony and proportion.[20] "A taste of this inferior beauty [even] in things
immaterial" [TV 41] does not in itself have any connection with true virtue.
The perception of secondary beauty even in spiritual or moral relations will
support rather than subvert the dominion of the higher law of spiritual
beauty only if it is subordinated or harnessed to a benevolent propensity toward being-in-general.

The authority of both the higher moral law of being's cordial consent to
being-in-general and of the natural (moral) law of proportion appears precarious because it is a law of beauty. The authority of beauty depends upon
its being perceived and enjoyed. But the appearance of instability in this is
deceiving, for it is precisely to this dependence that Edwards attributes the
reliability of the law of beauty.

The problem here is similar to the problem of formulating a law of freedom to which Immanuel Kant addressed himself. Kant's effort to formulate
such a law in terms of the concept of beauty, especially in Paragraph 59 of
the *Critique of Judgment*,[21] entitled "Beauty as the Symbol of Morality," is
significantly similar to Edwards' interpretation of the moral order in terms of
the concept of beauty. For Kant as for Edwards "the aesthetic dimension is

20. See Clyde A. Holbrook, "Edwards and the Ethical Question," *Harvard Theological Review,* 60 (1967), 163–75.

21. Kant, *Critique of Judgment* (New York, Hafner Publishing Co., 1951).

the medium in which the senses and the intellect meet . . . Moreover, the aesthetic dimension is also the medium in which nature and freedom meet."[22] The case of Kant is especially interesting because his situation is in some respects similar to Edwards'. His development of a philosophical alternative to the impasse of rationalism and empiricism is comparable to Edwards' development of a theological alternative to a polarized rationalism and sensationalism in religion. Both make significant use of the concepts of beauty and sensibility and of the relation of the aesthetic to the moral in developing these alternatives. The concept of beauty is important to both men's conceptions of objectivity and of freedom. Edwards' view that freedom has its only sufficient foundation in a perception of the beauty of the Divine Being and of divine things may have certain advantages over the similar but more formal Kantian formulation. In Edwards' view human freedom is necessarily theonomous because it is founded upon a sensible experience of the immediacy of God's presence and a perception of the transcendent beauty of God. The Kantian self achieves its freedom by virtue of its abstraction from concrete empirical involvements, while Edwards' self achieves both freedom and identity by virtue of the manner of its aesthetic-affectional engagement with reality.[23]

The force of the law of beauty in the moral world is firm for Edwards because of its universality with respect to intelligent perceiving beings. "Every being that has understanding and will," he argues, "necessarily loves happiness. For to suppose any being not to love happiness," he continues, in a characteristic fashion, "would be to suppose he did not love what was agreeable to him; which is a contradiction" [TV 101]. And happiness consists in the perception of beauty, as he says already in the "Notes on the Mind": "Happiness strictly consists in the perception of these three things: of the consent of being to its own being; of its own consent to being; and of being's consent to being" [Mind 1]. Whether the beauty perceived is true or false is, of course, a matter for investigation rather than definition.

22. These are Herbert Marcuse's words, speaking about Kant only (not Edwards) in *Eros and Civilization* (New York, Vintage Books, 1962), p. 163.

23. On Kant, in addition to the *Critique of Judgment*, see his *Observations on the Feeling of the Beautiful and Sublime*, trans. and intro. John T. Goldwait (Berkeley, University of California Press, 1960). See also John Silber's penetrating analysis of Kant's understanding of freedom in his Introduction to Kant's *Religion Within the Limits of Reason Alone* (New York, Harper, Torchbook, 1960), pp. lxxxvi–cxxxiv, and James Gustafson's analysis (*Treasure in Earthen Vessels* [New York, Harper, 1961], pp. 114–19) of the crucial distinction between the formal, noumenal self of Kant and the timeful historical self in Augustine and the "Augustinian stream" within which Edwards' thought moves.

The law of beauty is authoritative, furthermore, because it operates directly, without intermediaries or interpreters.

> Indirect agreeableness . . . is not beauty . . . The way we come by
> the idea of beauty is by immediate sensation of the gratefulness of
> the idea called beautiful; and not by finding out by argumentation
> any consequences, or other things with which it stands connected;
> any more than tasting the sweetness of honey, or perceiving the
> harmony of a tune, is by argumentation on connections and con-
> sequences. [TV 98–99]

The law of beauty is determinative, finally, because the perception of
beauty is a function of the self-disposition or inclination of a perceiving being. More precisely, the perception of beauty in the object is in necessary correspondence with the beauty and sensibility of the perceiving moral subject.
The passage just quoted continues:

> The manner of being affected with the immediate presence of the
> beautiful idea, depends . . . on the frame of our minds, whereby
> they are so made that such an idea, as soon as we have it, is grate-
> ful, or appears beautiful. [TV 99]

The writ of the law of beauty in the moral and spiritual (as well as the
external and material) world is secure. Although its authority depends
upon its being perceived and enjoyed, perception and enjoyment are neither
arbitrary nor indeterminate and accidental. Their structure and dynamics
are ordered, and it is the coordinate concepts of beauty and sensibility that
constitute for Edwards the decisive law of that order.

Edwards' "is as" volitional equation developed in *Freedom of the Will* is
relevant to an understanding of the divine governance of the moral world
as expressed in what I shall call the "beauty of virtue" formulation in *The
Nature of True Virtue*. Particularly if these two formulations are held together, the law of beauty appears to be a descriptive rather than a causal or
prescriptive one.[24] As we have seen, Edwards is quite explicit about the "is as"

24. I am distinguishing normative from prescriptive law. With beauty (and a corresponding sensibility) as the model of order in the moral life, Edwards' approach to ethics yields
norms for guidance and critical principles for moral discernment (sensibility) rather than
prescriptive rules for application. *The Nature of True Virtue,* his most significant and characteristic contribution to Christian ethics, is, as the title announces, an analysis of the nature
of virtue, not an ethical manual. The series of sermons delivered in 1738 and published

equation of the will; he does not mean that the will is caused by something other than its own pleasure—not even by the "apparent good." "The will always is as the greatest apparent good is" [FW 142]. This formulation focuses attention upon the "apparent good" side of the equation; and we have seen that it is the beauty of the apparent good that constitutes its attractive power. The "beauty of virtue" formulation, on the other hand, focuses attention upon the "will" side of the "is as" equation; it finds in the "frame of mind" of a perceiving moral being the determinant of what appears good or is perceived and enjoyed as beautiful. Although he speaks here of "the manner of being affected with the immediate presence of the beautiful idea" [TV 99] as depending on the "frame of mind," we have already seen in our analysis of the "is as" equation that for Edwards this really is an equation and not a causal or dependency relationship. What is gained by looking at both sides rather than simply one side of the equation is not the knowledge of causes but a greater descriptive and analytic knowledge.

The beauty of the subject, then, and the corresponding sensibility, which is always internally related to the beauty of intelligent perceiving subjects, is as the beauty perceived and enjoyed in the object is. The tendency of true virtue is always to see things as they are, that is, to see them as they are in themselves and with respect to their tendencies and connections with the universal system, to see their beauty and deformity according to the measure of primary beauty first and of secondary beauty rightly subordinate to it—and to be affected accordingly.

The interpretation Edwards offers of the departure from such a true perception of being and beauty is a descriptive rather than a causal account of sin. He finds that sin consists in privacy of affections, narrowness of views, and the deformity of "dissent from being," which is a necessary ingredient of any moral or spiritual self-definition by reference to a system of being that is less than universal.

> The reason why men are so ready to take these private affections for
> true virtue, is the narrowness of their views; and above all, that

---

under the title *Charity and its Fruits, or Christian Love as Manifest in the Heart and Life* (New York, Robert Carter and Brothers, 1856) is more pastoral in character and puts additional flesh on the bones of his analysis. These lectures or sermons bear about the same relation to his *The Nature of True Virtue* as do Kant's *Lectures on Ethics* to his *Critique of Practical Reason*. In *Charity and its Fruits* Edwards does not move a great deal closer to prescription, though he does fill out somewhat the content of the norms for guidance and the critical principles for moral discernment—as he does also in the *Religious Affections*.

they are so ready to leave the divine Being out of their view, and to neglect him in their consideration, or to regard him in their thoughts as though he did not properly belong to the system of real existence, but was a kind of shadowy, imaginary being. And though most men allow that there is a God, yet in their ordinary view of things, his being is not apt to come into the account, and to have the influence and effect of a real existence, as it is with other beings which they see, and are conversant with by their external senses. In their views of beauty and deformity, and in their inward sensations of displicence and approbation, it is not natural to them to view the Deity as part of the system, and as the head of it, in comparison of whom all other things are to be viewed with corresponding impressions. [TV 87]

The natural law of secondary beauty, then, may either serve and support the dominion of the higher law of primary beauty, or it may—if the partial is taken for the universal, if the image is taken for the substance of primary beauty—serve as a constitution for the setting up of private systems in dissention from the general system and from each other.

> The larger the number is, to which that private affection extends, the more apt men are, through the narrowness of their sight, to mistake it for true virtue; because then the private system appears to have more of the image of the universal. [TV 88]

The natural law of secondary beauty was meant by God to serve the dominion of primary beauty, not to reign in its place or independently of the higher law. The Fall consists in just that displacement of the master by the servant.

> Man did immediately set up himself, and the objects of his private affections and appetites, as supreme; and so they took the place of God. These inferior principles are like fire in a house; which we say is a good servant, but a bad master; very useful while kept in its place, but if left to take possession of the whole house, soon brings all to destruction. [OS 477]

Such an operation of the natural law of secondary beauty apart from the higher law of primary beauty is sin and introduces disharmony, deformity, and discord into the universal system of being and into the private system itself, whether the private system in question be the self alone (or even some aspect of the self) or a whole society. No partial principle can be universalized without self-contradiction or without introducing contradiction into the whole. Men may, "through the narrowness of their views . . . in judging of the beauty of affections and actions," take the private for the general, the partial for the universal. But that in no way alters the fact that they are in some way related to being-in-general and a part of the universal system. That is a matter of fact, not of choice; and unless the fact and choice correspond in cordial consent to being, there will be disharmony, discord, and deformity. Conformity to the law of beauty is, therefore, a requirement of consistency with self (or with any other private system), in which Edwards finds a secondary and limited beauty, as well as of consistency with being-in-general. "There is no other temper but this, whereby a man can agree with himself, or be without self-inconsistence" [TV 101]: a temper or "frame of mind" benevolently disposed to being-in-general.

The authority of the law of beauty in the moral world is, therefore, not heteronomous. That is, it is not imposed externally upon even a private system of being but is itself a condition of both the being and the perfection of even the most private system. For it includes a principle of self-consistency as well as of consistency with the universal system; it is of necessity in agreement with "the nature of things" [TV 99–107]; and it operates only in conformity with the frame of mind of the moral agent or subject. It is to that extent autonomously authoritative and a law of freedom. Ultimately, however, its authority is theonomous. For conformity to the law of beauty is indistinguishable from conformity to God and participation in His beauty. It is only in such primary spiritual beauty and in a corresponding spiritual sensibility that the fullness of freedom is to be found. That would be to have all things governed according to one's own pleasure.

Beauty is both the end or goal of redemption, and the principal means for the redemption of the moral or spiritual world. Beauty is both the end and the means of the redemption of the spiritual world; it is both the condition into which God seeks to restore the whole of His creation and the principal means of that restoration of the "primitive beauty" [Misc. 186] marred by the Fall. For God is Himself both the end and the means of redemption: it is His own beauty and glory that is God's end in view in all His actions, and it is not by brute force but by the attractive and creative power of His own beauty that He moves to achieve it, acting in accordance with the spiritual beauty that is the highest and most distinguishing of his own perfections.

Edwards comes early to find in the beauty of creation a type of the beauty of redemption.

> The old creation I believe was a type of the new. God's causing light to shine out of darkness is a type of his causing such spiritual light and glory by Jesus Christ . . . to arise out of the dreadful darkness of sin and misery. *His bringing the world into such beautiful form* out of a chaos without form and void, *typifies his bringing the spiritual world to such divine excellency and beauty* after the confusion, deformity, and ruin of sin. [Misc. 479, italics added]

If the beauty of the creation is to be restored, Edwards expects "it will undoubtedly be by way of immediate emanation from his [God's] beauty" [Misc. 187]. He finds that "rightly are grace, favour, and beauty one word in the Hebrew language and some others" [Misc. 220], for beauty is to him identical with the principal means and the substance of divine grace.

So consistently does Edwards regard the work of redemption as the greatest work of God, and so thoroughly does he identify spiritual beauty with the end sought in redemption, that, in a fascinating "Miscellany" entitled "Saints Higher in Glory Than the Angels," he speculates that the saints (who are the objects of the work of redemption) will be superior even to the angels in beauty and joy, though not in greatness.

> 'Tis not in all respects that the saints will be higher in glory than the angels, for *the angels will be superior in greatness, in strength, & wisdom,* & so in that honour that belongs to 'em on that account. *But they will not be superior in beauty and amiableness* and in being most beloved of God and most nearly united to him & [in] the fullest & sweetest enjoyment of him. It hath pleased God in his infinite wisdom that the superior *greatness* & the highest *beauty & blessedness* in the most intimate union with him & enjoyment of his love, should not go together; that creature greatness mayn't lift up itself; that it may appear that God don't depend on creature greatness, that creature greatness is nothing before God, and that all good is of God.
>
> . . . *the saints will be superior in goodness & happiness;* they will have the most excellent superiority: *goodness is more excellent than creature greatness;* 'tis more divine; God communicates him-

self more immediately in it; & therefore God is pleased to make
goodness the end of greatness, for he would make that in the creature which is properly belonging to the nature of the creature
subordinate to that which is of God or a communication of the divine nature in the creature, & accordingly has he disposed things
between the two kinds of intelligent creatures that he has made.
He has made the good creature the end of the great creature; he
has made saints the end of the angels rather than the angels the end
of the saints; he has subordinated that kind of creatures wherein is
most creature greatness to another sort of creatures that have *not
so much greatness but* are appointed to *more goodness, i.e., more
divine beauty & joy* in the communications of the Spirit of God.
[Misc. 824, italics added][25]

The communication to the creature of this "beauty and joy" is the goal of
redemption, and its consummation is contained within the fullness of the
divine glory, which is the single end governing all of God's action with
respect to the world. It consists in the restoration of the primary beauty of
the spiritual image of God in man and of the cordially consenting kingdom
of men in communion with one another and with the whole system of being
in God.

Just as being is bestowed by bestowing beauty, so also the system of being
is redeemed by a further manifestation and communication of God's own
beauty. The soteriological counterpart of Edwards' philosophical view that
beauty is the first principle of being-itself is that God's redemptive power, his
saving power, is most decisively present as the divine beauty. For God is present in the manner in which beauty is present and is most truly and fully
known in the perception and enjoyment of His beauty. Edwards finds in this
perception of beauty the key to the transforming, redeeming knowledge of
God. The redemption of the creature consists in the communication to him of
his greatest good, which is God Himself; and the fullest manifestation and

25. Note the way in which Edwards' language in this "Miscellany" illustrates several of
the relations between terms examined earlier in this study: e.g. the relation between greatness and goodness, and the corresponding relation—implicit but clear, since the subject is
the glory of both angels and saints—between the natural glory of the angels (including
their greatness, strength, and wisdom) and the spiritual glory of the saints (including their
beauty or goodness, and their happiness or joy or blessedness), and therefore the identification of beauty with the higher sort of glory (spiritual rather than natural).

communication of God is in His beauty. "The good of the creature," he says, consists in "its knowledge or view of God's glory and beauty, its union with God, conformity and love to him, and joy in him" [TV 25].

Nothing less than a manifestation and communication of the divine beauty itself has the creative, transforming, spiritual power sufficient to the reconciliation of the sinner with God.

> A sight of the awful greatness of God, may overpower men's strength, and be more than they can endure; but if the moral beauty of God be hid, the enmity of the heart will remain in its full strength, no love will be enkindled, all will not be effectual to gain the will, but that will remain inflexible; whereas the first glimpse of the moral and spiritual glory of God shining into the heart, produces all these effects, as it were with omnipotent power, which nothing can withstand. [RA 264–265]

Edwards follows this pattern with respect to the specific ingredients of the Christian life. For example, with respect to humility, he argues in *Charity and its Fruits* that

> a sense of the loveliness of God, is peculiarly that discovery of God that works humility. A sense or discovery of God's greatness, without the sight of his loveliness, will not do it, but it is the discovery of his loveliness that effects it, and that makes the soul truly humble. [CF 209]

Later, in the *Religious Affections,* he is more specific about the meaning of humility, distinguishing legal from evangelical humility and finding that the former is in large part distinguished from the latter in that it is from "a sense of the awful greatness, and natural perfections of God," while evangelical humility is from a sense and "discovery of the beauty of God's holiness and moral perfection" [RA 311]. Also,

> in a legal humiliation, men are made sensible that they are little and nothing before the great and terrible God, and that they are undone, and wholly insufficient to help themselves . . . but they have not an answerable frame of heart, consisting in a disposition to abase themselves, and exalt God alone: this disposition is given only in evangelical humiliation, by overcoming the heart, and

changing its inclination, by a discovery of God's holy beauty. [RA 311–12]

If nothing less than the divine beauty is sufficient to a reconciliation of the sinner with God, then a turning aside from that beauty will be a critical deflection of attention. Indeed, Edwards finds that this is one of the decisive marks of hypocrites in religion; they "take more comfort in their discoveries than in Christ discovered" and are much "affected with their affections" rather than with the supposed object of those affections. They "talk more of the discovery than of the thing discovered" [RA 252]. "What they are principally taken and elevated with, is not the glory of God, or beauty of Christ, but the beauty of their [own] experiences. They . . . put their experience in the place of Christ, and his beauty and fullness [RA 251]."

God exercises his sovereign power of redemption over intelligent perceiving beings not by the power of brute force but by the attractive and creative power of beauty. " 'Tis by a sight of the beauty and amiableness of God's holiness that the heart is transformed into the same image and strongly engaged to imitate God" [Misc. 1127]. It is by this divine beauty, perceived as a "*bonum formosum,* a beautiful good in itself . . . that the true saints have their hearts affected, and love captivated by the free grace of God in the first place" [RA 262–63]. The communication of God's own beauty is the decisive and definitive act of redemption.

Edwards' understanding of the manner in which the act is accomplished can be summarily expressed in terms of the same "is as" volitional equation by which the moral world is governed generally. It is accomplished by God's communicating His own beauty immediately to both sides of the equation. In the beauty of Jesus Christ God presents himself objectively as the creature's real good made manifest as the apparent good. "It is this sight of the divine beauty of Christ that bows the wills and draws the hearts of men."[26] On the other side of the moral equation God presents himself subjectively or inherently as the primary beauty and spiritual sensibility which is the gift of the indwelling Holy Spirit. It is in a "sight or sense" of the "divine and superlative beauty and loveliness of Jesus Christ" that "does fundamentally consist . . . the saving grace of God's Spirit."[27] The self-communication of God to this second side of the moral equation is objective as well as subjective or

26. "True Grace," *Works, 4,* 469–70.
27. Ibid., p. 469.

inherent, for the beauty and sensibility thereby given are not only from God but are something of God. The Holy Spirit is, substantially, the beauty and delight, the holiness and joy of God. The decisive work of redemption is accomplished, in sum, by the attractive power of God's beauty before men in Christ and by the creative power of His beauty and spiritual sensibility in men as the Holy Spirit.

With this formulation of divine governance and redemption Edwards is able to hold together the sovereign power of the Creator and the freedom and responsibility of the moral creature. He also unites an ontological theology in which beauty is the first principle of being and, as the Holy Spirit, is substantial to the internal life of God himself with an historical theology in which God offers himself to his free, responsible, spiritual creatures in the beauty of Jesus Christ as the apparent good, the real good become apparent. It would indeed have been interesting if Edwards had lived to carry out his projected theological program cast in an historical mold.

There are also other ways in which Edwards finds beauty to be a means of redemption. In addition to the decisive manifestation and communication of divine beauty in Jesus Christ and the Holy Spirit, the whole creation appears to him to be marshalled by God in the interest of the redemption of spiritual creatures. "The works of God are but a kind of voice or language of God to instruct intelligent beings in things pertaining to Himself" [Images 57]. And beauty is central to the vocabulary and syntax of that language; or rather, the pattern of articulation for the language of God is the aesthetic pattern of beauty. Both as reality and as language the system of being is articulated according to the principle of beauty. The natural as well as the moral world is seen by Edwards as itself one vast address to the creature, in which he is invited to read and hear the language of God in the forms of spiritual and natural beauty and in the "images or shadows of divine things" and to discern therein—and, discerning, to participate in—God's redemptive governance of the world toward its fulfillment in the beauty of the divine glory.

Edwards sees the whole natural world as ordered to this end, and the manner of that ordering is according to the natural law of secondary beauty.

> The reason, or at least one reason, why God has made this kind
> of mutual agreement of things beautiful and grateful to those in-
> telligent beings that perceive it, probably is, that there is in it some

image of the true, spiritual, original beauty . . . consisting in being's consent to being. [TV 30]

"There is symmetry and beauty in God's workmanship" [RA 365] not only because God enjoys it himself and is pleased "to observe analogy in his works" and so "has constituted the external world in analogy to the spiritual world" [TV 30] but also because the creature's enjoyment of natural beauty tends to support—though it does not itself produce, and may in fact, as we have seen, subvert—the dominion of spiritual beauty. Edwards thinks it probable,

> with regard to this image or resemblance which secondary beauty
> has of true spiritual beauty, that God has so constituted nature, that
> the presenting of this inferior beauty, especially in those kinds of it
> which have the greatest resemblance of the primary beauty, as the
> harmony of sounds and the beauties of nature, have [sic] a ten-
> dency to assist those whose hearts are under the influence of a truly
> virtuous temper to dispose them to the exercises of divine love, and
> enliven in them a sense of spiritual beauty. [TV 31]

An extension of the principle of secondary beauty will not itself produce primary beauty; the continuity between nature and grace is from the side of grace alone. But if, by the immediate presence of God, there is a direct communication of spiritual beauty and spiritual sensibility, then the communication and perception of secondary or natural beauty will be a means of redemption—by enriching the beauty and enlivening the corresponding sensibility of the creature to the highest spiritual beauty.

If beauty is not the only language in which God addresses his intelligent perceiving creatures and to which they ought to be attentive, it is nevertheless one that, if Edwards' account of things is correct, they neglect at their own peril, since beauty is the essential nature of God.

Beauty is the constitution of genuine community among men. The divine governance and redemption of intelligent, perceiving creatures operates as much to unite men in ever widening community with each other as to bind them in communion with God Himself. "A main difference between the intelligent and moral parts, and the rest of the world, lies in this, that the former are capable of knowing their Creator, and the end for which he made them, and capable of actively complying with his design" [EC 225]. The compliance of the creature with God, consisting empirically in the beauty of their active and cordial consent to the attractive beauty of His design, is understood theologically as consisting in a communion with the Holy Spirit, who "is himself the beauty and joy of the Creator" [Trinity 98], "the holiness and happiness of God," and therefore "the holiness and happiness of every holy or truly virtuous creature of God, in heaven or earth" [Grace 56]. Alternatively, the creature's compliance may be construed theologically as his conforming to the primary beauty that is the spiritual image of God in man [RA 256]. On the other hand, the creature's noncompliance with the design of God, his rebellion and dissention in constituting for himself alternative and lesser kingdoms, is nonetheless contained within the divine governance according to the same principle. For consent is, in Edwards' view, a constitutive principle of intelligent perceiving being. It is, for example, the creature's consent rather than any physical act or divine imputation that constitutes him as one with Adam in his sin [OS 483f]. It is what men consent to that defines who and what they are and locates them in the universal scheme of things. It is "by virtue of the full consent of the hearts of Adam's posterity to that first apostasy" that they are one with Adam in his sin; therefore, "the sin of the apostasy is not theirs merely because God imputes it to them; but it is truly and properly theirs, and on that ground, God imputes it to them" [OS 493]. So Edwards insists that God does and will treat men according to their consent or dissent. All who really consent to being-in-general will be regarded and treated as they therefore and therein are—as one with Christ in his cordial consent to God and to His design in the creation.

While theological explanations are not wanting, the major criterion of cordial consent among men to the dominion and design of God remains for Edwards the empirical one of Christian practice. "There may be several good evidences that a tree is a fig tree; but the highest and most proper evidence of it, is that it actually bears figs" [RA 443]. "Herein chiefly appears the power of true godliness, viz. in its being effectual in practice" [RA 393]. But the reason Christian practice is such a reliable test of cordial consent is once again theological. It has to do with the very nature of divine things, particularly that about them that is the peculiar object of holy religious affections—their beauty.

> The reason why gracious affections issue in holy practice, also further appears from the kind of excellency of divine things, that it has been observed is the foundation of all holy affection, viz. their moral excellency, or the beauty of their holiness. No won-

der that a love to holiness, for holiness' sake, inclines persons to practice holiness, and to practice everything that is holy . . . That which men love, they desire to have and to be united to, and possessed of. That beauty which men delight in, they desire to be adorned with. Those acts which men delight in, they necessarily incline to do. [RA 394]

Since delight is an essential ingredient of the apprehension of anything as beautiful, action according to one's own pleasure will be in conformity with the beauty that is the primary object of delight and love. The motive of Christian practice is, therefore, identical with the love of God, which is its foundation. "When God is loved aright, he is loved for his excellency, and the beauty of his nature . . . And all things that are loved with a truly holy love, are loved from the same respect to God. Love to God is the foundation of gracious love to men" [CF 7]. If God is loved for His beauty, the fruit of it will be Christian practice in conformity with the claims of that beauty, tending to build up the dominion of primary beauty in the world.

Christian practice, in these terms, will not be judged primarily according to distinct and isolated acts. It will consist rather in a continuing habit and disposition of the agent and will be judged primarily according to the pattern of the person's dispositions, actions, and relations. Those who love God will "have the whole image of Christ upon them" only if there is in them "something of the same beautiful proportion in the image, which is in the original" [RA 365]—namely, a "beautiful symmetry and proportion" with respect to both the whole of the object of their love and the whole of their own action through time. Respecting the object of love,

as there is a monstrous disproportion in the love of some, in its exercises towards different persons, so there is in their seeming exercises of love towards the same persons. Some men shew a love to others as to their outward man, they are liberal of their worldly substance, and often give to the poor; but have no love to, or concern for the souls of men. Others pretend a great love to men's souls, that are not compassionate and charitable towards their bodies. The making a great shew of love, pity, and distress for souls, cost 'em nothing; but in order to shew mercy to men's bodies, they must part with money out of their pockets. But a true Christian love to our brethren, extends both to their souls and bodies. [RA 369]

And respecting the whole of their own action through time, those who love God will not be "like comets, that appear for a while with a mighty blaze," but rather "like the fixed stars, which, though they rise and set, and are often clouded, yet are steadfast in their orb, and may truly be said to shine with a constant light" [RA 369f]. New men in Christ will endeavor to be "proportioned Christians" [CF 409]. There is in this both the primary beauty of cordial consent and the secondary beauty of proportion; the latter alone cannot constitute the foundation or even the sure sign of true virtue and holiness, but it is for Edwards a sign and an expression of the former. Anything that has primary beauty will therefore also possess secondary beauty, but the presence of the latter is in itself no sure sign of the former. True virtue or holiness will have a secondary beauty of proportion and harmony; but the critical pattern will be rather the beauty or the deformity manifest in the relations of consent and dissent among beings and systems of being in which the person is involved.

An even grander beauty than is manifest in personal virtue and holiness of individuals is the beauty embodied in the constitution and visible manifestation to others of genuine community among men. Other persons will be loved and enjoyed not so much with an eye for the moral beauty that is in them individually as with an eye (and taste) for the beauty that is manifest in their relations to other beings generally and especially to other spiritual beings. The communion of the saints in heaven is not the only form of fulfilment the divine promise can take. Edwards' postmillennialist reading of history disposed him to look for anticipations of the heavenly city on earth. He envisaged a time when in "the day of the gospel" Christ would set up His kingdom in all its power and beauty: "All the world shall then be as one church, one orderly, regular, beautiful society" [WR 493]. It will be

> a time wherein the whole earth shall be united as one holy city, one heavenly family, men of all nations shall as it were dwell together, and sweetly correspond one with another, as brethren and children of the same father . . . a time wherein this whole great society shall appear in glorious beauty, in genuine amiable Christianity, and excellent order, as *a city compacted together, the perfection of beauty, an eternal excellency* shining with a reflection of the glory of Jehovah *risen upon it,* which shall be attractive and ravishing to all kings and nations. [HA 446; italics original]

Short of that day there will be beauties enough to embody and display in the communities of men. In 1747, in response to a proposal by some ministers in Scotland that the churches on both sides of the Atlantic unite in a "concert of prayer" for yet further outpourings of the Holy Spirit, Edwards published a long essay in which he takes note of some forms of the beauty of community.

> How condecent, how beautiful, and of good tendency would it be, for multitudes of Christians, in various parts of the world, by explicit agreement, to unite in such prayer as is proposed to us.
>
> Union is one of the most amiable things that pertains to human society; yea, it is one of the most beautiful and happy things on earth, which indeed makes earth most like heaven. God has made of one blood all nations of men to dwell on the face of the earth; hereby teaching us this moral lesson, that it becomes mankind all to be united as one family . . . A civil union, or a harmonious agreement among men in the management of their secular concerns, is amiable; but much more a pious union and sweet agreement in the great business for which man was created, and had power given him beyond the brutes; even the business of religion; the life and soul of which is love. Union is spoken of in Scripture as the peculiar beauty of the church of Christ . . . As it is the glory of the church of Christ that in all her members, however dispersed, she is thus one, one holy society, one family, one body; so it is highly desirable that this union should be manifested, and become visible. [HA 462f]

Cordial union among men is good, and the visibility of it manifest in public celebration of that union makes it even better. "Union among God's people in prayer is truly beautiful," so "it must needs be desirable to Christians that such union be visible . . . for if it be not visible, it cannot be beheld" [HA 467f]. And wherein is the beauty of what cannot be beheld?

Primary beauty, it must be remembered, is defined by cordial consent to being rather than by harmony or proportion; the more cordial the consent and the larger the system of being to which the consent is extended, the greater the beauty. Thus the beauty of true virtue or holiness consists in benevolence to being-in-general and benevolence to any private system of being, however extended—even if it include mankind itself or the whole system of living beings—only in due subordination to and as a part of benevolence to the universal system and to God as the alpha and omega of that system. Furthermore, the beauty of true virtue or holiness consists, in the first instance, in benevolence rather than in complacence, in an active engagement of the self for the good of the widest possible system of being and beauty, and only secondarily in the enjoyment of the beauty of being. Such enjoyment or complacence is for Edwards necessarily and internally related to benevolence and is indeed an image in man of joy, which is one of the summary perfections of God. But if it were set above or apart from its appropriate objective foundation in benevolence to being-in-general, it would become a merely subjective and self-indulgent "complacence" in the pejorative sense of the term.

Captivated by the spiritual beauty of God, men of true virtue will be drawn, according to Edwards, to relate themselves to all things and to every limited system of things and persons in such a way as to affirm and celebrate and draw all things towards the larger systems of being to which they properly belong. They will attempt to build up and maximize the visibility of the image of the divine beauty in all creatures to whom that image properly belongs according to the will of their Creator and to overcome everything that breeds deformity among creatures. With a vision informed by the largest beauty, they will have a true measure for the discernment of such deformities.[28] Nor will they fail to both celebrate and respect (consent to) the secondary image of that same beauty in the natural world of things animate and inanimate. No parochial community will form for them a limit to their affection and consent; but neither will any small community or single person be scorned as beneath their high regard, for their consent will be to being as such and to the good of all beings as they are given to and encountered by the self in its personal and corporate relations of consent and dissent. The contrary possibilities of dissent carry with them destruction incalculable. But Edwards is confident that the power of God in all His splendid beauty will ultimately prevail and bring to nothing all the forces of dissension and deformity. Such a faith carries with it a confidence that men can and shall, by the grace of God, be reawakened to the reality of the divine beauty enough to consent and "actively comply" with that design.

If God undertakes to fulfill His purpose of redeeming the creation through the attractive and creative power of His own beauty, then those who love Him will respond in kind and according to the measure of their capacities,

28. "From a knowledge of divine excellencies follows a knowledge of spiritual deformities and is from the same principle; the same knowledge whereby he [the regenerate man] knows the excellency of holiness and the beauty of Jesus Christ, he also knows the deformity of sin"—especially his own. Sermon on I Cor. 2:14, Yale University Manuscript Collection.

not only to delight in the beauty of God and all things in Him but also to enlarge by their own cordial response the dominion of that beauty, constituting
ever wider communities in which a like beauty is embodied and from which
it might shine forth as a light to other men. Thus would be widened the circle
of those who would have ample occasion and liberty to glorify God (celebrate His being) and enjoy Him forever (delight in His beauty).

POSTSCRIPT

POSTSCRIPT

As an addendum to the foregoing essay I want to exhibit, by way of one example, something of what may be expected to follow for theological ethics and moral philosophy from the study of the place of beauty and sensibility in Edwards' thought.

One contemporary issue to which those dimensions of his thought are relevant is the continuing search for more adequate models in terms of which to construe the structure and dynamics of the moral life of free and responsible creatures. The models of self, world, and God that emerge out of Edwards' effort to construe those structures and dynamics have striking affinities with at least two recent efforts to deal with this problem. I have in mind the work of the contemporary philosopher Albert Hofstadter[1] and the late Christian moralist H. Richard Niebuhr.[2] One factor that suggests the fruitfulness of bringing Edwards, Hofstadter, and Niebuhr into conversation with each other as moral philosophers is the similarity of their conceptions of the unity of understanding and will in something like an aesthetic-affectional model of the self. Closely related to this is their general approach to ethics.

While the development of Niebuhr's thought shows him to be increasingly indebted to Edwards,[3] Hofstadter's thought is probably not informed by any direct acquaintance with him. Neither Niebuhr nor Hofstadter betray any

1. A major interest of Professor Hofstadter's has been aesthetics and its relevance to ethics. His ontological approach to art and beauty is developed in *Truth and Art* (New York, Columbia University Press, 1965).

2. The works of H. R. Niebuhr most relevant to what follows are *The Responsible Self* (New York, Harper and Row, 1963) and *Radical Monotheism and Western Culture* (New York, Harper and Brothers, 1960). See especially his essay on "The Center of Value," reprinted as a Supplementary Essay in the latter volume (pp. 100–13).

3. As Niebuhr himself writes in 1960, reflecting upon the direction of his own thought in the preceding decade, "I discover . . . a greater kinship with all theologians of Christian experience than with the theologians of Christian doctrine. So I find myself, though with many hesitations, closer to Edwards and Schleiermacher, Coleridge, Bushnell, and Maurice than to Barth and the dogmatic biblical theology current today in wide circles" (*How My Mind Has Changed,* ed. H. E. Fey [New York, Meridian, 1961], p. 76).

direct acquaintance with the other's thought. Yet their reflections about a common problem has led both of them to move in a direction closely related to that taken by Edwards. Hofstadter is led to a model of the self and of the moral order explicitly derived from his aesthetics and from his concept of beauty as the revelation of the validity and truth of spiritual being. Niebuhr is led to a model of the self as responsible, responding being and to a model of the moral order construed in terms of a relational value theory. Neither of Niebuhr's models is explicitly aesthetic in character, but they are closely related to aesthetic-affectional models such as those of Hostadter and Edwards. This is more obviously the case with respect to his model of the self as primarily responding being. With respect to Niebuhr's conception of the moral order, however, the relation to an aesthetic model is more direct, though less obvious, for his relational value theory was developed in part out of continuing intellectual dialogue with Edwards' more aesthetically conceived reflections about the same matters. Niebuhr's models of the self and the moral order remain essentially moral rather than aesthetic, but it is helpful to a right understanding of both him and Edwards to emphasize the close relation between the moral and the aesthetic. Niebuhr himself frequently warned his students against reifying the distinctions between them and conceiving of them as independent realms.

The paths Niebuhr and Hofstadter take in their search for new and more adequate models of man as a moral creature and of the world as a moral order are related by a common motive. They both set out from a dissatisfaction with the adequacy of the models offered by the two major approaches into which ethics has traditionally been divided—deontology and teleology.[4] Edwards addresses himself to a similar and even more unsatisfactory set of polarized alternatives—legalism and (theological) utilitarianism,[5] alterna-

4. Deontology begins by asking about "that which is binding" (Greek: *deon*); its first questions are about obligations, duties, laws, rules, and about obedience to them in right action. Teleology begins by asking about ends (Greek: *telos*); its first questions are about goals, values, purposes, ideals, and goods to be envisaged, sought, and achieved.

5. In his doctoral dissertation on "The Ethics of Jonathan Edwards" (unpublished Ph.D. dissertation, Yale University, 1944), written, incidentally, under the direction of H. R. Niebuhr, Clyde A. Holbrook distinguishes between "theological objectivism" and "theological utilitarianism" and finds that a large measure of the permanent validity of Edwards' ethic consists in his repudiation of "theological utilitarianism."

William K. Frankena, in his Foreword to a recent edition of *The Nature of True Virtue* (Ann Arbor, University of Michigan Press, 1960, p. viii), makes the curious assertion that:

Edwards' essay was the beginning of a tradition of teleological and utilitarian thinking which strongly opposed the deontological intuitionism prevailing in American

tives that might properly be construed as corrupt forms, respectively, of deontology and teleology. Neither Niebuhr nor Hofstadter rejects deontology and teleology as irrelevant or unilluminating; they reject them only as the source of the primary models for their approaches to moral philosophy.

Like Edwards, both Niebuhr and Hofstadter try to ground their conceptions of the perfection of being in nothing less than an adequate conception of being-itself. That is, they both try to articulate the conviction that whatever the things that are good and ought to be and the things that are right and ought to be done, they have their only sure foundation in the things that *are*. As Niebuhr expresses it, "radical monotheism dethrones all absolutes short of the principle of being itself . . . Its two great mottoes are: 'I am the Lord thy God; thou shalt have no other gods before me' and 'Whatever is, is good.'" Such radical monotheism finds its "value-center" in "the principle of being itself" and "is less than radical if it makes a distinction between the principle of being and the principle of value." Three essential "notes" of radically monotheistic faith, then, according to Niebuhr, are the conviction "that the valuing, saving power in the world is the principle of being itself," that is, that "God is nothing less than being"; confidence "that the ultimate

---

ethics in the nineteenth century. For over a hundred years the Edwardian ethics was stated and restated by such men as Samuel Hopkins, Joseph Bellamy, Timothy Dwight, N. W. Taylor, C. G. Finney, Mark Hopkins, and J. H. Fairchild. Through them Edwards may have been at least partly responsible for the textbook vogue enjoyed in the early 1800's by William Paley's utilitarian *Principles of Moral and Political Philosophy,* and for the eventual triumph of teleological ethics at the opening of the present century.

It is not all unreasonable to regard Edwards' ethics as teleological. But his whole program is so thoroughly opposed to utilitarianism in every form that it makes little sense to identify teleological and utilitarian ethics with each other. The extent to which utilitarianism developed in American ethics, even among so-called Edwardseans, cannot be taken as constituting a tradition begun by Edwards. It must, in fact, more properly be taken as a measure of his failure to impress his influence upon later ethics. If Paley was employed for moral instruction by Edwards' would-be followers in the nineteenth century, it only goes to show how far they had traveled from Edwards' aesthetic-teleological vision of the moral order as governed by the laws of beauty according to God's pleasure to Paley's mechanical-teleological vision of the moral order as governed by the laws of mechanical contrivance in the interest of man's happiness. Edwards is not unmindful of mechanics, and he occasionally employs the image of the world as a complicated system of wheels [e.g. EC 204, 244]. But it is beauty rather than mechanics that provides his central clue to order in the world. The difference between Edwards' and Paley's approaches to the discernment of order in the world finds corresponding expression in the difference between Paley's mechanical and Edwards' aesthetic model of the relation of God to the world, and in the difference between the Deistic and the Edwardsean visions of the nature and character of God.

principle of being gives and maintains and reestablishes worth," that is, that "being is God, namely, valuer and savior"; and some concrete challenge or call to men "to make the cause of that God their cause."[6]

Hofstadter's way of affirming that nothing less than the principle of being is an adequate foundation for the principle of the perfection of being is to argue in terms of a more Hegelian metaphysics.

> In his search for a grounding of his practical action and life, man looks in the two directions already mentioned: the axiological or teleological and the deontological. That is, he looks either to goods and ends to be accomplished or to obligations, duties, and laws to be obeyed—or to some combination of the two. And in both directions he finds himself confronted by the limitation of practical existence as such.

Hofstadter finds this limitation in the fact that "about any ends or goods the practical question can always be raised again" and that similarly,

> if I come to the point at which a decision rests on some concept of duty, as e.g. the duty to fulfill my promises, the question can always be asked: But is this my duty? And if this is pushed back to another duty, more ultimate, such as the duty to realize my moral self or the duty to treat others as ends and not as mere means, the question reappears: But is this my duty? Ought I to try to realize myself or to treat others as ends?[7]

He concludes that the "practical life cannot be its own foundation. The question of what justifies the will in its final decisions is not answerable by another decision of the will." The practical will "does not have the capacity to set its own boundary or end." "What could remove arbitrariness from freedom would be a knowledge that is competent to tell it what its bounds should be, thus providing it with a truth that is appropriate to it as freedom, as will." It would have to do so, therefore, "not by violence—which can always be questioned anew—but by the power of persuasion." The question he asks, then, is whether there is such a truth. "Is there a form of truth and knowledge that would make the person competent to break the infinitude of the merely practical will and give measure to it?"[8]

---

6. Niebuhr, *Radical Monotheism,* pp. 37, 32, 43.
7. Hofstadter, *Truth and Art,* pp. 123, 124.
8. Ibid., pp. 125, 127, 128, 124, 128.

Hofstadter's affirmative answer to this question is bound up with conceptions of levels of truth—"truth-about" (e.g. truth of statement), "thing-truth," and "truth of being" (e.g. truth of spirit)[9]—and of the relation of understanding, which aims at uncovering the existent, and will, which aims at governing the existent, in a higher aesthetic-affectional unity of the self as personal being.[10] These conceptions need not detain us here, but their relation to Edwards' and Niebuhr's conceptions of the self and of the moral order will be of interest later. What is of interest in the present context is that Hofstadter finds in beauty the model for such a truth—a truth that is at once the truth or validity of objective being and the truth or validity of the subjective, personal being of a free, responsible agent. Hofstadter finds in beauty the disclosure of the unity of being and perfection of being, of being and being good, or, as Niebuhr expresses it, of being and value, without which there would be no reliable foundation for the moral life.

Both Niebuhr and Hofstadter, starting out from a shared dissatisfaction with deontological and teleological models of the self and the moral order, move in different but related ways toward aesthetic-affectional models of the self and of the moral order that have a good deal in common with the models developed by Edwards in terms of his concepts of beauty and sensibility. Both Niebuhr and Hofstadter see themselves as cutting between and perhaps transcending—though not leaving behind or discarding as irrelevant—the models emerging out of the polarized alternatives of deontological and teleological approaches to moral philosophy or ethics. Hofstadter sees his path carrying him closer to deontology than to teleology, for it is from the former that he picks up the concept of validity, which is decisive for his conception of beauty. For Niebuhr and Edwards, on the other hand, teleology lies closer than deontology to the paths they take towards their primary models. But the very effort to fix such distinctions serves to remind one of the fact that these approaches and their related models are not usually encountered in moral

9. "When something is truly, as that thing, it has truth of being. It is as its own essence requires it to be; it has an essence that requires it to be itself. Man's essence is spirit. His truth is truth of spirit. For man, to be truly is to be truly as a spiritual being, in his finitude. Spirit includes cognition, and hence truth in the first sense, as truth-about, is included in truth of spiritual being. But truth of spiritual being goes beyond cognition to the actuality of being itself" (*Truth and Art,* p. viii).

10. "This means that we are asking about the possibility of a mode of human existence that encompasses the two previous forms of existence within itself. Man exists as the aim to uncover the existent; he exists as the aim to govern the existent. Now we ask whether and how it is possible for man to exist in such a way as to comprehend both uncovering and governing, both understanding and will, in the unity of a new truth" (Ibid., p. 128).

philosophy as clear and sharp alternatives but rather as differences of emphasis. As Hofstadter says, the teleological and deontological spheres "overlap, since there are rules concerning means-ends and goods, and there are
values belonging to rules. Nevertheless the concepts are distinct and they distinguish different aspects of things."[11] Deontology and teleology are both present in the thought of all three of these men, as they are in any serious ethic,
though for all three the primary and formative models are derived from
other approaches in which different aspects of human experience and reality
are taken as yielding the primary clue to the character of the whole.

Hofstadter begins by identifying axiology with teleology, and rejects therefore the concept of value as a clue to the aesthetic realm from which he takes
his primary model of self and world. His own approach is more closely related to deontology, with its emphasis upon the concept of the right and the
priority of rightness over goodness. His approach to aesthetics is through the
concept of validity rather than that of value, which he finds to be inappro-
priate to the discipline of aesthetics. He relies heavily upon the distinction
between validity and value and upon a brief etymological analysis of the two
terms; validity consists in "the power of rightness and the rightness of
power,"[12] while value moves in "a somewhat different semantic region." "The
emphasis in the concept of value is on the presence in the object of something good, useful, desirable, or estimable" and has to do more with the evaluative response of the subject than with a judgment about the object itself.
"To value something is to appreciate or prize it, estimate its worth, rate or
grade, appraise it with regard to some valued quality"; it is to judge the object
with respect to some relation to self or to things in which the self has an interest. On the other hand, he finds that "the emphasis in the concept of validity is on the combination of rightness and power in the object" and is therefore a judgment respecting the properties of the object itself rather than of its
relation to the projects and values (aesthetic and otherwise) of other beings. The distinction between validity and value is one of emphasis rather
than a sharp disjunction. But the difference of emphasis is one that Hofstadter feels is crucial for aesthetics and therefore also for his conception of
self and world in terms of a model derived from the aesthetic realm. "Nothing," he says, "is as fatal to aesthetic discernment and to philosophy of the
aesthetic as [the] tendency to confuse the beautiful—the central aesthetic

11. Ibid., p. 111.
12. Albert Hofstadter, "Validity Versus Value: An Essay in Philosophical Aesthetics,"
The Journal of Philosophy, 59 (1962), 613.

phenomenon—with the good, validity with value." He argues that this tendency leads to making the aesthetic derive from what is essentially non-aesthetic by regarding something as aesthetically valuable because it conduces to values that are themselves nonaesthetic—for aesthetic objects can be valuable on many grounds besides their beauty. Hofstadter would have aesthetics as a discipline abandon such expressions as "aesthetic value" and "aesthetic goodness" and attend rather to beauty. "Aesthetic thinking has been shunted, in its concern with finding values, away from the specifically aesthetic character of the work, its beauty, to the sources in it of the attribution of value to it."[13]

The result of the focus Hofstadter finds in much contemporary aesthetic theory upon the sources in the work of art of its value is, in substance, that any theory about the identity of those sources reflects the values of the theorist's epoch and culture. If it is a good theory, relatively speaking, it may be recognized for its "authenticity as a genuine manifestation of the living art-reality of a period," but what it provides is only a "limited *aesthetic* rather than a comprehensive *aesthetics.*"

> The history of aesthetics is littered with doctrines that, like expression theory, were the conceptualized voices of the art impulse of their day . . . Such doctrines, each an *aesthetic* in the sense of being an option for one among the many possibilities opened up in the form of being constituted by art and each, therefore, constituting the conceptual counterpart of a possible form of art, are products of authentic spiritual forces. But they must not be confused with *aesthetics,* or with the *theory of fine art,* whose aim it is not to speak for a single kind of art but to understand art in all its forms and dimensions.[14]

Properly conceived aesthetics would look for validity rather than value and would find it manifest in the beauty of its object.

Approaching aesthetics through validity rather than value, Hofstadter finds in the concept of validity not only the key to aesthetics as a discipline but also the key to a new model of the self and of the moral order. "Aesthetic validity is the revelation of spiritual validity, which is itself the validity of being at the level of spirit." Hofstadter therefore agrees with Edwards that beauty is the model of ontological and spiritual or moral excellence as well as

13. Ibid., pp. 608, n. 1, 609, 610.
14. Hofstadter, *Truth and Art,* pp. 18, 17, 21.

of aesthetic validity or excellence. "Beauty," he says, "is the revelation of the truth of (spiritual) being."

> It is just this relation of identity between beauty and the validity of (spiritual) being that makes beauty philosophically important. If beauty were simply the capacity to give us satisfying or delightful or otherwise valuable experience, it would, like perfume, be valuable and worth a price, but philosophically insignificant. And in a parallel way, it is because beauty is truth regarding the validity of spiritual being that he who seeks to live in a valid way will try to understand and live with beauty. But also, for the same reason, he will try to live beyond beauty.[15]

H. Richard Niebuhr is also dissatisfied with teleological and deontological models, so he develops a model of the self as responsible and a model of the structure and dynamics of the moral order in terms of a relational theory of value. In *The Responsible Self* he explores the illuminative capacity of the idea of responsibility, of "the image of man-the-answerer, man engaged in dialogue, man acting in response to action upon him." He finds that "this idea makes some aspects of our life as agents intelligible in a way that the teleology and deontology of traditional thought cannot do."[16]

The idea of responsibility is to Niebuhr's understanding of the self as the idea of sensibility is to Edwards'. Niebuhr's model of the moral agent and religious man as primarily a responding (response-able) being bears close affinity to Edwards' aesthetic-affectional model. For example, Niebuhr distinguishes within "reasoning faith" between aesthetic reason and analytic reason and finds in the former the essential "sensible element" that we have seen to be so fundamental to Edwards' conception of religious knowledge.

> Reason is present in this faith. First of all it appears as a kind of aesthetic reason which intuits the intention of the divine artist in the wholeness of his masterpieces; but it is present also as analytic, comparing, and relating reason, as distinguishing and question-raising, even as doubting reason. Reasoning faith, confident in God as the source of the glory as well as of the being [Edwards might have said "of the beauty as well as of the being"] of all creatures,

15. Hofstadter, "Validity Versus Value," p. 615 and n. 7.
16. Niebuhr, *The Responsible Self,* pp. 56, 67.

makes its distinctions and comparisons among celestial and mundane, human and subhuman beings.[17]

The aesthetic element appears also in Niebuhr's interpretation of virtue. Where Edwards regards virtue as a form of inherent beauty (being's consent to being) and of sensibility to objective being and beauty, Niebuhr interprets virtue as a form of value and as consisting in responsive relations of the self to other beings.

> The gifts which we call theological virtues . . . are given not as states of character but as relations to other beings and particularly as relations to God. They are given with and in the gift of the object toward which as actions of the self they are directed . . . Love is given with the gift of the lovely, the love-attracting; it is called forth by the gift of God himself as the supremely and wholly desirable good; by the gift of the neighbor, as the one beloved by God, as lovely, and as loving the self. Hereby we not only know love but conceive love, that God makes himself known in his beauty, as Jonathan Edwards would say.[18]

What the moral agent is responsive to in his responsibility—the reality to which he is related—is interpreted by Niebuhr as always encountered at once as being and as value. "Value," he says, "is present wherever being confronts being . . . It is not a function of being as such but of being in relation to being." The reverence for being and beauty, which is central to Edwards' whole theological-philosophical-moral program, is shared by Niebuhr, for whom "the starting point of all inquiry lies in the recognition of *that which is*" and "the solid founding of value on the nature of being." Niebuhr makes it clear that his relational theory of value is based upon his understanding of the manner in which selves encounter reality—as being and value, as being and good, or, in Edwards' terms, as being and beauty. He is also quite explicit about the close relation between this conception and Edwards' conception of the same encountered reality as at once being and beauty.

> The basis of this relational value theory is not the relation of existence to essence, it is that of self to other. Philosophically, it is more

---

17. Niebuhr, *Radical Monotheism,* p. 14. See also Niebuhr's analysis of the relation of the affections and the imagination to reason in *The Meaning of Revelation* (New York, Macmillan, 1952), esp. Ch. III, pp. 91–137, on "Reasons of the Heart."

18. Niebuhr, "Reflections on Faith, Hope, and Love" (unpublished manuscript).

indebted to G. H. Mead than to Aristotle; theologically, it is closer,
I believe, to Jonathan Edwards ("consent of being to being") than
to Thomas Aquinas.[19]

Niebuhr does not begin (as Hofstadter does) by identifying axiology with
teleology; he does not identify the term value with teleological terms such
as end and goal. He is therefore free, as Hofstadter is not, to employ the concept of value in constructing his response model as an alternative emphasis to
the primacy of teleology as well as of deontology. He employs the concept
of value primarily to designate one of the two fundamental aspects of reality
as it is encountered by, and as it shapes the character of, moral and religious
creatures—reality as being and as good.

The concepts of beauty and sensibility, then, are to Edwards' thought as
the concepts of value and responsibility are to Niebuhr's. Niebuhr's categories are more distinctively moral, as compared with Edwards' more aesthetic categories. But Edwards' definition of beauty and sensibility in terms
of consent suggests a relevance to political life that may be as great as Niebuhr's model of responsibility—and the political is a dimension of being human that aesthetic models of the self and of the moral life tend to neglect or
distort. It may be that we are in need of a model of human excellence at once
aesthetic and political. If so, Edwards' aesthetic-affectional model of the self
may have some advantages over Niebuhr's model of responsibility, with
which it nonetheless has so much in common. Consent is a political as well as
an aesthetic concept. It may also have the advantage of more active connota-
tions than the more passive symbol of response, with which Niebuhr works.
This is a direction and a possibility that the study of Jonathan Edwards can
help us to explore.

19. Niebuhr, *Radical Monotheism*, pp. 107, 111, 105, n. 1.

BIBLIOGRAPHY

Bibliographical Essay

It may be useful to call the reader's attention to the work of those who have contributed most to my own understanding of Edwards. Although I have had to mention some of the qualifications that must be made in his interpretation of Edwards, Perry Miller must be mentioned first not only because of his own achievements but also because he has been a seminal influence in generating serious Edwards scholarship. Douglas Elwood's book appeared after the argument of this essay had taken shape but not too late to be very instructive. John E. Smith's Introduction to the *Religious Affections* (Yale Edition) has been especially helpful in understanding Edwards' work as a whole and not only that volume. My interpretation of Edwards' "is as" volitional equation owes something to the stimulation of Paul Ramsey's Introduction to the *Freedom of the Will* (Yale Edition). The unpublished doctoral dissertations of Clyde A. Holbrook (Yale, 1944), John Clayton Feaver (Yale, 1949), and Thomas A. Schafer (Duke, 1951) have been especially instructive. I have had occasion to express some reservations about Alan Heimert's systematic interpretation of Edwards, but as cultural history his book opens up whole new dimensions to the study of Edwards and of the Edwardseans, and I benefited greatly from reading the doctoral dissertation (Harvard, 1960) that was an earlier draft of his book. Although Joseph Haroutunian has not written extensively on Edwards, he has in occasional articles been pointing for some decades in the general direction taken by this essay. Although Conrad Cherry's book is primarily concerned with other dimensions of Edwards' thought—his approach is through his understanding of faith— I would be missing an opportunity if I did not take this occasion to recommend it for its comprehensive grasp of Edwards.

Among the Edwards manuscript materials there were few surprises in the unpublished sermons, though some of them are cited in this essay. The "Miscellanies," however, proved to be an even richer resource than I had expected, and I have drawn heavily upon them. They are important not because they contain unexpected ideas but because they give further support and substance to my conviction of the essential unity and continuity of Edwards' thought as well as to my view that an important key to that unity is to be found in the twin aesthetic concepts of beauty and sensibility. The central themes of Edwards' thought are already present in his earliest "Notes" and "Miscellanies" and are for the most part only developed rather than transformed by later "Miscellanies," manuscripts, and published works.

Collected Works by Edwards

The Works of President Edwards, ed. Samuel Austin, 8 vols. Worcester, Mass., 1808–09.

The Works of President Edwards, ed. Sereno E. Dwight, 10 vols. New York, 1829–30.

The Works of President Edwards, a reprint of the Worcester edition of 1808–09 with some additions, 4 vols. New York, Leavitt & Allen, 1843.

The Works of Jonathan Edwards, gen. ed. Perry Miller, New Haven, Yale University Press. Vol. 1, 1957; Vol. 2, 1959.

Additional Works by Edwards

"A Treatise on Grace," in *Selections From the Unpublished Writings of Jonathan Edwards of America,* ed. A. B. Grosart, Edinburgh, 1865.

An Unpublished Essay of Edwards on the Trinity, ed. G. P. Fisher, New York, 1903.

Charity and its Fruits, ed. Tryon Edwards, New York, Robert Carter & Brothers, 1856.

Freedom of the Will, ed. with intro. Paul Ramsey, New Haven, Yale University Press, 1957.

Images or Shadows of Divine Things, ed. with intro. Perry Miller, New Haven, Yale University Press, 1948.

Jonathan Edwards: Selections, ed. with intro. Clarence H. Faust and Thomas H. Johnson, rev. ed. New York, Hill and Wang, 1962.

"Notes on the Mind," in *The Philosophy of Jonathan Edwards From His Private Notebooks,* ed. Harvey G. Townsend, Eugene, University of Oregon Press, 1955.

Religious Affections, ed. with intro. John E. Smith, New Haven, Yale University Press, 1959.

The Nature of True Virtue, foreword William K. Frankena, Ann Arbor, University of Michigan Press, Ann Arbor Paperback, 1960.

Edwards Manuscripts

"Interleaved Bible," Yale Collection of Edwards Manuscripts, Yale University Library.

"Miscellanies" Journal, Yale Collection of Edwards Manuscripts, Yale University Library. The "Miscellanies" consist of ten notebooks containing 1,360 entries, about half of which have been published in various collections; the most useful and accessible is the selection in Harvey G. Townsend, ed., *The Philosophy of Jonathan Edwards From His Private Notebooks,* Eugene, University of Oregon Press, 1955. Thomas A. Schafer is editing what will be a definitive and first complete edition, soon to be published in several volumes of the new Yale University Press edition of Edwards' collected works.

Sermons, Yale Collection of Edwards Manuscripts, Yale University Library. About half the 1,150 manuscripts in this collection are full-length. Five volumes of sermons are projected for the new Yale University Press edition of Edwards' collected works.

Books About Edwards

Aldridge, Alfred Owen, *Jonathan Edwards,* New York, Washington Square Press, 1964.

Allen, A. V. G., *Life and Writings of Jonathan Edwards,* Edinburgh, T. & T. Clark, 1889.

Cherry, Conrad, *The Theology of Jonathan Edwards: A Reappraisal,* Garden City, N.Y., Doubleday, Anchor Books, 1966.

Dwight, Sereno E., *The Life of President Edwards,* in *The Works of President Edwards,* Vol. 1, New York, 1829–30.

Elwood, Douglas J., *The Philosophical Theology of Jonathan Edwards,* New York, Columbia University Press, 1960.

Feidelson, Charles, *Symbolism and American Literature,* Chicago, University of Chicago Press, 1953.

Gardiner, H. Norman, ed., *Jonathan Edwards: A Retrospect,* Boston, Houghton Mifflin, 1901.

Gaustad, Edwin Scott, *The Great Awakening in New England,* New York, Harper, 1957.

Haroutunian, Joseph, *Piety Versus Moralism: the Passing of the New England Theology,* New York, Holt, 1932.

Heimert, Alan, *Religion and the American Mind: From the Great Awakening to the Revolution,* Cambridge, Harvard University Press, 1966.

Howard, Leon, *"The Mind" of Jonathan Edwards: A Reconstructed Text,* Berkeley, University of California Press, 1963.

Johnson, Thomas H., *The Printed Writings of Jonathan Edwards, 1703–1758, A Bibliography,* Princeton, Princeton University Press, 1940.

Lewis, R. W. B., *The American Adam,* Chicago, University of Chicago Press, 1955.

McGiffert, Arthur C., Jr., *Jonathan Edwards,* New York, Harper, 1932.

Miller, Perry, *Errand Into the Wilderness*, Cambridge, Harvard University Press, 1956.

———, *Jonathan Edwards*, New York, Meridian Books, 1959.

———, *Nature's Nation*, Cambridge, Harvard University Press, 1967.

———, *Orthodoxy in Massachusetts*, Cambridge, Harvard University Press, 1933.

———, *The New England Mind: The Seventeenth Century*, New York, Macmillan, 1939.

Schneider, Herbert W., *A History of American Philosophy*, New York, Columbia University Press, 1947.

———, *The Puritan Mind*, Ann Arbor, University of Michigan Press, Ann Arbor Paperback, 1958.

Smith, James Ward, and A. Leland Jamison, eds., *The Shaping of American Religion*, Princeton, Princeton University Press, 1961.

Smyth, E. C., ed., *Exercises Commemorating the Two-hundredth Anniversary of the Birth of Jonathan Edwards*, Andover, Mass., Andover Press, 1904.

Townsend, Harvey G., *Philosophical Ideas in the United States*, New York, American Book, 1934.

Winslow, Ola E., *Jonathan Edwards*, New York, Macmillan, 1941.

Wright, Conrad, *The Beginnings of Unitarianism in America*, Boston, Starr King, 1955.

Articles About Edwards

Aldridge, A. O., "Edwards and Hutcheson," *Harvard Theological Review*, 44 (1951), 35–53.

Alexis, Gerhard T., "Jonathan Edwards and the Theocratic Ideal," *Church History*, 35 (1966), 328–43.

Beach, Waldo, "The Recovery of Jonathan Edwards," *Religion in Life*, 27 (1958), 286–89.

Cady, E. H., "The Artistry of Jonathan Edwards," *New England Quarterly*, 22 (1949), 61–72.

Carpenter, F. I., "The Radicalism of Jonathan Edwards," *New England Quarterly*, 4 (1931), 629–44.

Curtis, Matoon Munroe, "Kantian Elements in Jonathan Edwards," in *Festschrift fur Heinze*, Berlin, 1906.

Gardiner, H. N., "The Early Idealism of Jonathan Edwards," *Philosophical Review*, 9 (1900), 573–96.

Goen, C. C., "Edwards' New Departure in Eschatology," *Church History*, 28 (1959), 25–40.

Haroutunian, Joseph, "Jonathan Edwards: A Study in Godliness," *Journal of Religion*, 11 (1931), 400–19.

———, "Jonathan Edwards: Theologian of the Great Commandment," *Theology Today, 1* (1944), 361–77.

———, "Review Article on Perry Miller: *Jonathan Edwards*," *Theology Today, 7* (1951), 554–56.

Holbrook, Clyde A., "Jonathan Edwards and His Detractors," *Theology Today, 10* (1953), 384–96.

———, "Edwards and the Ethical Question," *Harvard Theological Review,* 60 (1967), 163–75.

Johnson, Thomas H., "Jonathan Edwards' Background of Reading," *Publications of the Colonial Society of Massachusetts, 28,* Transactions 1930–1933.

Miller, Perry, "Jonathan Edwards on the Sense of the Heart," *Harvard Theological Review, 41* (1948), 123–45.

Morris, William S., "Jonathan Edwards Reconsidered," *New England Quarterly, 30* (1957), 515–25.

Murphy, Arthur E., "Jonathan Edwards on Free Will and Moral Agency," *Philosophical Review, 68* (1959), 181–202.

Nichols, James H., "Perry Miller's *Jonathan Edwards*," *Church History,* 20 (1951), 75–82.

Park, Edwards Amasa, "Remarks of Jonathan Edwards on the Trinity," *Bibliotheca Sacra, 38* (1881), 147–87, 333–69.

Rice, Howard C., Jr., "Jonathan Edwards at Princeton; with a survey of Edwards materials in the Princeton University Library," *Princeton University Library Chronicle, 15* (1954), 69–89.

Schafer, Thomas A., "Jonathan Edwards and Justification by Faith," *Church History,* 20 (1951), 55–67.

———, "Jonathan Edwards' Conception of the Church," *Church History,* 24 (1955), 51–66.

Smith, Claude A., "Jonathan Edwards and the Way of Ideas," *Harvard Theological Review, 59* (1966), 153–73.

Smyth, E. C., "Jonathan Edwards' 'Idealism'," *American Journal of Theology, 1* (1897), 950–64.

Suter, Rufus, "A Note on Platonism in the Philosophy of Jonathan Edwards," *Harvard Theological Review, 52* (1959), 283–84.

———, "An American Pascal: Jonathan Edwards," *Scientific Monthly,* May, 1949, 338–42.

———, "The Concept of Morality in the Philosophy of Jonathan Edwards," *Journal of Religion, 14* (1934), 265–72.

———, "The Strange Universe of Jonathan Edwards," *Harvard Theological Review, 54* (1961), 125–28.

Tomas, Vincent, "The Modernity of Jonathan Edwards," *New England Quarterly, 25* (1952), 60–84.

Townsend, Harvey G., "Jonathan Edwards' Later Observations of Nature," *New England Quarterly, 13* (1940), 510–18.

———, "The Will and the Understanding in the Philosophy of Jonathan Edwards," *Church History, 16* (1947), 210–20.

Whittemore, Robert C., "Jonathan Edwards and the Theology of the Sixth Way," *Church History, 35* (1966), 60–75.

Wright, Conrad, "Edwards and the Arminians on the Freedom of the Will," *Harvard Theological Review, 35* (1942), 241–61.

Other Books Used or Cited

Arendt, Hannah, *Between Past and Future,* New York, Viking Press, 1961.

———, *The Human Condition,* Garden City, N.Y., Doubleday, Anchor Books, 1960.

Augustine, *An Augustine Synthesis,* ed. Erich Przywara, New York, Harper and Brothers, Torchbook, 1958.

Barth, Karl, *Church Dogmatics,* II/1, Edinburgh, T. & T. Clark, 1957.

Berdyaev, Nicolas, *The Destiny of Man,* London, Geoffrey Bles, 1937.

Bixler, J. S., R. L. Calhoun, and H. R. Niebuhr, eds., *The Nature of Religious Experience: Essays in Honor of Douglas Clyde Macintosh,* New York, Harper and Brothers, 1937.

Burke, Edmund, *A Philosophical Enquiry Into the Origin of Ideas of the Sublime and Beautiful,* ed. J. T. Boulton, London, Routledge & Kegan Paul, 1958.

Bushnell, Horace, *God in Christ,* Hartford, 1849.

———, *The Vicarious Sacrifice, Grounded in Principles of Universal Obligation,* New York, 1866.

Chambers, Ephraim, *Cyclopaedia,* 2nd ed. rev., 2 vols. London, 1728.

Cross, Barbara M., *Horace Bushnell: Minister to a Changing America,* Chicago, University of Chicago Press, 1958.

Fey, Harold E., ed., *How My Mind Has Changed,* New York, Meridian Books, 1961.

Grove, Henry, *A System of Moral Philosophy,* 2 vols. London, 1749.

Gustafson, James, *Treasure in Earthen Vessels,* New York, Harper, 1961.

Hofstadter, Albert, *Truth and Art,* New York, Columbia University Press, 1965.

Hopkins, Mark, *The Law of Love and Love as Law,* 4th ed., New York, Scribner's, 1881.

Hutcheson, Francis, *An Inquiry Into the Original of Our Ideas of Beauty and Virtue,* London, 1725.

Jones, O. R., *The Concept of Holiness,* London, George Allen & Unwin, Ltd., 1961.

Kant, Immanuel, *Critique of Judgment,* trans. with intro. J. H. Bernard, New York, Hafner Publishing Co., 1951.

———, *Observations on the Feeling of the Beautiful and Sublime,* trans. with intro. John T. Goldwait, Berkeley, University of California Press, 1960.

———, *Religion Within the Limits of Reason Alone,* trans. with intro. Theodore M. Greene and Hoyt H. Hudson, and intro. essay by John R. Silber, New York, Harper, Torchbook, 1960.

Kitto, H. D. F., *The Greeks,* Baltimore, Penguin Books, 1957.

Langer, Suzanne K., *Feeling and Form,* New York, Scribner's, 1953.

———, *Philosophy in a New Key,* New York, New American Library, 1952.

Lovejoy, Arthur O., *The Great Chain of Being,* New York, Harper, Torchbook, 1961.

Lynch, William F., *Christ and Apollo: The Dimensions of the Literary Imagination,* New York, Sheed and Ward, 1960.

Marcuse, Herbert, *Eros and Civilization,* New York, Vintage Books, 1962.

Maritain, Jacques, *Creative Intuition in Art and Poetry,* New York, Pantheon Books, 1953.

———, *Man and the State,* Chicago, University of Chicago Press, 1951.

Maurer, Armand A., *Medieval Philosophy,* New York, Random House, 1962.

Monk, Samuel H., *The Sublime,* Ann Arbor, University of Michigan Press, 1960.

Niebuhr, H. Richard, *Radical Monotheism and Western Culture,* New York, Harper and Brothers, 1960.

———, *The Kingdom of God in America,* New York, Harper and Brothers, 1937.

———, *The Meaning of Revelation,* New York, Macmillan, 1952.

———, *The Responsible Self,* New York, Harper and Row, 1963.

Nygren, Anders, *Agape and Eros,* London, S.P.C.K., 1953.

Passmore, J. A., *Ralph Cudworth,* Cambridge, England, Cambridge University Press, 1951.

Ramsey, Paul, ed., *Faith and Ethics: the Theology of H. Richard Niebuhr,* New York, Harper and Brothers, 1957.

Selby-Bigge, L. A., ed., *British Moralists,* Indianapolis, Bobbs-Merrill, 1964.

Shaftesbury [Anthony Ashley Cooper, Third Earl of Shaftesbury], *Characteristics,* London, 1711.

Sherburne, Donald W., *A Whiteheadian Aesthetic,* New Haven, Yale University Press, 1961.

Skelton, Philip, *Ophiomaches: or Deism Revealed,* 2 vols. London, 1749.

Smith, H. Shelton, *Horace Bushnell,* New York, Oxford University Press, 1965.

Sontag, Frederick, *Divine Perfection: Possible Ideas of God,* New York, Harper and Brothers, 1962.

Tillich, Paul, *Love, Power, and Justice,* New York, Oxford University Press, 1954.

van der Leeuw, Gerardus, *Sacred and Profane Beauty: The Holy in Art,* New York, Holt, Rinehart and Winston, 1963.

Whitehead, Alfred North, *Adventures of Ideas,* New York, Macmillan, 1933.
——, *Essays in Science and Philosophy,* New York, Philosophical Library, 1947.
——, *Religion in the Making,* Cleveland, World Publishing Company, Meridian Books, 1960.
Wieman, Henry Nelson, *The Source of Human Good,* Chicago, University of Chicago Press, 1946.

Other Articles Used or Cited

Battenhouse, Roy W., "The Doctrine of Man in Calvin and in Renaissance Platonism," *Journal of the History of Ideas, 9* (1948), 447–71.
Haroutunian, Joseph, "Theology and American Experience," *Criterion, 3,* No. 1 (Winter 1964), 3–9.
Hofstadter, Albert, "Validity Versus Value: An Essay in Philosophical Aesthetics," *The Journal of Philosophy, 59* (1962), 607–17.
Niebuhr, Richard R., "Dread and Joyfulness: The View of Man as Affectional Being," *Religion in Life, 31* (1962), 443–64.

Other Unpublished Materials

Alexis, Gerhard Theodore, "Calvinism and Mysticism in Jonathan Edwards," unpublished Ph.D. dissertation, University of Minnesota, 1947.
Bushnell, Horace, "God Reigns for the Largest Love," manuscript sermon, Manuscript Collection, Yale Divinity School Library, 1870.
Carse, James P., "Incarnation and Atonement in the Theology of Jonathan Edwards," unpublished S.T.M. thesis, Yale Divinity School, 1963.
Feaver, John Clayton, "Jonathan Edwards' Concept of God as Redeemer," unpublished Ph.D. dissertation, Yale University, 1949.
Heimert, Alan E., "American Oratory: From the Great Awakening to the Election of Jefferson," unpublished Ph.D. dissertation, Harvard University, 1960.
Holbrook, Clyde A., "The Ethics of Jonathan Edwards," unpublished Ph.D. dissertation, Yale University, 1944.
Niebuhr, H. Richard, class lecture in Christian ethics, 26 March 1954, as transcribed in my notes.
——, "Reflections on Faith, Hope, and Love," unpublished manuscript, n.d.
Schafer, Thomas A., "The Concept of Being in the Thought of Jonathan Edwards," unpublished Ph.D. dissertation, Duke University, 1951.
Scott, Lee Osborne, "The Concept of Love as Universal Disinterested Benevolence in the Early Edwardseans," unpublished Ph.D. dissertation, Yale University, 1952.

INDEX

Actualism, 69, 168, 182, 192

Aesthetic, priority of, vii, 10, 41, 103, 111–14, 219 n.

Aesthetic-affectional self. *See* Self

Aestheticism, rejected by Edwards, 3, 25, 51, 62. *See also* Objectivism

Aesthetics, 222–24

Affections, 128; and will, 5 f., 94

Aquinas, Thomas, 118

Arendt, Hannah, 47 n.

Arête, 64

Augustine, 29, 85, 118, 163, 191

Axiology, 220, 222, 226

Barth, Karl, 119–22, 135 f.

Beauty: definition of, 15–26; summary definition of, 20 f.; general and particular, 21; objective, structural, relational concept of, 4, 8, 22–24, 26, 64 f., 79, 103, 105, 166 f., 191; primary and secondary, 9, 17–19, 24, 26, 31 f., 51, 88 f., 105, 112 f., 132, 192–94, 206 f., 210 f.; true and false, 20; universal and partial, 20; and being, 1 f., 27–57, 104–14, 188, 203; and excellence, 58–67, 94; and goodness, 67–99; as measure of goodness, 71–79; as objective foundation of goodness, 71, 79–85; as attractive power of good, 71, 85–98; and knowledge, 72 f., 126, 131 f.; and perception of being, 48 f., 112–14; and perfection of being, 3, 58, 64, 67, 79, 99, 104; and sensibility, correspondence of, 3 f., 67, 80, 82 f., 126, 145,

Beauty (*Cont.*)
153, 160, 172 f., 177 f., 198, 226; and the sublime, 146 f.; and truth of being, 53–56, 221, 223 f.; and unity of being, 56 f.; and unity of being and good, 104–11; and value, 99–103; as category of being, 29, 104 f.; as category of interpretation, 29, 104 f.; as constitutive of community, 207–13; as creative principle, 25 f., 46 f., 108, 168 f.; as divine perfection, 79, 117–47; as goal of redemption, 201–06, 212 f.; as means of redemption, 135, 201–06 f., 212 f.; as model of order, 1 f., 104, 111–14, 167, 184; of community, 10 f., 207, 210–13; of holiness, 50, 118 n., 124, 126; of the world, 180, 185–87, 206 f.; ontological priority of, 1 f., 27–57, 104, 166, 188; perception of, 27, 48, 61 f., 72–74, 88 f., 95, 97, 113 f., 126 f., 188, 195–98; sense of, 3, 90–92, 124–28, 158, 205; primary beauty as beautifying, 25 f.; primary beauty as higher law of moral world, 196–201; secondary beauty as law of natural world, 184–88; secondary beauty as natural law of moral world, 192–96. *See also* Excellence; Good

Being: aesthetic articulation of, 41 f.; fullness of, 34, 45 ff.; and good, coordinate orders of, 8, 30 f., 35; and "nothing," 44–47, 171; philosophy of, 27–57, 104–14. *See also* Beauty

Benevolence, 78, 100